DK SMITHSONIAN

Children's Illustrated
ATLAS

Writer and consultant Andrew Brooks
Senior editor Marie Greenwood
Senior designer Jim Green

US editor Margaret Parrish
Map illustrator Jeongeun Park
Illustrators Maltings Partnership,
Daniel Long
Senior editors Gill Pitts, Cécile Landau
Project art editor Hoa Luc
Designer Emma Hobson
Design assistant Rhea Gaughan
Cartography Ed Merritt, Simon Mumford
Index Helen Peters
Pre-production Dragana Puvacic
Production Srijana Gurung
Managing editor Laura Gilbert
Managing art editor Diane Peyton Jones
Art director Martin Wilson
Publisher Sarah Larter
Publishing director Sophie Mitchell

First American Edition, 2016
Published in the United States by DK Publishing
345 Hudson Street, New York, New York 10014

Copyright © 2016 Dorling Kindersley Limited
DK, a Division of Penguin Random House LLC
16 17 18 19 20 10 9 8 7 6 5 4 3 2 1
001-196405-Aug/2016

A catalog record for this book is available from the Library of Congress.
ISBN: 978-1-4654-3555-2

DK books are available at special discounts when purchased in bulk for sales
promotions, premiums, fund-raising, or educational use. For details, contact: DK
Publishing Special Markets, 345 Hudson Street, New York, New York 10014
SpecialSales@dk.com

Printed and bound in Hong Kong

A WORLD OF IDEAS:
SEE ALL THERE IS TO KNOW
www.dk.com

CONTENTS

HOW TO READ THE MAPS

A map is a drawing that gives an instant impression of a place. The maps in this book show many of the world's countries plotted with rivers, mountains, forests, and plains.

Picture symbols
You will find picture symbols of a country's produce, industry, sports, and activities plotted on each country map. Look at the key to find what each symbol means

Picture features
Pictures with text pick out a country's special features, including historic sites, animals, and natural wonders

Capital
A country's capital city is marked with a red outline

Bordering countries
Around the edges of the map you can see all the bordering countries

Flag
On every country, you'll find the country's flag

History and culture
These photographs show historical and cultural features that are unique to that country

Places of interest
These photographs zoom in on a city, building, or landscape and show where it is on the map

Produce
Close-up photographs show food, drink, and other goods that a country produces

Page numbers
The color of the circle matches the continent opener and tells you which continent you are in

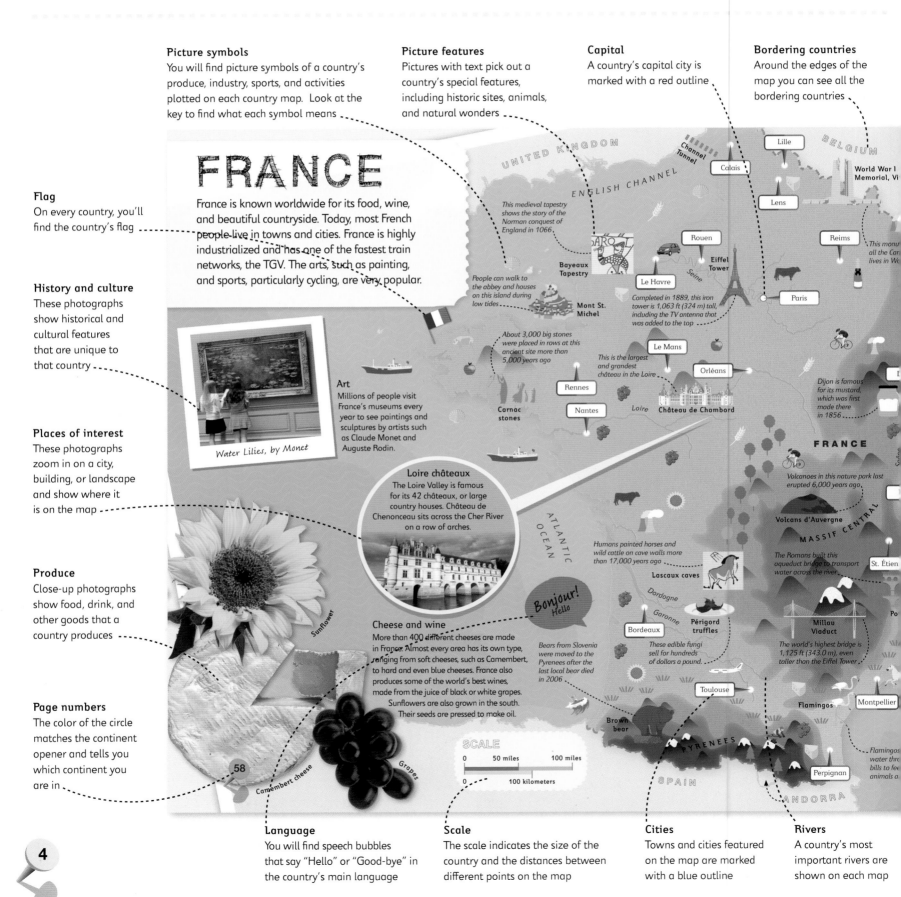

FRANCE

France is known worldwide for its food, wine, and beautiful countryside. Today, most French people live in towns and cities. France is highly industrialized and has one of the fastest train networks, the TGV. The arts, such as painting, and sports, particularly cycling, are very popular.

UNITED KINGDOM

ENGLISH CHANNEL

Channel Tunnel

Calais

Lille

BELGIUM

World War I Memorial, Vi

Lens

This monu all the Ca lives in Wo

This medieval tapestry shows the story of the Norman conquest of England in 1066

Bayeaux Tapestry

Rouen

Reims

People can walk to the abbey and houses on this island during low tides

Le Havre

Seine

Eiffel Tower

Paris

Mont St. Michel

Completed in 1889, this iron tower is 1,063 ft (324 m) tall, including the TV antenna that was added to the top

Art
Millions of people visit France's museums every year to see paintings and sculptures by artists such as Claude Monet and Auguste Rodin.

Water Lilies, by Monet

About 3,000 big stones were placed in rows at this ancient site more than 5,000 years ago

Rennes

Carnac stones

Nantes

This is the largest and grandest château in the Loire

Le Mans

Orléans

Loire

Château de Chambord

Dijon is famous for its mustard, which was first made there in 1856

FRANCE

Loire châteaux
The Loire Valley is famous for its 42 châteaux, or large country houses. Château de Chenonceau sits across the Cher River on a row of arches.

ATLANTIC OCEAN

Volcanoes in this nature park last erupted 6,000 years ago

Volcans d'Auvergne

MASSIF CENTRAL

Bonjour! Hello

Humans painted horses and wild cattle on cave walls more than 17,000 years ago

Lascaux caves

The Romans built this aqueduct bridge to transport water across the river

St. Étien

Cheese and wine
More than 400 different cheeses are made in France. Almost every area has its own type, ranging from soft cheeses, such as Camembert, to hard and even blue cheeses. France also produces some of the world's best wines, made from the juice of black or white grapes. Sunflowers are also grown in the south. Their seeds are pressed to make oil.

Sunflower

Dordogne

Garonne

Bordeaux

Périgord truffles

Bears from Slovenia were moved to the Pyrenees after the last local bear died in 2006

These edible fungi sell for hundreds of dollars a pound.

Millau Viaduct

The world's highest bridge is 1,125 ft (343.0 m), even taller than the Eiffel Tower

Po

Toulouse

Flamingos

Montpellier

Brown bear

Flamingos water thr bills to fee animals a

Camembert cheese

Grapes

PYRENEES

Perpignan

SPAIN

ANDORRA

SCALE

0   50 miles   100 miles

0   100 kilometers

58

Language
You will find speech bubbles that say "Hello" or "Good-bye" in the country's main language

Scale
The scale indicates the size of the country and the distances between different points on the map

Cities
Towns and cities featured on the map are marked with a blue outline

Rivers
A country's most important rivers are shown on each map

Country borders

Borders
The borders between countries are shown with a red broken line.

Disputed borders
Some countries disagree about where the border between them should be. These borders are shown with a dotted line.

Compass
The compass always points north (N) in line with the map and also shows the direction of south (S), east (E), and west (W)

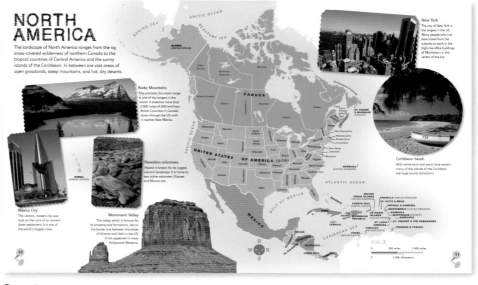

The landscape of North America ranges from the icy, snow-covered wilderness of northern Canada to the tropical countries of Central America and the sunny islands of the Caribbean. In between are vast areas of open grasslands, steep mountains, and hot, dry deserts.

New York
The city of New York is the largest in the US. Many people who live here travel from the suburbs to work in the high-rise office buildings of Manhattan in the center of the city.

Rocky Mountains
This dramatic mountain range is one of the longest in the world. It stretches more than 3,000 miles (4,800 km) from British Columbia in Canada down through the US until it reaches New Mexico.

Hawaiian volcanoes
Hawaii is known for its rugged, volcanic landscape. It is home to two active volcanoes: Kilauea and Mauna Loa.

Mexico City
This vibrant, modern city was built on the ruins of an ancient Aztec settlement. It is one of the world's biggest cities.

Monument Valley
This valley, which is famous for its amazing rock formations, lies on the border line between the states of Arizona and Utah in the US. It has appeared in many Hollywood Westerns.

Caribbean beach
With white sand and warm blue waters, many of the islands of the Caribbean are huge tourist attractions.

Continent maps

The continent maps are colored to show every country in each continent. Photographs show the continent's major features.

Au revoir
Good-bye

Strasbourg

GERMANY

SWITZERLAND

live

Alpine ibex

ITALY

French street market

Outdoor markets
Every French village and town has an outdoor market that opens at least one day a week. People can buy fresh fruit and vegetables grown at nearby farms and local produce, such as cheese.

Café culture
French people enjoy meeting up with their friends in cafés. They often have a croissant (a flaky pastry) and coffee for breakfast. In the evenings, popular drinks include beer, wine, or champagne (a fizzy wine).

A popular café in Paris

Tour de France
The world's most famous bicycle race lasts for three weeks and passes through the Alps and Pyrenees before finishing in Paris.

KEY

PRODUCE
- Vineyards
- Sunflowers
- Beef cattle
- Wheat
- Apples
- Cheese
- Champagne
- Shellfish
- Pigs

INDUSTRY
- Nuclear power
- Aircraft manufacture
- Fishing
- Cars

ACTIVITIES
- Mountain climbing
- Skiing
- Cycling
- Surfing

Nice

MONACO

Monaco is a small country that is independent from France

TGV

Toulon

French Riviera

wild horses marshes of ue

High-speed trains connect France's major cities

The southeast coast is famous for its seaside resorts and the Cannes Film Festival

Corsica

Napoleon Bonaparte was born in Corsica in 1769. He became Emperor of France in 1804 and died in 1821

MEDITERRANEAN SEA

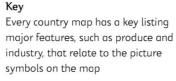

Independent states
Small independent states, such as Monaco, are shown with a red border and a solid red dot, and the name is in capital letters.

Key
Every country map has a key listing major features, such as produce and industry, that relate to the picture symbols on the map

Habitats

These colors and symbols show the different habitats, or landscapes, of each country.

Hot deserts
Hot deserts are dry and sandy areas and few plants grow here.

Cold deserts
Cold deserts, such as the Gobi in Asia, are cold, dry stretches of land.

Snow and ice
Frozen areas are found high in the mountains and at the North and South poles.

Mountains
High, rugged mountainous areas are often covered with snow.

Oceans and seas
Huge stretches of water surround the seven continents.

Scrubland
Low-lying plants and grasses grow in scrubland areas, such as in southern Spain.

Wetland
Wetlands are marshy, swampy areas, such as the Pantanal in Brazil.

Grassland
Grasslands are flat, grassy plains with few trees, such as the savanna of Africa

Tropical
Green rain forests, such as the Amazon, get a lot of rain and so trees grow very tall.

Deciduous forests
These forests have trees that lose their leaves in the fall and winter.

Coniferous forests
Evergreen trees that do not lose their leaves in winter are found in coniferous forests.

NORTH AMERICA

North America
This huge continent lies
wholly in the northern half
(hemisphere) of the world.
It includes Greenland, which
lies above the Arctic Circle.

ATLANTIC
OCEAN

Equator
This continent lies mainly in
the southern hemisphere of
the world. North, Central, and
South America are together
known as the Americas.

PACIFIC
OCEAN

South America
This continent lies mainly in
the southern hemisphere of
the world. North, Central, and
South America are together
known as the Americas.

SOUTH AMERICA

ATLANTIC
OCEAN

THE WORLD

This is a flat map of our round Earth. Land covers
about a third of Earth's surface. This land is broken
up into seven large blocks called continents. Water
makes up the rest of the Earth and is divided into
five major areas, called oceans.

Antarctica
This is the most southern of
all the continents. It is
covered in frozen ice and
hardly anybody lives here.

SOUTHERN OCEAN

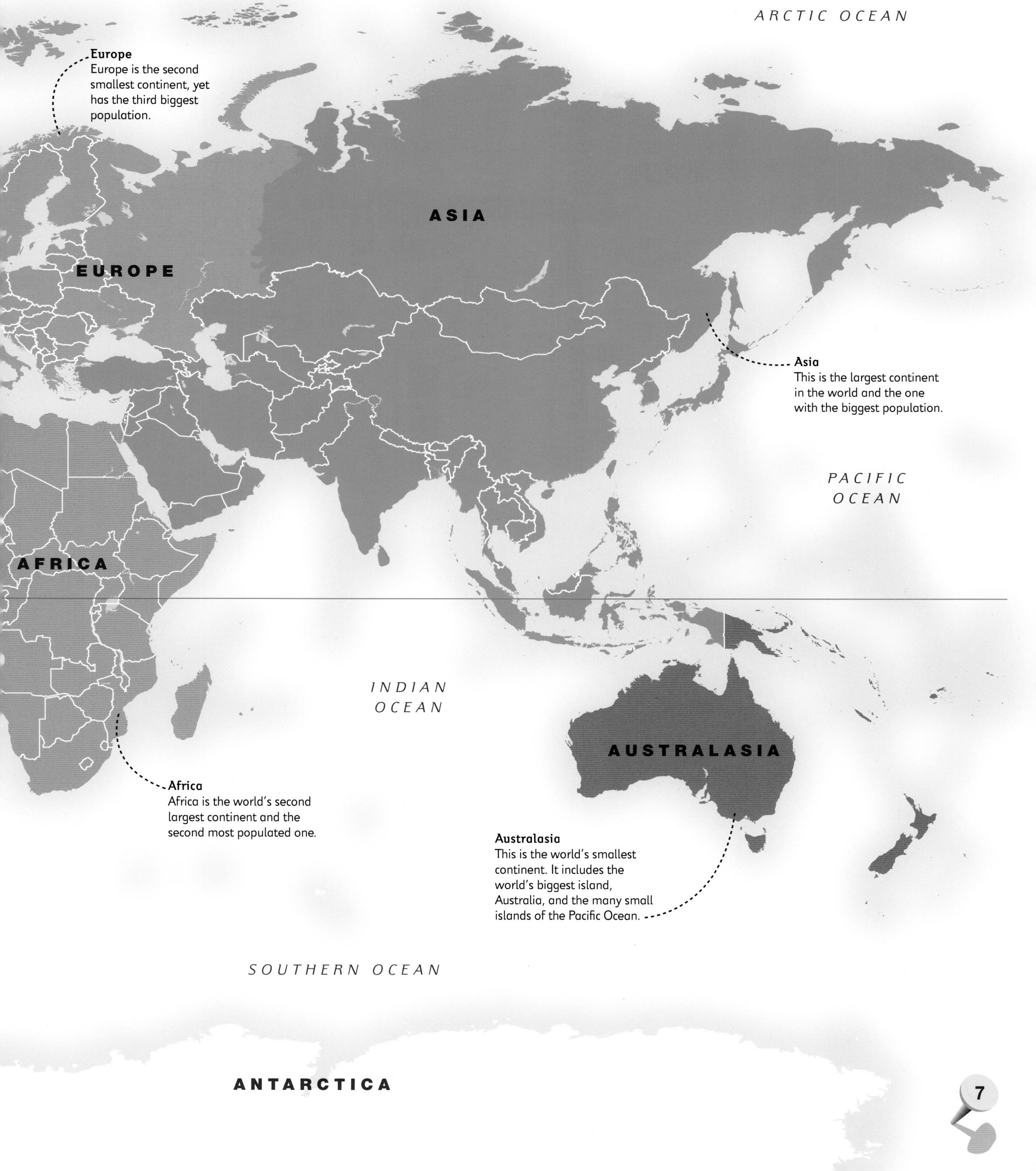
ARCTIC OCEAN
Europe
Europe is the second smallest continent, yet has the third biggest population.
ASIA
EUROPE
Asia
This is the largest continent in the world and the one with the biggest population.
PACIFIC OCEAN
AFRICA
INDIAN OCEAN
AUSTRALASIA
Africa
Africa is the world's second largest continent and the second most populated one.
Australasia
This is the world's smallest continent. It includes the world's biggest island, Australia, and the many small islands of the Pacific Ocean.
SOUTHERN OCEAN
ANTARCTICA

2. The merengue is the national dance of which Caribbean country?

3. In which Canadian city is the CN Tower found?

1. Into which mountain is this sculpture carved?

4. In which country would you find this ancient Pyramid of the Sun?

NORTH AMERICA

Canada, the United States of America (USA), Mexico, Central America, and the Caribbean islands make up North America. This vast continent was first settled by American Indian people before the arrival of Europeans and people from other parts of the world.

8. Which canal connects the world's two biggest oceans?

7. Who were the first people to settle in northern Canada?

6. Which river flows through the Grand Canyon?

5. In which American city will you see yellow taxis?

You can find all the answers and more quizzes on pages 120-121.

NORTH AMERICA

The landscape of North America ranges from the icy, snow-covered wilderness of northern Canada to the tropical countries of Central America and the sunny islands of the Caribbean. In between are vast areas of open grasslands, steep mountains, and hot, dry deserts.

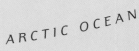

ARCTIC OCEAN

BERING SEA

BEAUFORT SEA

ALASKA
(UNITED STATES)

Yukon
Territory

Northwe
Territorie

British Columbia

Alberta

PACIFIC OCEAN

Washington

Mont

Oregon

Idaho

UNITED STAT

Nevada

California

Utah

Arizona

Rocky Mountains

This dramatic mountain range is one of the longest in the world. It stretches more than 3,000 miles (4,800 km) from British Columbia in Canada down through the US until it reaches New Mexico.

HAWAII
(UNITED STATES)

Hawaiian volcanoes

Hawaii is known for its rugged, volcanic landscape. It is home to two active volcanoes: Kilauea and Mauna Loa.

Mexico City

This vibrant, modern city was built on the ruins of an ancient Aztec settlement. It is one of the world's biggest cities.

Monument Valley

This valley, which is famous for its amazing rock formations, lies on the border line between the states of Arizona and Utah in the US. It has appeared in many Hollywood Westerns.

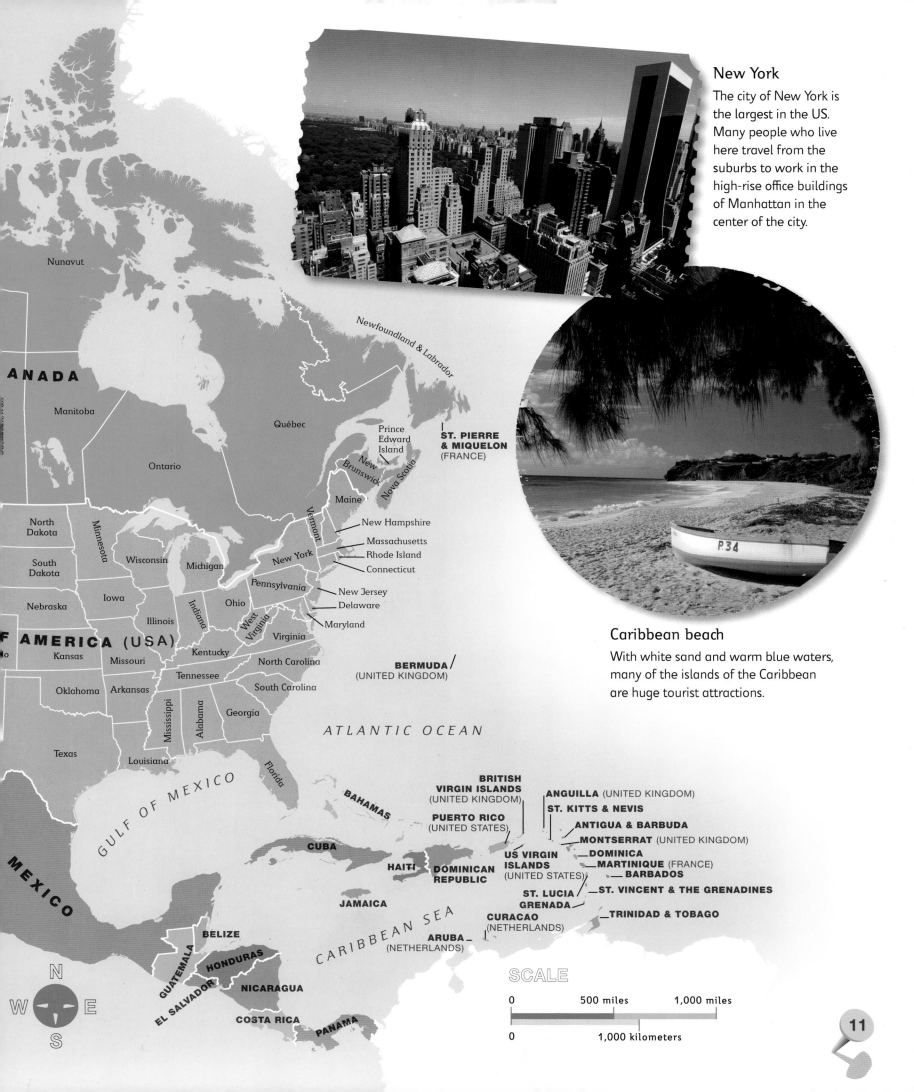

New York

The city of New York is the largest in the US. Many people who live here travel from the suburbs to work in the high-rise office buildings of Manhattan in the center of the city.

Caribbean beach

With white sand and warm blue waters, many of the islands of the Caribbean are huge tourist attractions.

Nunavut

C A N A D A

Manitoba

Québec

Ontario

Newfoundland & Labrador

Prince Edward Island

New Brunswick

Nova Scotia

Maine

Vermont

ST. PIERRE & MIQUELON (FRANCE)

North Dakota

Minnesota

Wisconsin

Michigan

New Hampshire

Massachusetts

Rhode Island

Connecticut

South Dakota

Iowa

Illinois

Indiana

Ohio

New York

Pennsylvania

New Jersey

Delaware

Maryland

Nebraska

F A M E R I C A (U S A)

Kansas

Missouri

Kentucky

West Virginia

Virginia

North Carolina

Oklahoma

Arkansas

Tennessee

South Carolina

BERMUDA (UNITED KINGDOM)

Texas

Mississippi

Alabama

Georgia

Louisiana

Florida

ATLANTIC OCEAN

GULF OF MEXICO

BAHAMAS

BRITISH VIRGIN ISLANDS (UNITED KINGDOM)

ANGUILLA (UNITED KINGDOM)

PUERTO RICO (UNITED STATES)

ST. KITTS & NEVIS

ANTIGUA & BARBUDA

MONTSERRAT (UNITED KINGDOM)

CUBA

US VIRGIN ISLANDS (UNITED STATES)

DOMINICA

MARTINIQUE (FRANCE)

HAITI

DOMINICAN REPUBLIC

BARBADOS

ST. VINCENT & THE GRENADINES

JAMAICA

ST. LUCIA

GRENADA

CURACAO (NETHERLANDS)

TRINIDAD & TOBAGO

M E X I C O

CARIBBEAN SEA

ARUBA (NETHERLANDS)

BELIZE

GUATEMALA

HONDURAS

N
W E
S

EL SALVADOR

NICARAGUA

COSTA RICA

PANAMA

SCALE

0   500 miles   1,000 miles

0   1,000 kilometers

11

CANADA AND ALASKA

Canada is the world's second largest country. It has huge mountain ranges, wide and vast forests, and bustling cities. It is also rich in oil and mineral resources, as is Alaska, the biggest state in the US.

Defending the net

Ice hockey
This fast-moving sport is very popular in Canada and can be played on ice rinks or frozen lakes. Both the women's and men's teams have won more Olympic gold medals than any other nation.

ARCTIC OCEAN

Grizzly bear
In the rivers of Alaska and western Canada, grizzly bears catch salmon as the fish swim and leap upstream in the fall.

BEAUFORT SEA

Oil is carried across Alaska from the north coast to the south by the Trans-Alaska Pipeline

Prudhoe Bay

Trans-Alaska Pipeline

KEY

PRODUCE

- Wheat
- Dried beans and legumes
- Corn

INDUSTRY

- Gold
- Coal
- Silver
- Oil
- Lumber
- Uranium
- Technology
- Aircraft
- Gas
- Fishing
- Diamonds
- Aluminum
- Paper mills
- Cars

ACTIVITIES

- Hiking
- Skiing

At 20,310 ft (6,190 m) Denali is the highest mountain in North America

A l a s k a (U S A) Yukon

Mackenzie

The Inuit were the first people to settle in north Canada; they play drums at special events and celebrations

Inuit drummers

Fairbanks

Alaskan rivers are full of trout and other fish

Line fishing

Denali

Anchorage

Valdez

Great Bear Lake

ROCKY MOUNTAINS

Pelly

Yellowknife

The Mounties police force wear red jackets on special occasions

Great Slave Lake

The Alaskan coast is home to groups of sea otters, which rest floating on their backs

Sea otter

Whitehorse

Juneau

Canadian Mountie

More than one million people come to this big rodeo festival every July

COAST MOUNTAINS

Haida portrait figures made from wood

Haida figurines

PACIFIC OCEAN

Vancouver coast
Vancouver is an exciting, international city that is surrounded by nature. It is often voted as one of the best places in the world to live.

The first people of Canada carved wooden totem poles to show their cultural beliefs

Totem pole

Calgary Stampede

Edmonton

Curling

Dinosaur Provincial Park

First people
The Haida were among the first people to live in Canada before the arrival of Europeans. "Haida" means "person," and they live on the Pacific Northwest Coast.

Victoria

Vancouver

Calgary

SCALE

0	250 miles
0	250 kilometers

This sport is played with sliding stones on a sheet of ice

Well-preserved dinosaur fossils have been found in this park

12

Canadian goods

Canada is famous for its maple syrup, which is made from the sap of the sugar maple tree. Canola oil is used for cooking, flax is grown for its seeds and fibers, and lobsters live in the cool waters off the east coast.

Flax

Flax seeds

Lobster

Canola oil

Maple syrup

GREENLAND

BAFFIN BAY

The Arctic Circle marks the edge of the Arctic region

Arctic Circle

CANADA

Iqaluit

Street cycling

Tour de l'Île de Montréal

Every year the French Canadian city of Montréal celebrates the Tour de l'Île de Montréal, a series of major street cycling events.

Beaver

Beavers fell trees and build dams across rivers

HUDSON BAY

Bonjour!
Hello

A male moose's antlers may span 6½ ft (2 m)

Hello!

Moose

This popular sport is similar to football in the US, but played by teams of 12

This author wrote children's books about the orphan girl Anne of Green Gables, and most were set in Prince Edward Island

St. John's

Lucy Maud Montgomery

This grand hotel stands just inside the walls of Old Québec City. It opened in 1893

Château Frontenac

Charlottetown

Prince Edward Island

Fredericton

Lacrosse

Canadian football

Lake Superior

Québec City

Montréal

Ottawa

Halifax

Bay of Fundy

Niagara Falls

On the border of Canada and the US are the huge Niagara Falls. Water flows over the Horseshoe, American, and Bridal Veil waterfalls.

Winnipeg

This Toronto landmark gives fantastic views of the city

Lake Huron

CN Tower

Toronto

London

Lake Erie

UNITED STATES OF AMERICA

Players use a lacrosse stick to catch and hold a rubber ball in this team sport

This bay has the highest tides in the world, which have created amazing rock shapes

Golden Gate Bridge

This huge suspension bridge spans the Golden Gate strait (narrow sea channel) between San Francisco Bay and the Pacific Ocean. It is San Francisco's most famous landmark.

Bald eagle

This large majestic eagle is a symbol of the US

CANADA

SCALE

0 — 200 miles
0 — 200 kilometers

Seattle

ROCKY MOUNTAINS

Columbia

Yellowstone is the world's oldest national park and inside the park is a huge geyser called "Old Faithful"

Yellowstone National Park

This sculpture carved into a mountain shows the faces of four US presidents

GREAT BASIN DESERT

Snake

Big powerful bison once roamed the plains in large herds

American Bison

Mount Rushmore

GREAT PLA

This is the highest waterfall in Yosemite National Park

PACIFIC OCEAN

Cable cars run up and down the steep hills of San Francisco

San Francisco

Cable cars

Yosemite Falls

These golden-leaved trees grow throughout North America

Quaking aspen

Salt Lake City

Denver

UNITED STATE

Tornado Alley is so named because lots of tornadoes occur here

Giant sequoia trees grow in this national park

Sequoia National Park

Stars fitted into the sidewalks of Hollywood celebrate famous entertainers

Hollywood's Walk of Fame

Grand Canyon

This steep-sided canyon was carved by the Colorado River

Colorado

Santa Fe

Tornado Alley

Los Angeles

This is Walt Disney's original theme park; it features rides, displays, and characters from Disney films

Disneyland Park

San Diego

Phoenix

Rio Grande

Cowboys are skilled horse riders who herd cattle

Pueblo Eagle Dance

Pecos

Cowboy

Navajo girls in traditional clothes

American Indians

American Indians were the first people to live in America. The Navajo, from Arizona and New Mexico, are the largest tribe.

This dance performed by the Pueblo people of Colorado represents the flight of eagles

USA

The United States of America (USA) is a huge and powerful country with 50 states. It has wide stretches of wilderness as well as big, modern cities. The landscape is a mix of vast plains, high mountain ranges, dry deserts, and wetlands. Many people from all over the world have made their home here.

Hawaii

The islands of Hawaii, in the Pacific Ocean, became the 50th US state in 1959

Honolulu

MEXICO

Hawaii

Aloha!
Hello or good-bye

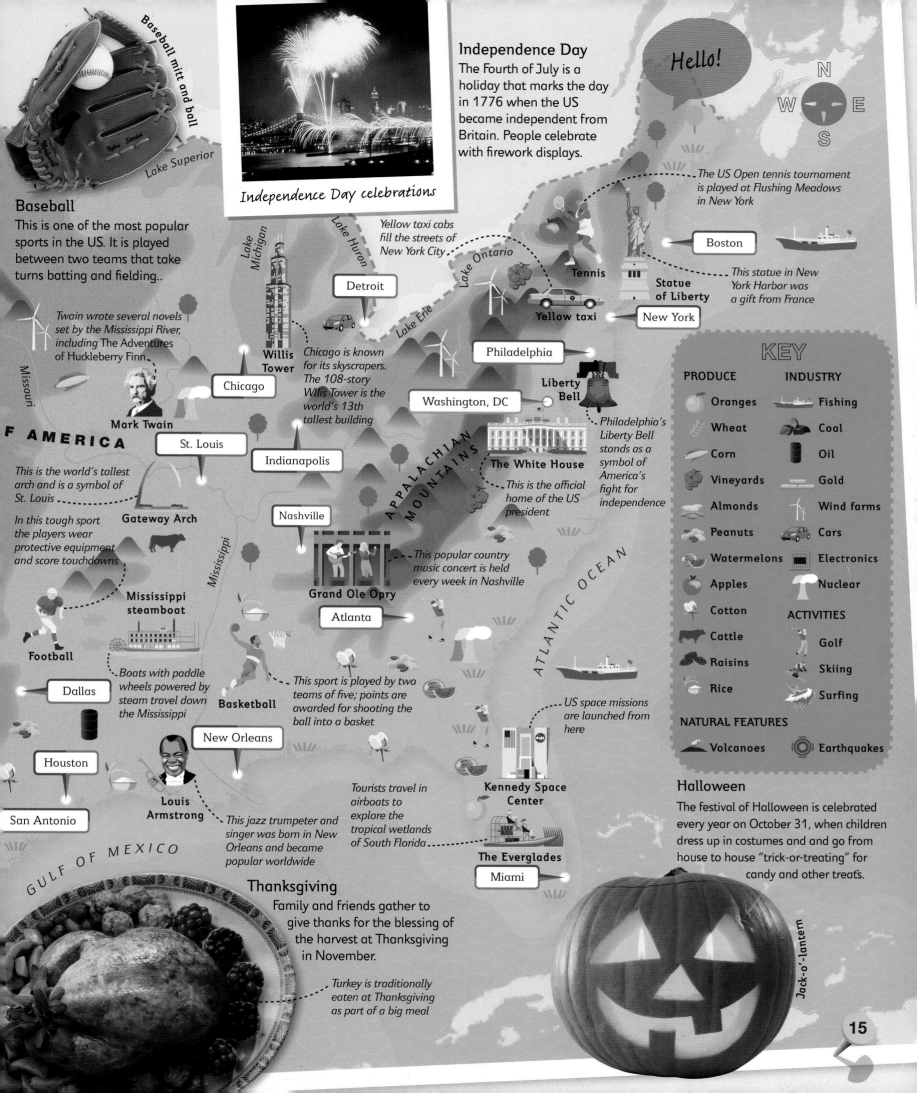

Baseball mitt and ball

Baseball
This is one of the most popular sports in the US. It is played between two teams that take turns batting and fielding..

Independence Day celebrations

Independence Day
The Fourth of July is a holiday that marks the day in 1776 when the US became independent from Britain. People celebrate with firework displays.

Hello!

The US Open tennis tournament is played at Flushing Meadows in New York

Lake Superior

Twain wrote several novels set by the Mississippi River, including The Adventures of Huckleberry Finn

Lake Michigan

Lake Huron

Yellow taxi cabs fill the streets of New York City

Lake Ontario

Lake Erie

Detroit

Tennis

Boston

Statue of Liberty

This statue in New York Harbor was a gift from France

Willis Tower

Chicago is known for its skyscrapers. The 108-story Willis Tower is the world's 13th tallest building

Chicago

Mark Twain

St. Louis

Indianapolis

Yellow taxi

New York

Philadelphia

Washington, DC

Liberty Bell

Philadelphia's Liberty Bell stands as a symbol of America's fight for independence

The White House

This is the official home of the US president

F AMERICA

Missouri

This is the world's tallest arch and is a symbol of St. Louis

Gateway Arch

In this tough sport the players wear protective equipment and score touchdowns

Nashville

APPALACHIAN MOUNTAINS

Grand Ole Opry

This popular country music concert is held every week in Nashville

Mississippi

Football

Mississippi steamboat

Atlanta

Basketball

Boats with paddle wheels powered by steam travel down the Mississippi

This sport is played by two teams of five; points are awarded for shooting the ball into a basket

Dallas

New Orleans

Houston

Louis Armstrong

San Antonio

This jazz trumpeter and singer was born in New Orleans and became popular worldwide

ATLANTIC OCEAN

US space missions are launched from here

Kennedy Space Center

Tourists travel in airboats to explore the tropical wetlands of South Florida

The Everglades

Miami

KEY

PRODUCE		INDUSTRY	
Oranges		Fishing	
Wheat		Coal	
Corn		Oil	
Vineyards		Gold	
Almonds		Wind farms	
Peanuts		Cars	
Watermelons		Electronics	
Apples		Nuclear	
Cotton			

ACTIVITIES

Cattle	Golf
Raisins	Skiing
Rice	Surfing

NATURAL FEATURES

Volcanoes	Earthquakes

Halloween
The festival of Halloween is celebrated every year on October 31, when children dress up in costumes and and go from house to house "trick-or-treating" for candy and other treats.

Thanksgiving
Family and friends gather to give thanks for the blessing of the harvest at Thanksgiving in November.

GULF OF MEXICO

Turkey is traditionally eaten at Thanksgiving as part of a big meal

Jack-o'-lantern

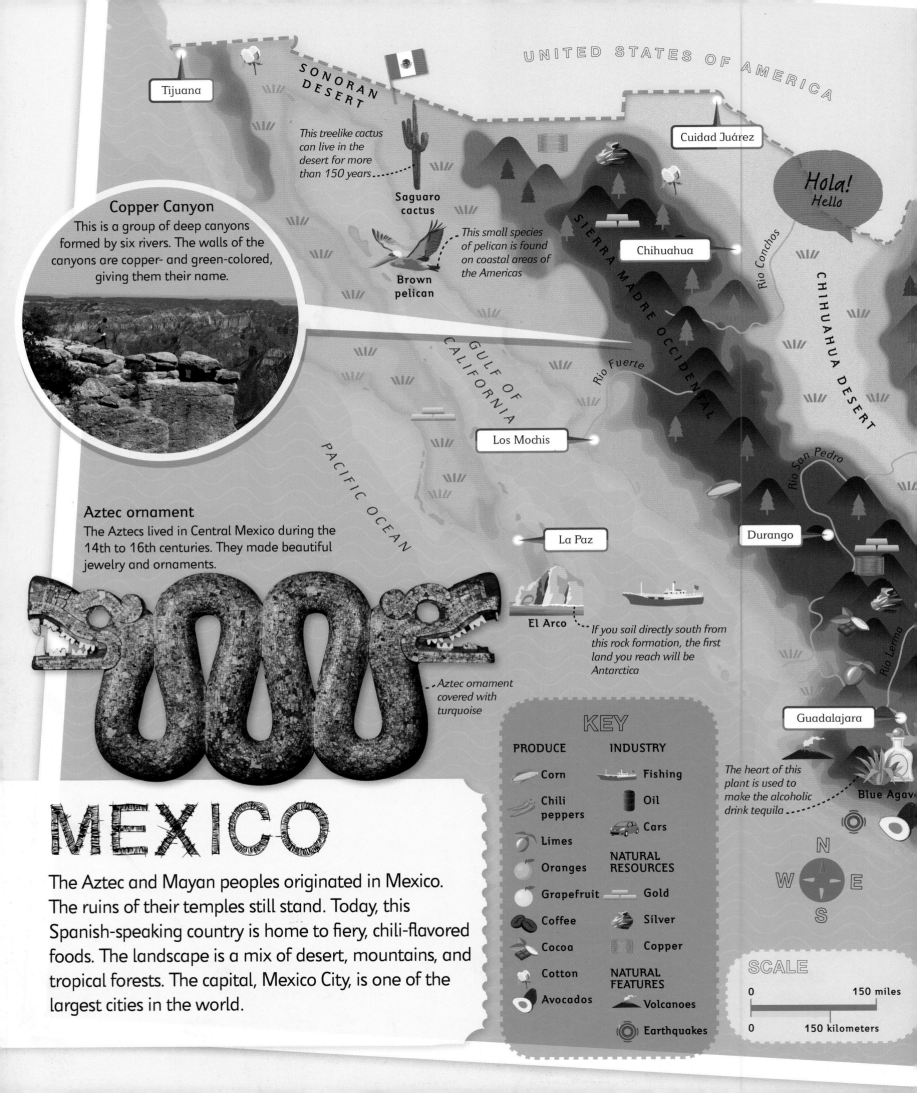

Tijuana

SONORAN DESERT

This treelike cactus can live in the desert for more than 150 years...

Saguaro cactus

Cuidad Juárez

Hola!
Hello

Copper Canyon
This is a group of deep canyons formed by six rivers. The walls of the canyons are copper- and green-colored, giving them their name.

This small species of pelican is found on coastal areas of the Americas

Brown pelican

SIERRA MADRE OCCIDENTAL

Chihuahua

Rio Conchos

CHIHUAHUA DESERT

GULF OF CALIFORNIA

Rio Fuerte

Los Mochis

Rio San Pedro

PACIFIC OCEAN

Aztec ornament
The Aztecs lived in Central Mexico during the 14th to 16th centuries. They made beautiful jewelry and ornaments.

La Paz

Durango

El Arco

If you sail directly south from this rock formation, the first land you reach will be Antarctica

Rio Lerma

Aztec ornament covered with turquoise

Guadalajara

The heart of this plant is used to make the alcoholic drink tequila...

Blue Agave

MEXICO

The Aztec and Mayan peoples originated in Mexico. The ruins of their temples still stand. Today, this Spanish-speaking country is home to fiery, chili-flavored foods. The landscape is a mix of desert, mountains, and tropical forests. The capital, Mexico City, is one of the largest cities in the world.

KEY

PRODUCE	INDUSTRY
Corn	Fishing
Chili peppers	Oil
Limes	Cars
Oranges	**NATURAL RESOURCES**
Grapefruit	Gold
Coffee	Silver
Cocoa	Copper
Cotton	**NATURAL FEATURES**
Avocados	Volcanoes
	Earthquakes

N
W   E
S

SCALE

0 ———— 150 miles

0 ———— 150 kilometers

Butterfly reserve

Every year in the fall, thousands of monarch butterflies migrate (move) from northern North America to Mexico. The Monarch Butterfly Biosphere Reserve, northwest of Mexico City, protects these butterflies during the winter.

Monarch butterflies

Spicy food

Mexican food is often very spicy and includes tacos, which are corn tortillas (flatbread) filled with meat or seafood. Refreshing limes and creamy avocados are grown in many parts of Mexico.

Tacos

Limes

Avocados

Lucha Libre

Lucha Libre, which means "free wrestling," is a special type of wrestling. Fighters wear dramatic costumes, including masks, to hide their identity.

Masked wrestlers

Río Grande

Boxing is a major sport and Mexico has produced many world champion boxers

Boxing

Monterrey

SIERRA MADRE ORIENTAL

MEXICO

Armadillos are protected by their bony armor and leathery skin

Armadillo

GULF OF MEXICO

Palenque

This ruined Mayan city in southern Mexico thrived from 500–700 CE. Many of the ruins are still covered by jungle.

Cancùn

El Castillo

This temple was built by the Mayan civilization more than 1,000 years ago

León

This pyramid is one of the largest ancient buildings in the Americas

Metropolitan Cathedral

Pyramid of the Sun

Veracruz

Puebla

Mexico City

This volcano is the highest mountain in Mexico

These giant stone heads were carved 3,000 years ago.

Campeche

YUCATAN PENINSULA

GUATEMALA

BELIZE

Skeleton puppet

Pico de Orizaba

Olmec heads

Acapulco

Oaxaca

This is the largest cathedral in the Americas

These candies in the shape of skulls are given to celebrate the Day of the Dead

Day of the Dead

On this Mexican holiday, family and friends gather to pray and remember people who have died. Parades are held and colorful puppets are made in the shape of skeletons.

17

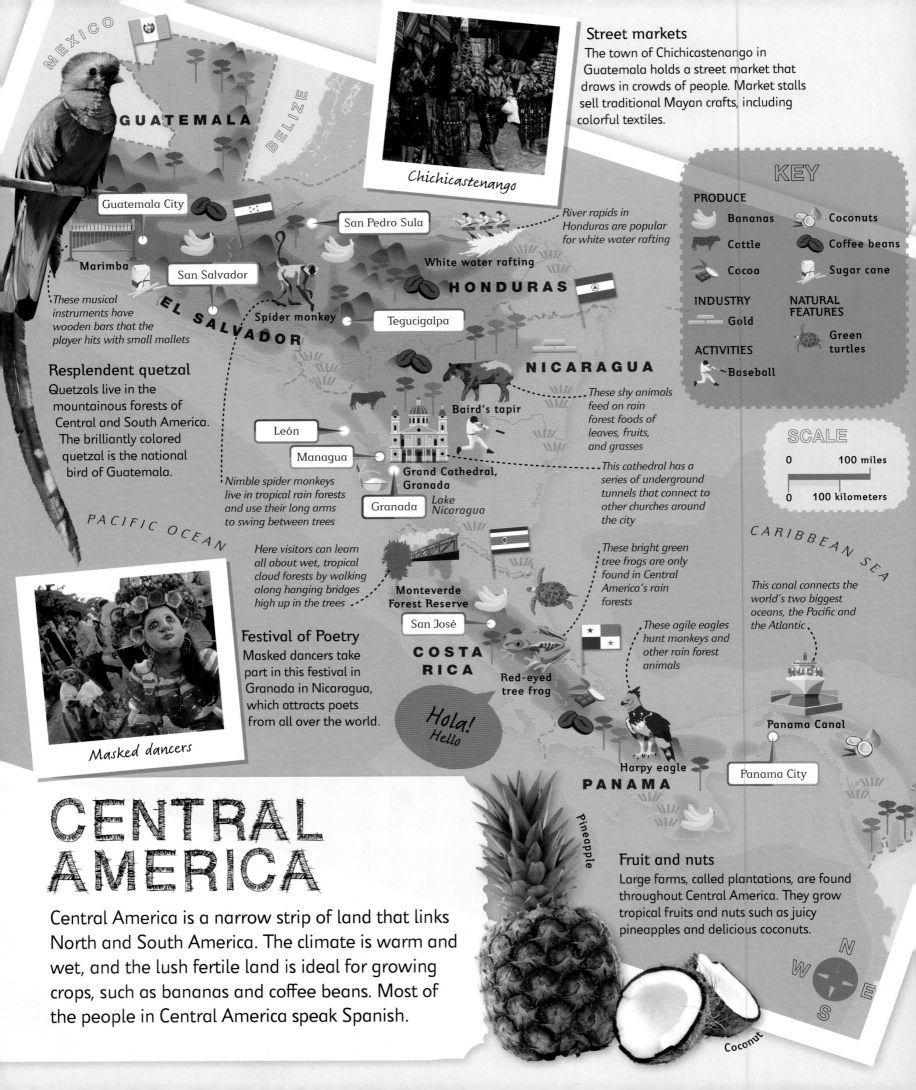

MEXICO

GUATEMALA

BELIZE

Street markets
The town of Chichicastenango in Guatemala holds a street market that draws in crowds of people. Market stalls sell traditional Mayan crafts, including colorful textiles.

Chichicastenango

Guatemala City

San Pedro Sula

River rapids in Honduras are popular for white water rafting

White water rafting

Marimba

San Salvador

EL SALVADOR

Spider monkey

HONDURAS

Tegucigalpa

NICARAGUA

These musical instruments have wooden bars that the player hits with small mallets

Resplendent quetzal
Quetzals live in the mountainous forests of Central and South America. The brilliantly colored quetzal is the national bird of Guatemala.

KEY

PRODUCE
Bananas   Coconuts
Cattle   Coffee beans
Cocoa   Sugar cane

INDUSTRY   **NATURAL FEATURES**
Gold   Green turtles

ACTIVITIES
Baseball

These shy animals feed on rain forest foods of leaves, fruits, and grasses

Baird's tapir

León

Managua

Grand Cathedral, Granada

Granada   *Lake Nicaragua*

Nimble spider monkeys live in tropical rain forests and use their long arms to swing between trees

This cathedral has a series of underground tunnels that connect to other churches around the city

SCALE

0   100 miles

0   100 kilometers

PACIFIC OCEAN

CARIBBEAN SEA

Here visitors can learn all about wet, tropical cloud forests by walking along hanging bridges high up in the trees

Monteverde Forest Reserve

San José

These bright green tree frogs are only found in Central America's rain forests

This canal connects the world's two biggest oceans, the Pacific and the Atlantic

Festival of Poetry
Masked dancers take part in this festival in Granada in Nicaragua, which attracts poets from all over the world.

COSTA RICA

Hola!
Hello

Red-eyed tree frog

These agile eagles hunt monkeys and other rain forest animals

Panama Canal

Masked dancers

Harpy eagle

PANAMA

Panama City

CENTRAL AMERICA

Central America is a narrow strip of land that links North and South America. The climate is warm and wet, and the lush fertile land is ideal for growing crops, such as bananas and coffee beans. Most of the people in Central America speak Spanish.

Pineapple

Fruit and nuts
Large farms, called plantations, are found throughout Central America. They grow tropical fruits and nuts such as juicy pineapples and delicious coconuts.

N E S W

Coconut

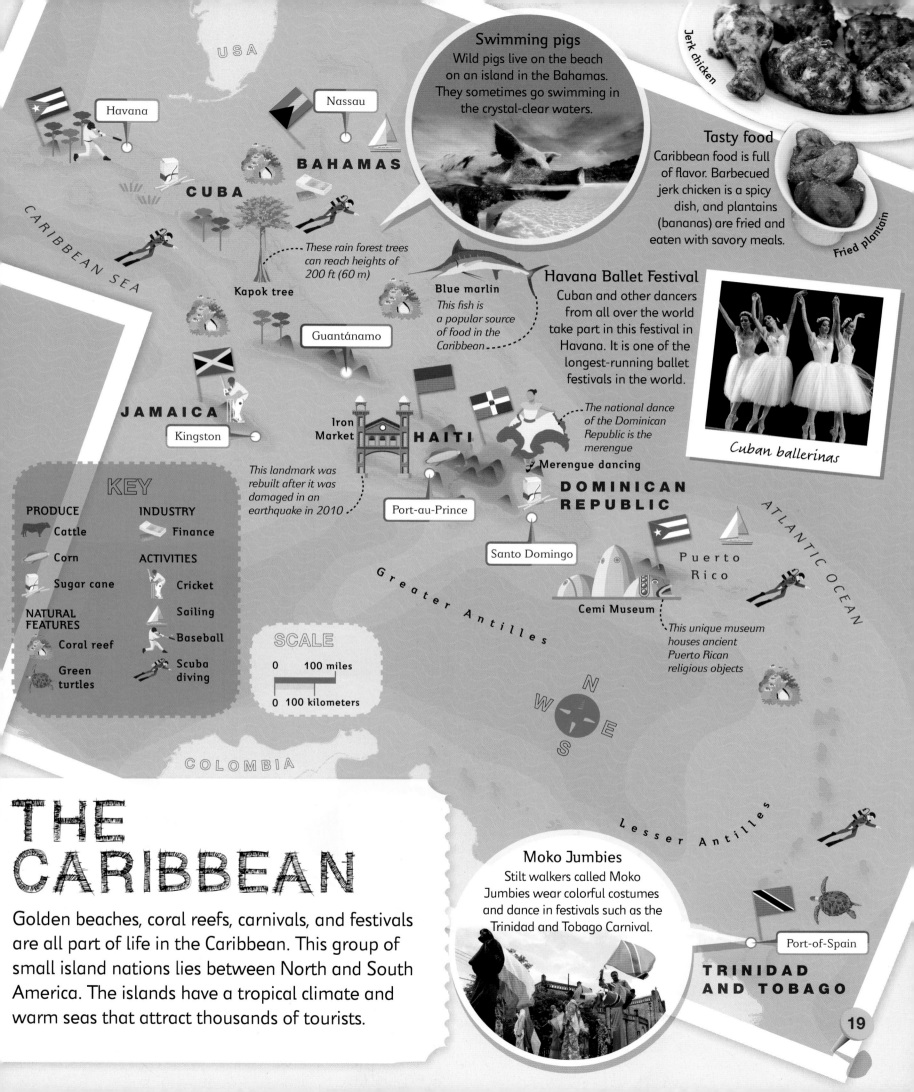

Swimming pigs
Wild pigs live on the beach on an island in the Bahamas. They sometimes go swimming in the crystal-clear waters.

Jerk chicken

Tasty food
Caribbean food is full of flavor. Barbecued jerk chicken is a spicy dish, and plantains (bananas) are fried and eaten with savory meals.

Fried plantain

USA

Havana

Nassau

BAHAMAS

CUBA

CARIBBEAN SEA

These rain forest trees can reach heights of 200 ft (60 m)

Kapok tree

Blue marlin
This fish is a popular source of food in the Caribbean

Guantánamo

Havana Ballet Festival
Cuban and other dancers from all over the world take part in this festival in Havana. It is one of the longest-running ballet festivals in the world.

Cuban ballerinas

JAMAICA

Kingston

Iron Market

HAITI

This landmark was rebuilt after it was damaged in an earthquake in 2010

Port-au-Prince

The national dance of the Dominican Republic is the merengue

Merengue dancing

DOMINICAN REPUBLIC

Santo Domingo

ATLANTIC OCEAN

Puerto Rico

Cemi Museum

This unique museum houses ancient Puerto Rican religious objects

Greater Antilles

KEY

PRODUCE
Cattle
Corn
Sugar cane

NATURAL FEATURES
Coral reef
Green turtles

INDUSTRY
Finance

ACTIVITIES
Cricket
Sailing
Baseball
Scuba diving

SCALE
0   100 miles
0   100 kilometers

N W E S

COLOMBIA

THE CARIBBEAN

Golden beaches, coral reefs, carnivals, and festivals are all part of life in the Caribbean. This group of small island nations lies between North and South America. The islands have a tropical climate and warm seas that attract thousands of tourists.

Lesser Antilles

Moko Jumbies
Stilt walkers called Moko Jumbies wear colorful costumes and dance in festivals such as the Trinidad and Tobago Carnival.

Port-of-Spain

TRINIDAD AND TOBAGO

19

CLIMATES

The weather that is typical of an area is called a climate. Climates vary around the world. The polar regions at the top and bottom of the Earth are the coldest places. Moving toward the equator, the climate gets warmer. Different animals and plants are suited to different types of climate.

The world is getting warmer. The average temperature has risen by 1.4°F (0.8°C) since 1880.

COLDEST CONTINENT

Antarctica is the coldest continent in the world. Temperatures here can drop as low as -128.5°F (-89.2°C).

KEY

POLAR AND SUBARCTIC	TEMPERATE
DESERT	SUBTROPICAL
MEDITERRANEAN	TROPICAL

POLAR AND SUBARCTIC

The climate around the North and South Poles is freezing cold and icy. Subarctic regions lie south of the North Pole, where the climate is a little warmer and some plants can survive.

DESERT

A desert climate is dry, with very little rainfall each year. Many deserts are very hot in the day and cold at night. Only a few plants and animals can survive in this harsh climate.

MEDITERRANEAN

Regions close to the Mediterranean Sea have hot, dry summers and cool, wet winters. This type of climate also describes places with similar weather patterns, such as California.

TEMPERATE

Areas with a temperate climate, such as the British Isles, have warm summers and cool winters. This kind of climate suits deciduous trees, which lose their leaves in winter.

SUBTROPICAL

Hot regions of the world with dry and rainy seasons have a subtropical climate. African savannas, which are large grasslands with few trees, have this kind of climate.

TROPICAL

A tropical climate is hot and rainy. Regions with this kind of climate are near the equator. Dense rain forests grow here. The Amazon rain forest is an example of a tropical region.

20

Five rainiest places

A state called Meghalaya in India has the world's highest rainfall each year. Here, seasonal winds called monsoons bring heavy rains. Other very wet places in the world are in rain forests or lush, hilly countryside.

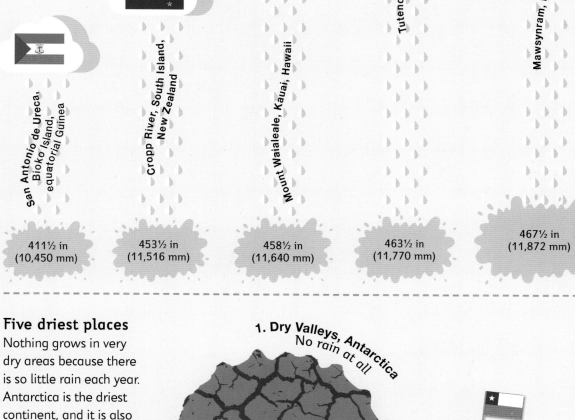

San Antonio de Ureca, Bioko Island, equatorial Guinea
411½ in (10,450 mm)

Cropp River, South Island, New Zealand
453½ in (11,516 mm)

Mount Waialeale, Kauai, Hawaii
458½ in (11,640 mm)

Tutendo, Colombia
463½ in (11,770 mm)

Mawsynram, Meghalaya state, India
467½ in (11,872 mm)

Five driest places

Nothing grows in very dry areas because there is so little rain each year. Antarctica is the driest continent, and it is also the coldest and windiest.

1. Dry Valleys, Antarctica
No rain at all

2. Atacama Desert, Chile
0.03 in (0.76 mm)

3. Al-Kufrah, Libya
0.0338 in (0.860 mm)

4. Aswan, Egypt
0.0339 in (0.861 mm)

5. Luxor, Egypt
0.034 in (0.862 mm)

Death Valley, California
134°F (56.7°C)

Kebili, Tunisia
131°F (55°C)

Tirat Tsvi, Israel
129°F (54°C)

Sulaibiya, Kuwait
128.3°F (53.5°C)

Mohenjo-daro, Pakistan
128.3°F (53.5°C)

Snag, Yukon, Canada
-81.4°F (-63°C)

Oymyakon, Russia
-90°F (-67.7°C)

Klinck, Greenland
-93.3°F (-69.6°C)

South Pole, Antarctica
-117°F (-82.8°C)

Vostok Station, Antarctica
-128.5°F (-89.2°C)

Hot and cold places

The hottest places on Earth are in desert regions. They are hotter than tropical areas, because there are no clouds to block the Sun. The coldest places are polar regions. They get less sunlight than other places.

21

SOUTH AMERICA

South America blends together Latin culture and the traditions of its native peoples. Spanish is the main language of most countries, because the first Europeans to arrive came from Spain. The exception is Brazil, where Portuguese people settled, bringing their own language.

5. Which country has won the soccer World Cup the most times?

You can find all the answers and more quizzes on pages 120-121.

6. In which country can you see this flightless bird?

8. Which country is this popular pet a native of?

7. What is the name of this Peruvian bear?

SOUTH AMERICA

South America stretches from the tropical Caribbean Sea in the north to the icy Southern Ocean in the south. The world's largest forest, the Amazon rain forest, covers most of Brazil and the northern part of the continent.

CARIBBEAN SEA

VENEZUEL

COLOMBIA

GALÁPAGOS ISLANDS (ECUADOR)

ECUADOR

PERU

BOLIV

Lake Titicaca

This deep lake, high up in the Andes mountains, sits on the border between Bolivia and Peru. There are several inhabited islands on the lake, including some floating, man-made islands, built from reeds. The way of life here has changed little over the centuries.

PACIFIC OCEAN

CHILE

ARGENTINA

Amazon river

This giant river flows through the Amazon rain forest, out into the Atlantic Ocean. It carries more water than any other river in the world.

Andes mountains

This mountain range runs like a spine down the west side of South America. It is the world's longest mountain range, stretching from the north of Colombia to the southern tip of Chile.

DRAKE PASSA

São Paulo

More people live in São Paulo than in any other city in South America. It started as a tiny, isolated village, which was founded by Portuguese settlers in the 16th century. After gold was discovered nearby in the 1690s, it grew, and this bustling city is now Brazil's main business center.

FRENCH
GUIANA
(FRANCE)

SURINAME

ATLANTIC OCEAN

BRAZIL

N
W · E
S

RAGUAY

URUGUAY

Pampas

This vast, grassy plain stretches over the eastern part of Argentina, most of Uruguay and the extreme south of Brazil. Parts are now farmed and huge quantities of wheat and vegetables grow here. The grasslands are perfect for rearing animals, including sheep and cattle. Argentine beef is some of the best in the world.

SCALE

| 0 | 500 miles | 1,000 miles |
| 0 | 1,000 kilometers | |

KLAND ISLANDS
TED KINGDOM)

SCOTIA SEA

COLOMBIA AND VENEZUELA

Colombia and Venezuela lie in the northwest corner of South America. To the north is the Caribbean Sea and to the south is the Amazon rain forest. These Spanish-speaking countries are rich in emeralds, diamonds, and gold.

Scarlet macaw
This large, noisy parrot lives in the rain forests of both Colombia and Venezuela. It eats nuts, seeds, and fruit.

Angel Falls
The Angel Falls is the world's highest waterfall. Water plunges 3,212 ft (979 m) into the rain forest.

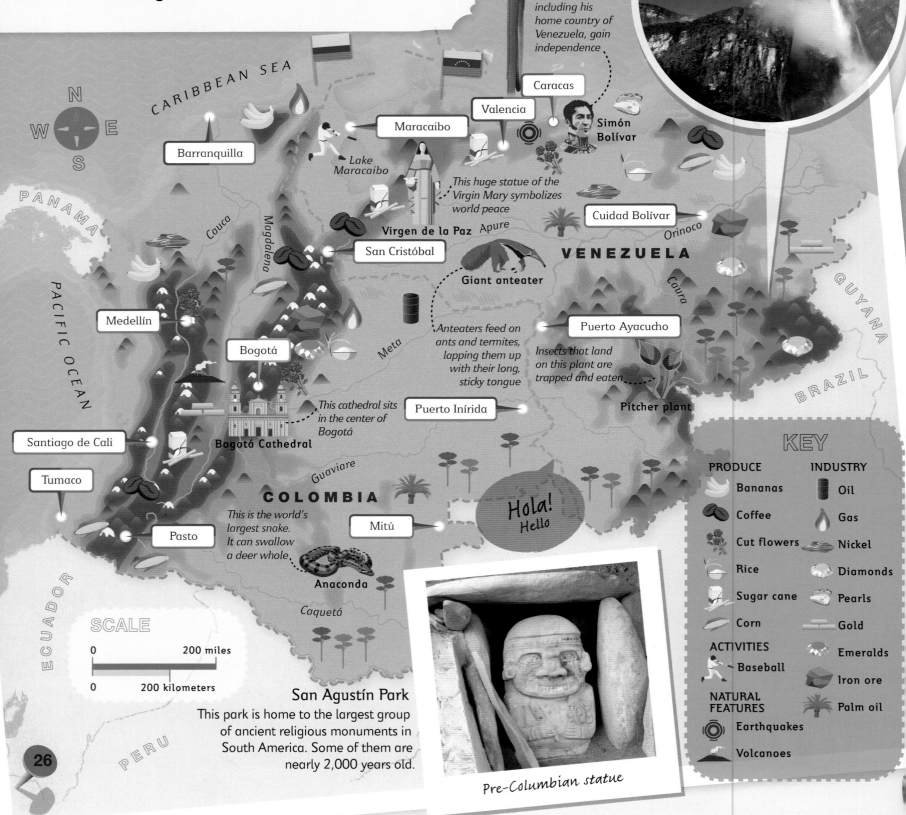

Bolívar helped several South American countries, including his home country of Venezuela, gain independence

CARIBBEAN SEA

N W E S

PANAMA

PACIFIC OCEAN

Barranquilla

Maracaibo

Lake Maracaibo

Valencia

Caracas

Simón Bolívar

This huge statue of the Virgin Mary symbolizes world peace

Virgen de la Paz   Apure

San Cristóbal

Cuidad Bolívar

Orinoco

VENEZUELA

Cauca   Magdalena

Giant anteater

Anteaters feed on ants and termites, lapping them up with their long, sticky tongue

Medellín

Bogotá

Meta

Puerto Ayacucho

Insects that land on this plant are trapped and eaten

Pitcher plant

Caura

GUYANA

BRAZIL

This cathedral sits in the center of Bogotá

Bogotá Cathedral

Puerto Inírida

Santiago de Cali

Tumaco

Guaviare

COLOMBIA

This is the world's largest snake. It can swallow a deer whole

Mitú

Hola! Hello

Pasto

Anaconda

Caquetá

ECUADOR

PERU

SCALE

0 _____ 200 miles

0 _____ 200 kilometers

San Agustín Park
This park is home to the largest group of ancient religious monuments in South America. Some of them are nearly 2,000 years old.

Pre-Columbian statue

KEY

PRODUCE
- Bananas
- Coffee
- Cut flowers
- Rice
- Sugar cane
- Corn

ACTIVITIES
- Baseball

NATURAL FEATURES
- Earthquakes
- Volcanoes

INDUSTRY
- Oil
- Gas
- Nickel
- Diamonds
- Pearls
- Gold
- Emeralds
- Iron ore
- Palm oil

PERU

Peru has some stunning scenery, ranging from dense rain forest to snow-capped peaks. The Andes mountain range runs the length of the country and is a popular destination for hiking. Peru is known for its brightly colored, traditional textiles and its delicious fish and potato dishes.

San Pedro market

Craft market
The native Quechua people live on traditional farms high up in the Andes. Cuzco's San Pedro market sells colorful Quechua textiles.

Adiós! Goodbye

This large-winged bird lives in the Andes mountains

Andean condor

Emperor tamarin
This monkey lives in the Amazon rain forest. Both male and female adults have long, white mustaches.

Machu Picchu
Machu Picchu is an ancient Inca city in the Andes. Its ruins are one of the world's most popular tourist attractions.

The tarka is a traditional Andean wooden flute

The cream around this bear's eyes make it look like it is wearing glasses

Chiclayo

Trujillo

PERU

Pucallpa

Flute

This native of Peru is now a popular pet worldwide

Iquitos

Amazon

BRAZIL

COLOMBIA

ECUADOR

Yurimaguas

Some structures at this site are nearly 3,000 years old

Chavin archeological site

Guinea pig

Spectacled bear

Urubamba

Boats made from dried reeds are used for fishing

PACIFIC OCEAN

Lima

This magnificent monastery was built by the Spanish

Monastery of San Francisco

ANDES

Cuzco

Lake Titicaca

Reed boats

Potatoes
Potatoes are native to Peru. More than 4,000 varieties grow here and come in many different sizes, shapes, and colors, including pink, purple, orange, and yellow.

Llama

Llamas are kept for their meat, wool, and carrying loads

Arequipa

BOLIVIA

CHILE

SCALE

0 — 200 miles

0 — 200 kilometers

KEY

PRODUCE
- Asparagus
- Coffee
- Sugar cane
- Quinoa

INDUSTRY
- Fishing
- Lumber
- Gold
- Silver
- Copper
- Cotton
- Iron ore

ACTIVITIES
- Hiking

NATURAL FEATURES
- Earthquakes

BRAZIL

Brazil is the largest country in South America and has a great variety of people and cultures. Most Brazilians live in big, crowded cities and speak Portuguese, the country's official language, while more than 200 tribal groups have their own unique languages.

Coffee and oranges

Brazil is the world's largest producer of oranges and coffee beans. About 75 percent of the orange crop is turned into juice and exported. There are about 300,000 coffee farms across the country, and Brazilians drink half of the coffee they produce.

Coffee beans

Oranges

Rain forest people

People have lived in the Amazon rain forest for thousands of years. The Yanomami are one of the largest tribes. They live in large, circular huts with palm leaf roofs.

Rain forest life

The vast Amazon rain forest is packed with plant and animal life.
An amazing number of insect species live there—about 2.5 million!

The bright blue upper wings help these large butterflies to see each other in the dark forest

Morpho butterfly

SCALE

0   200 miles   400 miles

0   400 kilometers

Some people use canoes to travel along the Amazon. Larger boats are used for tourists and trade

Canoes

VENEZUELA

COLOMBIA

GUYANA

SURINAME

FRENCH GUIANA (FRANCE)

ATLANTIC OCEAN

N
W   E
S

Fortaleza

Recife

Maceió

São Luís

Belém

Negro

Amazon

Xingu

Tocantins

Araguaia

São Francisco

AMAZON RAIN FOREST

Porto Velho

Manaus

This rare dolphin likes clean rivers with plenty of fish to eat

Pink river dolphin

Amazon Theater

Manaus, in the heart of the jungle, opened its opera house in 1896

These fish use their razor-sharp teeth to eat meat. Local people catch them for food

Piranha

A toucan's huge, colorful bill has many uses, including picking forest fruit

Toco toucan

This tree grows in Brazil's Cerrado, a vast grassland region

Qualea grandiflora

PERU

ATLANTIC OCEAN

Brasília replaced Rio as the capital in 1960. The modern cathedral looks like a crown of thorns

Belo Horizonte

Christ the Redeemer
This giant statue overlooks the city and is one of Rio's main landmarks

Rio de Janeiro

Sugar Loaf Mountain
This domed mountain rises above Rio. Stunning views of the city can be enjoyed by people who take a cable car to the top. Rio was chosen to host the Summer Olympics in 2016.

Brasília

Goiânia

São Paulo

Curitiba

Porto Alegre

Olá!
Hello

Lagoa dos Patos

São Miguel Mission
Built in 1687, this Catholic church is now a ruin

BOLIVIA

PARAGUAY

URUGUAY

ARGENTINA

PANTANAL

Capybara

This rodent is as big as a large dog and lives in marchy areas like the Pantanal

Paraná

Soccer
Brazilians love soccer. Brazil has won the World Cup more times (five) than any other country. Many famous players come from Brazil, including Pelé, one of the greatest players of all time.

Soccer on the beach

Iguaçu Falls
This spectacular series of waterfalls stretches across the border between Brazil and Argentina. The forests surrounding the falls are protected by two national parks.

Every jaguar has a unique pattern of spots on its coat

Jaguar
This big cat lives in the Amazon rain forest. Jaguars are strong swimmers and have a powerful bite.

Capoeira
This martial art involves music, dance, and acrobatics. Capoeira was developed in Brazil 500 years ago by people from West Africa, and it is a fun form of exercise.

Acrobatic moves

KEY

PRODUCE
- Coffee
- Oranges
- Bananas
- Soybeans
- Dried beans
- Sugar cane
- Rice

RESOURCES
- Gold
- Iron
- Diamonds
- Oil
- Hydroelectric power

ACTIVITIES
- Soccer

29

ARGENTINA AND CHILE

These two countries stretch across the southern part of South America. Between them lie the Andes mountains. Argentina's dramatic landscape includes the rugged hills of Patagonia, while Chile is a long, thin country with both desert and fertile farmland.

Argentine tango
This Latin American style of dance originated in Buenos Aires. Dancers hold one another close and walk together in time to the music, with one partner taking the lead.

Tango dancers

Highest vineyard
The highest vineyard in the world lies at 10,200 ft (3,111 m) in the Calchaqui Valley in northern Argentina.

Maned wolves look like a small wolf or a large red fox, but are a different species, unique to the grasslands of South America

This mine is one of the largest open-cast (surface) copper mines in the world

Atacama Desert
The Atacama Desert is one of the driest places on Earth. This strip of land between the Pacific Ocean and the Andes mountains receives little rainfall, because the mountains block the rain.

One of the world's most powerful observatories, which captures images of objects in outer space, is based in the Atacama Desert

Salt lakes and other deposits formed in the Atacama Desert when lakes dried out

The snowy slopes of the Andes are perfect for skiing

Fertile land
The land of Central Chile is rich and fertile. Here, fruits, such as juicy peaches, are grown in orchards. Grapes also flourish, and Chilean wine is exported all over the world

Tall species of flowering grass grow in the lowland grasslands of the Pampas

The successful Argentinian soccer team has a big rivalry with neighboring Brazil

Rodeo is Chile's national sport—pairs of riders known as "Huasos" work together to read up cattle

Pampas grass

Soccer

Maned wolf

San Miguel de Tucumán

Salta

Chiquicamata copper mine

ALMA space observatory

Salt lakes

Antofagasta

Córdoba

Mendoza

Santiago

Valparaíso

Huaso rodeo

Skiing

Aconcagua

PERU

BOLIVIA

PARAGUAY

URUGUA

BRAZIL

ARGENTINA

CHILE

ATACAMA DESERT

PACIFIC OCEAN

Bermejo

Loa

Paraná

Maipo

This museum in Buenos Aires features many spectacular art exhibits

Buenos Aires

Río de la Plata

MALBA Museum of Modern Art

Polo

Polo players compete in teams on horseback to score goals against each other by hitting a ball with a mallet.

This large, flightless bird hunts for reptiles and insects in the grasslands.

Rhea

Beef steak and sauce

Argentina is well known for producing top-quality beef. Chimichurri sauce, made from fresh herbs, garlic, and olive oil, is often served with steak.

ATLANTIC OCEAN

Welsh people settled in the remote region of Patagonia in the 1800s. They speak their own special dialect of Welsh.

Patagonian Welsh

Hola!
Hello

Lake Argentino

Ice flows into Lake Argentino from the Perito Moreno Glacier

This is one of seven species of penguin that live in South America

Perito Moreno Glacier

Magellanic penguins

Punta Arenas

Talcahuano

Bío Bío

KEY

PRODUCE
Vineyards
Onions
Corn
Beef cattle
Sunflowers
Peaches
Soybeans
Sheep
Apples and pears
Wheat

INDUSTRY
Hydroelectric power
Copper
Lumber
Zinc
Lead
Iron
Fishing
Oil
Tin

NATURAL FEATURES
Volcanoes
Earthquakes

Gaucho herding cattle

Cattle herding

Beef cattle is an important industry on the flat, treeless plains of the Pampas. Argentine cowboys, known as "gauchos," herd the cattle on huge ranches.

SCALE

0   200 miles

0   200 kilometers

Stone heads

Easter Island

This Chilean island lies in the Pacific Ocean, 2,290 miles (3,686 km) west of the mainland. It is known for its huge stone statues, called moai, that were carved by local people hundreds of years ago.

Alpacas

Alpacas are kept in herds high in the mountains of northern Chile. Their thick hair can be woven to make blankets, hats, and sweaters.

POPULATION

The number of people living in the world is growing fast. In 1800, the world's population was about 1 billion. Today, there are more than 7.3 billion people worldwide. More than half of these people live in cities, rather than in the countryside. The population is growing because of healthier eating and better health care, which means that people are living longer.

Emptiest country

The emptiest country in the world is Mongolia, with an average of about five people for every square mile of land (about two people per square kilometer).

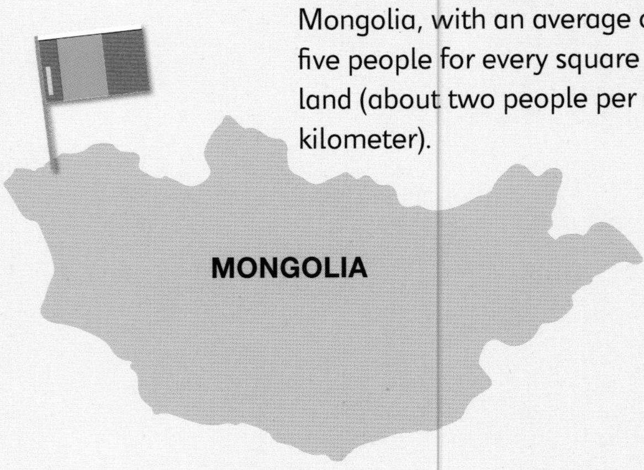

MONGOLIA

Most populated countries

These five countries have the biggest populations in the world. They are all large countries with plenty of farmland for growing crops to feed people.

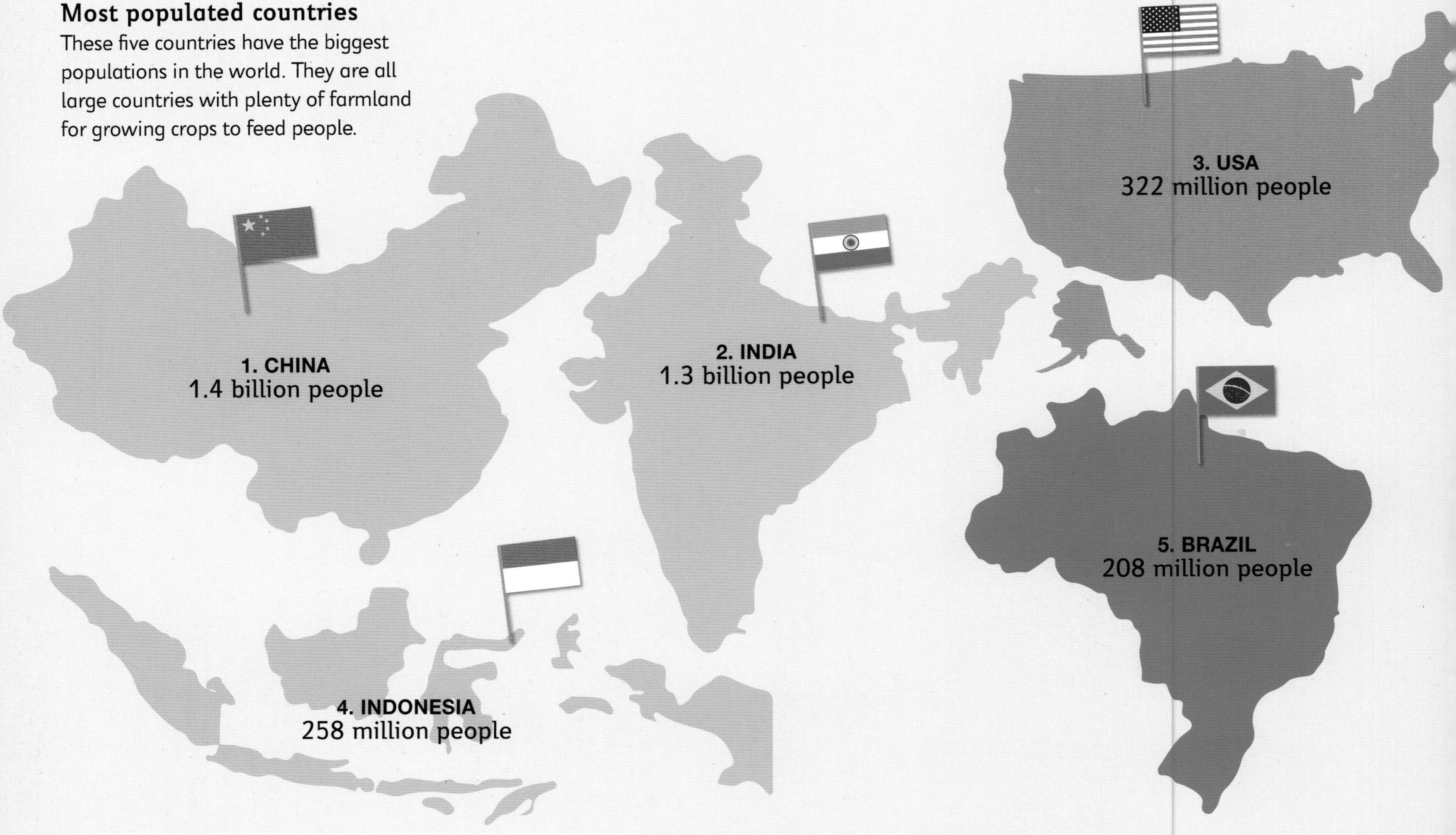

1. CHINA
1.4 billion people

2. INDIA
1.3 billion people

3. USA
322 million people

5. BRAZIL
208 million people

4. INDONESIA
258 million people

Who lives where?

This chart shows the percentage of the world's population in each continent. Asia is by far the world's most populated continent.

ASIA
60%

Most populated cities

The biggest city in most countries is usually, but not always, its capital city. A huge, sprawling city is also known as a metropolis. This chart shows the most populated city in each continent.

The Greater Tokyo area has nearly the same population as the whole of Canada!

Tokyo, Japan, Asia
38 million people

Mexico City, Mexico, North America
21 million people

São Paulo, Brazil, South America
21 million people

Cairo, Egypt, Africa
19 million people

Moscow, Russia, Europe
12 million people

Sydney, Australia, Australasia
5 million people

City versus countryside

In many parts of the world, cities are growing fast. People are moving, or migrating, from rural areas (the countryside) into towns and cities. Worldwide, about 54 percent of people live in cities and about 46 percent live in the countryside.

City 48% / Country 52%
ASIA

Country 29% / City 71%
AUSTRALASIA

City 40% / Country 60%
AFRICA

Country 17% / City 83%
SOUTH AMERICA

Country 20% / City 80%
NORTH AMERICA

Country 26% / City 74%
EUROPE

LARGEST CHILD POPULATION

India is the country with the most children. It has about 450 million children. This is about 40 percent of India's population.

AFRICA 16%

NORTH AMERICA 8%

AUSTRALASIA 1%

EUROPE 10%

SOUTH AMERICA 5%

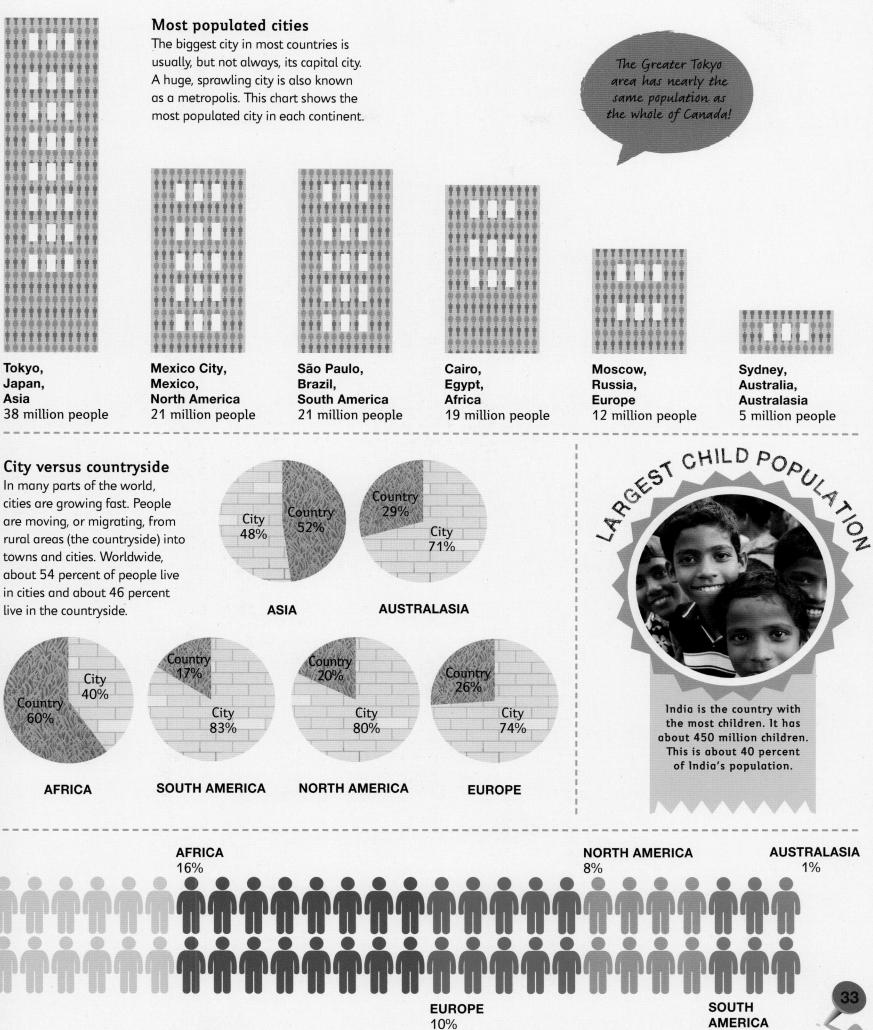

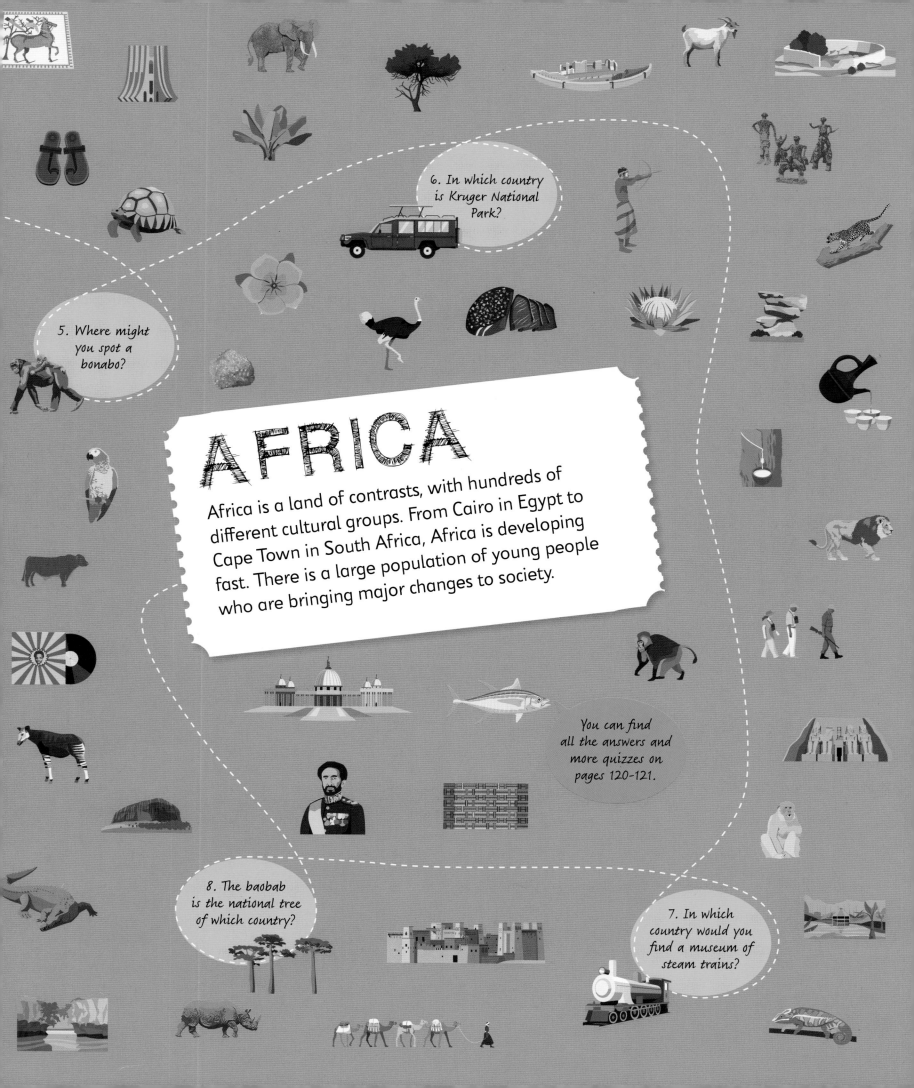

AFRICA

Africa is a land of contrasts, with hundreds of different cultural groups. From Cairo in Egypt to Cape Town in South Africa, Africa is developing fast. There is a large population of young people who are bringing major changes to society.

5. Where might you spot a bonabo?

6. In which country is Kruger National Park?

7. In which country would you find a museum of steam trains?

8. The baobab is the national tree of which country?

You can find all the answers and more quizzes on pages 120-121.

AFRICA

Africa is the world's second largest continent. The dry countries bordering the Mediterranean Sea in the north are cut off from the rest of Africa by the Sahara Desert. South of the Sahara are grassy plains and tropical rain forests, where many unique wild animals live.

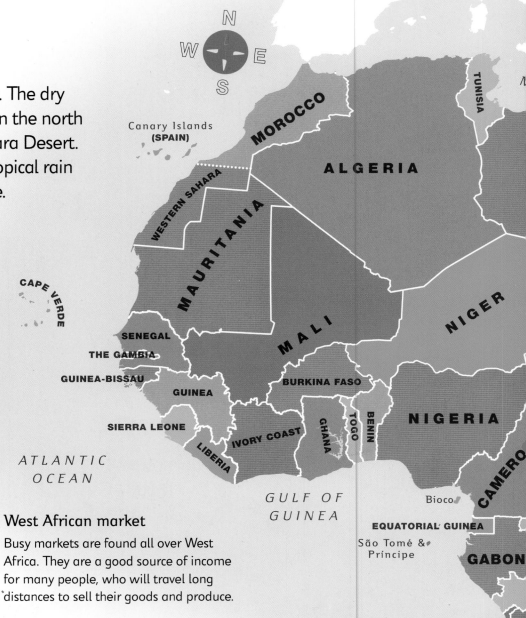

Canary Islands (SPAIN)

MOROCCO

TUNISIA

ALGERIA

WESTERN SAHARA

MAURITANIA

CAPE VERDE

NIGER

MALI

SENEGAL

THE GAMBIA

GUINEA-BISSAU

BURKINA FASO

GUINEA

NIGERIA

SIERRA LEONE

IVORY COAST

GHANA

TOGO

BENIN

LIBERIA

ATLANTIC OCEAN

GULF OF GUINEA

Bioco

EQUATORIAL GUINEA

São Tomé & Príncipe

CAMERO

GABON

West African market

Busy markets are found all over West Africa. They are a good source of income for many people, who will travel long distances to sell their goods and produce.

Sahara Desert

The Sahara is the world's largest hot desert. It stretches from Mauritania in the west to Sudan in the east. Camels are still used to carry goods across the sandy dunes.

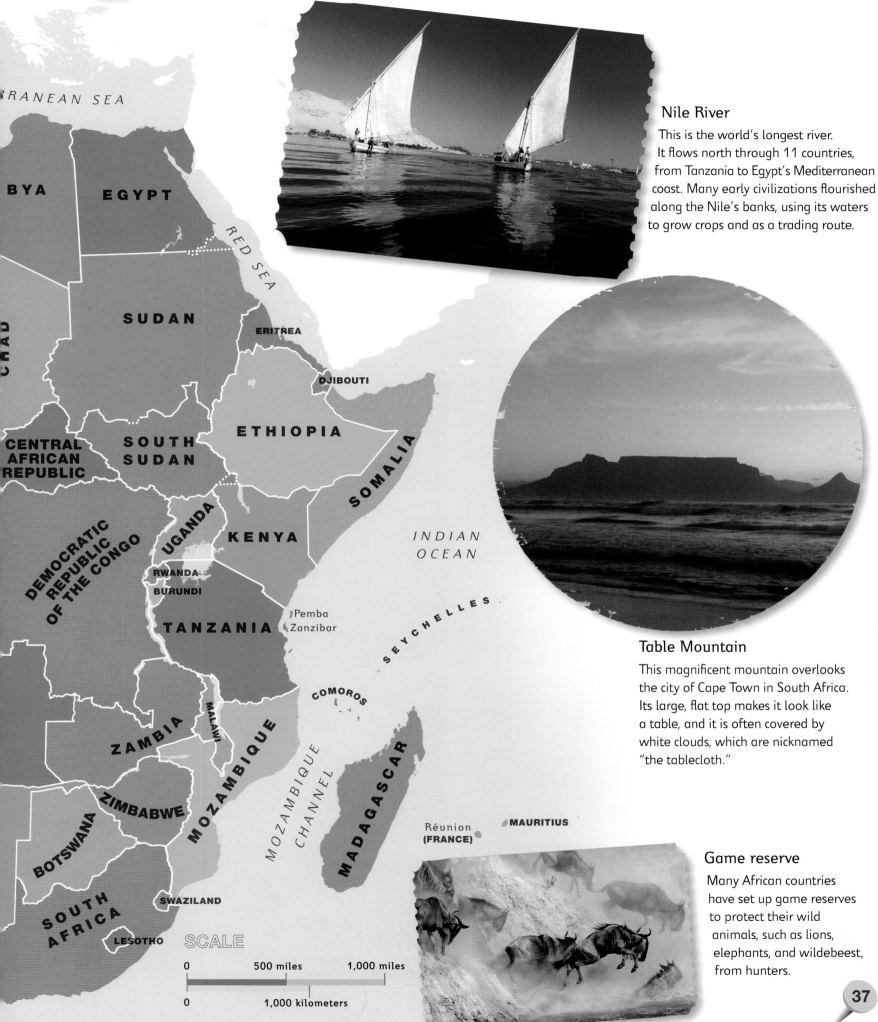

RRANEAN SEA

BYA

EGYPT

RED SEA

SUDAN

ERITREA

DJIBOUTI

ETHIOPIA

SOMALIA

CHAD

CENTRAL
AFRICAN
REPUBLIC

SOUTH
SUDAN

DEMOCRATIC
REPUBLIC
OF THE CONGO

UGANDA

KENYA

RWANDA

BURUNDI

TANZANIA

Pemba
Zanzibar

INDIAN
OCEAN

SEYCHELLES

ZAMBIA

MALAWI

COMOROS

ZIMBABWE

MOZAMBIQUE

MOZAMBIQUE
CHANNEL

MADAGASCAR

Réunion
(FRANCE)

MAURITIUS

BOTSWANA

SWAZILAND

SOUTH
AFRICA

LESOTHO

SCALE

| 0 | 500 miles | 1,000 miles |

| 0 | 1,000 kilometers |

Nile River

This is the world's longest river. It flows north through 11 countries, from Tanzania to Egypt's Mediterranean coast. Many early civilizations flourished along the Nile's banks, using its waters to grow crops and as a trading route.

Table Mountain

This magnificent mountain overlooks the city of Cape Town in South Africa. Its large, flat top makes it look like a table, and it is often covered by white clouds, which are nicknamed "the tablecloth."

Game reserve

Many African countries have set up game reserves to protect their wild animals, such as lions, elephants, and wildebeest, from hunters.

37

NORTH AFRICA

The four countries of Morocco, Algeria, Tunisia, and Libya sit side by side at the northern end of Africa. Towns and cities are dotted along the Mediterranean coast, where lively markets are found alongside ancient ruins. Vast areas of North Africa are sandy desert, with rich oil reserves in some places.

SPAIN

Tangier

Markets all over Morocco sell traditional leather goods

Rabat

Casablanca

Fès

Leather goods

Meknès

Marrakesh

Aït Benhaddou

ATLAS MOUNTAINS

Barbary macaque

Bechar

These monkeys mainly live in the Atlas Mountains

SCALE

0		200 miles
0		200 kilometers

ATLANTIC OCEAN

MOROCCO

This ancient fortified town is built from red clay

These small, venomous snakes live in the deserts of North Africa

Horned viper

Salam!
Hello

Laâyoune

Tindouf

Western Sahara

Medina
Many North African cities have ancient walled areas, with mazelike, narrow alleyways, called medinas. The Marrakesh medina contains Morocco's largest traditional market.

SAHARA DESERT

The Tuareg are a desert people, who traditionally wear blue robes

Hassan II Mosque
This huge mosque stands on the edge of the city of Casablanca in Morocco. More than 100,000 worshipers can gather here for prayer. Its 689-ft (210-m) minaret tower is the tallest in the world.

MALI

Tuareg blue robes

MAURITANIA

North African cuisine
Tagine, a type of stew usually made with lamb, is eaten in many parts of North Africa. Refreshing mint tea is the most popular drink.

Tagine

Mint tea

Mint leaves

Striped hyena
These hyenas are found throughout North Africa. They live in caves or dig dens, coming out to search for food at night.

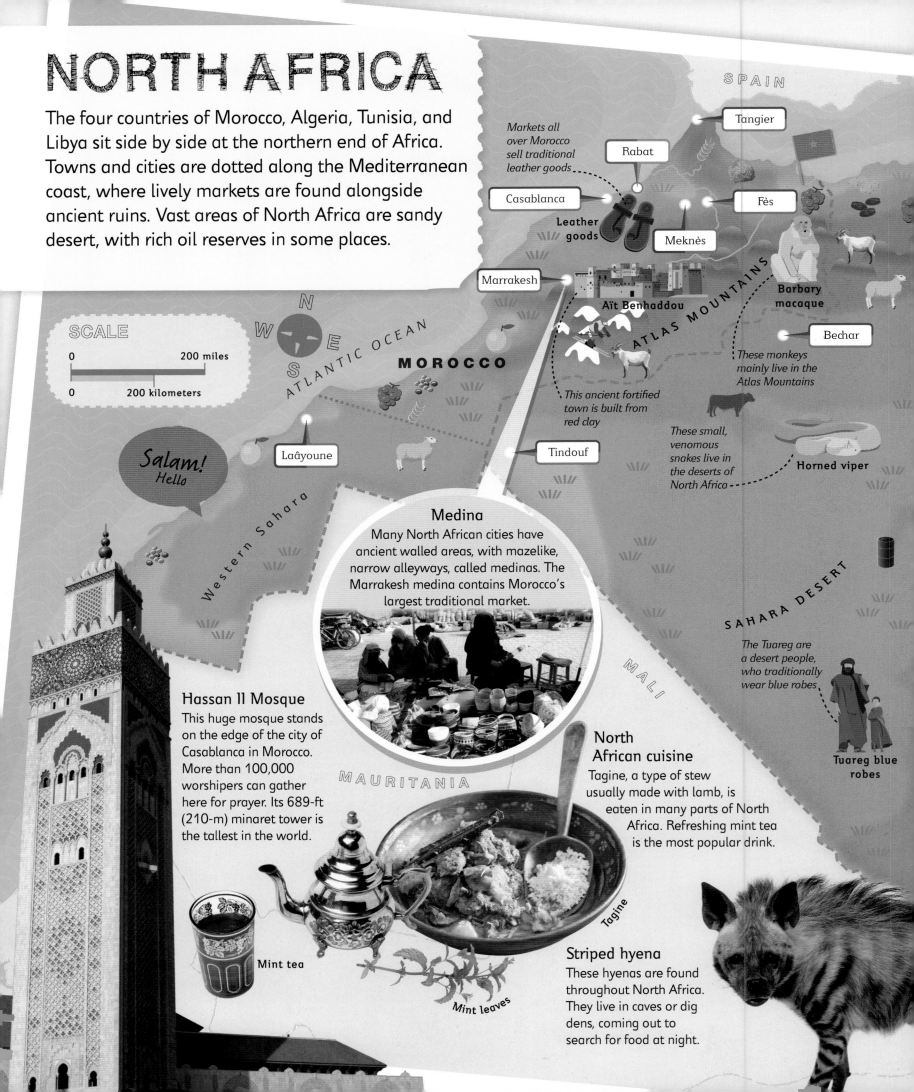

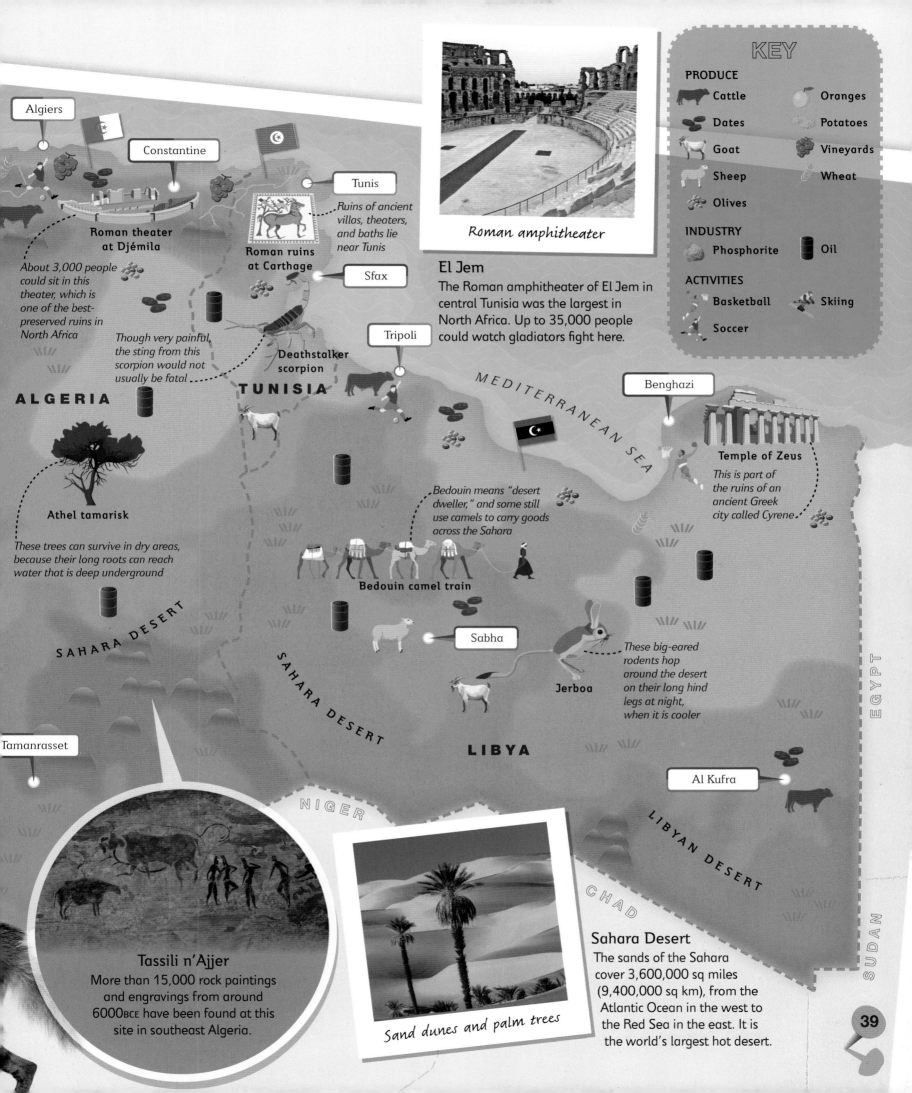

Algiers

Constantine

Tunis

Ruins of ancient villas, theaters, and baths lie near Tunis

Roman theater at Djémila

About 3,000 people could sit in this theater, which is one of the best-preserved ruins in North Africa

Roman ruins at Carthage

Sfax

Though very painful, the sting from this scorpion would not usually be fatal

Deathstalker scorpion

Tripoli

ALGERIA

TUNISIA

KEY

PRODUCE
- Cattle
- Dates
- Goat
- Sheep
- Olives
- Oranges
- Potatoes
- Vineyards
- Wheat

INDUSTRY
- Phosphorite
- Oil

ACTIVITIES
- Basketball
- Soccer
- Skiing

Roman amphitheater

El Jem
The Roman amphitheater of El Jem in central Tunisia was the largest in North Africa. Up to 35,000 people could watch gladiators fight here.

Benghazi

Temple of Zeus

This is part of the ruins of an ancient Greek city called Cyrene.

Athel tamarisk

These trees can survive in dry areas, because their long roots can reach water that is deep underground

Bedouin means "desert dweller," and some still use camels to carry goods across the Sahara

Bedouin camel train

MEDITERRANEAN SEA

SAHARA DESERT

SAHARA DESERT

Sabha

Tamanrasset

LIBYA

Jerboa

These big-eared rodents hop around the desert on their long hind legs at night, when it is cooler

EGYPT

Al Kufra

NIGER

LIBYAN DESERT

CHAD

SUDAN

Tassili n'Ajjer
More than 15,000 rock paintings and engravings from around 6000BCE have been found at this site in southeast Algeria.

Sand dunes and palm trees

Sahara Desert
The sands of the Sahara cover 3,600,000 sq miles (9,400,000 sq km), from the Atlantic Ocean in the west to the Red Sea in the east. It is the world's largest hot desert.

EGYPT

Much of Egypt is made up of dry, sandy desert, and so most people live along the banks of the Nile River. This river, the longest in the world, is a vital source of water for drinking and farming. Thousands of years ago, pharaohs (kings) built pyramids along the Nile, some of which are still standing.

Mummy case
Ancient Egyptians preserved, or mummified, bodies. The specially treated body was wrapped in bandages and the mummy was then placed in a decorated case.

KEY

PRODUCE	INDUSTRY
Rice	Oil
Wheat	Fishing
Oranges	**ACTIVITIES**
Dates	Scuba diving
Cotton	**NATURAL FEATURES**
	Coral reef

Pyramids
These massive structures were built as tombs for the bodies of dead pharaohs and their queens. The three most famous pyramids are at Giza.

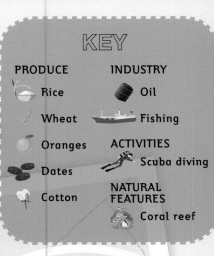

SCALE

0   100 miles   200 miles

0   200 kilometers

MEDITERRANEAN SEA

Port Said

This huge sandstone statue has a lion's body and a human head

Alexandria

Suez

Cairo

Great Sphinx

Giza

SINAI PENINSULA

GULF OF SUEZ

EASTERN DESERT

WESTERN DESERT

LIBYA

Large crocodiles live in the Nile, eating all kinds of animals, from fish to cattle

Nile crocodile

EGYPT

RED SEA

SAUDI ARABIA

Rescued ruins
When the Aswan Dam was built, it created a large reservoir called Lake Nasser. Two ancient temples had to be moved from the area that was flooded.

Some pharaohs were buried in tombs in the Valley of the Kings near Luxor

Valley of the Kings

Nile

Luxor

Salam!
Hello

This snake is one of the most venomous in Africa. One bite can kill a human in minutes

These two huge temples were important places of worship in Ancient Egypt

Feluccas are traditional wooden sailing boats, still used along the Nile

Aswan Dam

This dam opened in 1970; it generates hydroelectricity and controls flood water

Lake Nasser

Cotton tunic

Egyptian cobra

Great Temples at Abu Simbel

Felucca

SUDAN

Cotton
Cool and comfortable cotton tunics are a common form of dress in this hot country. Egyptian cotton is known for its high quality.

Camels
Camels are still used for transportation in Egypt because they can survive in very dry conditions, and so can travel long distances across the desert.

Yellowfin tuna
Huge yellowfin tuna swim in the Indian Ocean, off the coast of Kenya. Large numbers are caught and exported to markets all over the world.

Yellowfin tuna

Church of St. George
This important place of pilgrimage for the Ethiopian Orthodox Christian Church was carved out of solid rock.

ERITREA

SUDAN

These baboons are only found in the Ethiopian Highlands

Mek'ele

Lake Tana

Bahir Dar

Blue Nile

Gelada

ETHIOPIAN HIGHLANDS

Awash

Lalibela

YEMEN

DJIBOUTI

Ethiopian food
Ethiopians eat lots of enjera. This spongy bread is an important part of most meals and is used, instead of a spoon or fork, to scoop up food.

SOUTH SUDAN

Addis Ababa

ETHIOPIA

Dire Dawa

Omo

GREAT RIFT VALLEY

Salam! Hello

Enjera

SCALE
0   100 miles   200 miles

0   200 kilometers

Hawassa

Coffee culture

In Ethiopia, strong, dark coffee is made and served in a special ceremony

Shebelle

SOMALIA

UGANDA

Huge flocks of pink flamingos gather to feed in Kenya's lakes

Lake Turkana

Lesser flamingo

Lion

Groups of these big cats roam the plains of Kenya

Many of the world's best long-distance runners are from Kenya

The Maasai
The Maasai people live in southern Kenya and northern Tanzania. Their warriors perform traditional dances.

KENYA

Roses and other flowers grown in Kenya are exported for sale in Europe

Roses

Nakuru

Lake Victoria

Long-distance runner

Tana

Giraffes enjoy munching the leaves of this thorny tree

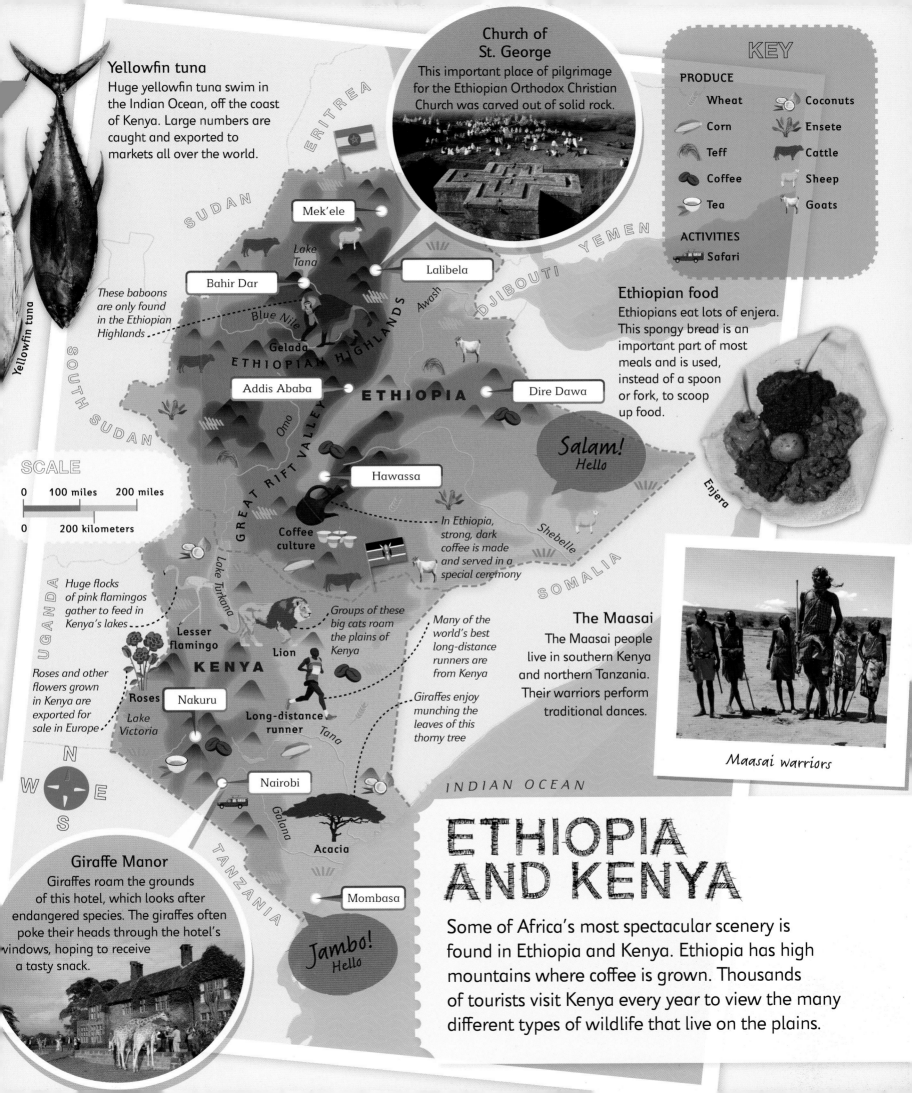

Maasai warriors

N W E S

Nairobi

Galana

Acacia

INDIAN OCEAN

TANZANIA

Mombasa

Jambo! Hello

Giraffe Manor
Giraffes roam the grounds of this hotel, which looks after endangered species. The giraffes often poke their heads through the hotel's windows, hoping to receive a tasty snack.

ETHIOPIA AND KENYA

Some of Africa's most spectacular scenery is found in Ethiopia and Kenya. Ethiopia has high mountains where coffee is grown. Thousands of tourists visit Kenya every year to view the many different types of wildlife that live on the plains.

NIGERIA

About 175 million people live in Nigeria, more than in any other African country. Many different tribal groups live here, each with its own colorful traditions, handicrafts, and music. Nigeria is also Africa's largest producer of oil, and has several oil rigs in the Gulf of Guinea.

Tribal traditions

The Yoruba are one of Nigeria's largest tribal groups. Their traditional dress includes brightly patterned fabrics and beautiful, finely carved ivory bracelets.

Ivory bracelet

Yoruba cloth

KEY

PRODUCE
- Cocoa
- Rubber
- Palm oil
- Peanuts
- Yams
- Cotton
- Cattle
- Goats

INDUSTRY
- Oil
- Hydroelectric power

NIGER

Hello!

CHAD

Sokoto

Sokoto

Hadejia

Kano

Maiduguri

This huge rock rises 2,379 ft (725 m) above the countryside to the north of the capital

Gongola

N I G E R I A

Lake Kainji

Kaduna

Jos

Zuma rock

Abuja

Sacred Yoruba statues stand among the trees in this area of thick jungle

Falling 492 ft (150 m), Farin Ruwa is one of the highest waterfalls in Nigeria

Benue

Niger

BENIN

Ogbomosho

Osun-Osogbo Sacred Grove

Ibadan

Farin Ruwa waterfall

SHEBSHI MOUNTAINS

Wooden mask

GOTEL MOUNTAINS

Ritual masks

Wooden masks are traditionally worn in parts of Nigeria to ward off evil spirits.

Afrobeat

Benin bronzes

Benin City

Afrobeat music combines jazz with chanting and drumming

Lagos

More than 1,000 bronze plaques once decorated the Royal Palace of the kingdom of Benin

CAMEROON

Aba

Pepper sauce

Street food

Nigerian street food includes some spicy dishes. Jollof rice contains chili, and suya is strips of barbequed meat on a stick with different spices in the seasoning.

GULF OF GUINEA

SCALE

0	100 miles	200 miles

0	200 kilometers

Port Harcourt

N W E S

Jollof rice

Suya

42

GHANA AND THE IVORY COAST

Ghana was once known as the Gold Coast because of its plentiful gold; the Ivory Coast used to be a center for the trade in ivory (elephant tusks). Today, both countries grow cocoa beans, which are used to make some of the world's finest chocolate.

Plantain and okra

West Africa has lots of fertile farming land. Plantains, a type of banana used in cooking, are grown. Another common crop is okra. This is a long, thin vegetable that is often known as "ladies' fingers."

Plantain

Okra

KEY

PRODUCE

Coffee		Corn	
Cocoa		Coconuts	
Bananas		Yams	
Pineapples		Cassavas	
Rubber		Cattle	
Palm oil		Goats	
Rice			

INDUSTRY

Iron		Oil	
Gold		Natural gas	
Bauxite		Diamonds	

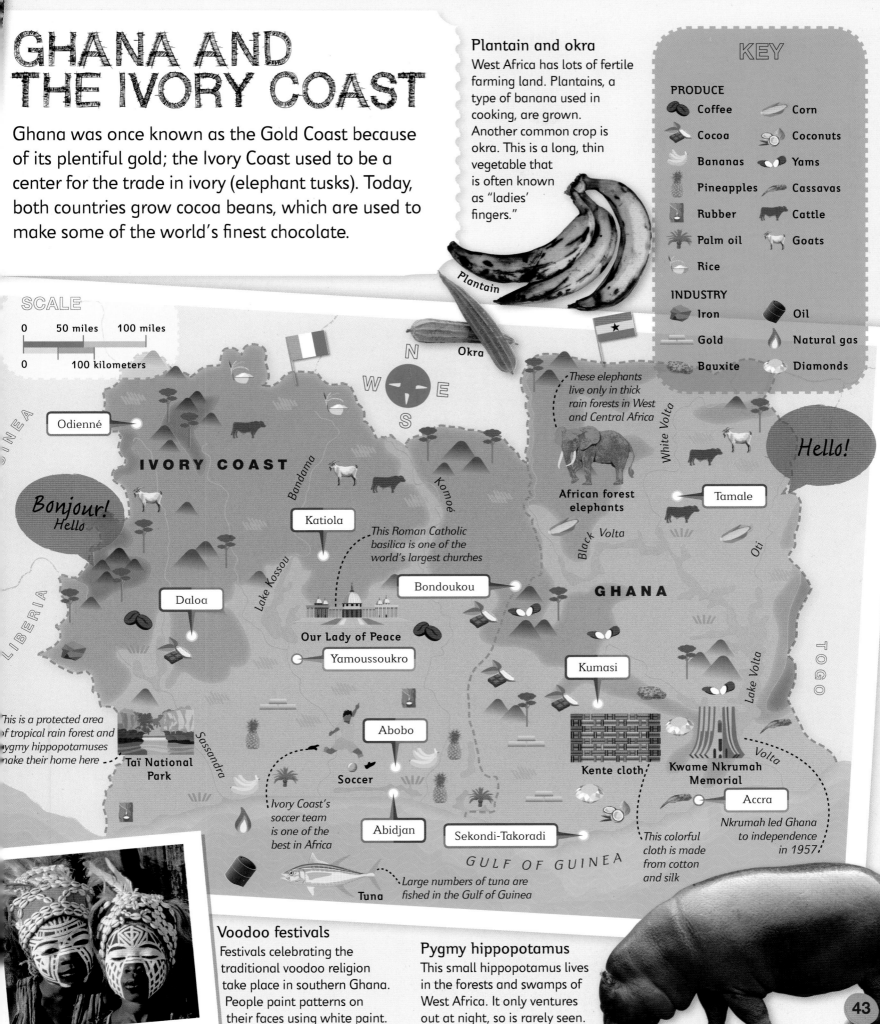

GUINEA

Odienné

IVORY COAST

Bonjour!
Hello

Bandama

Katiola

Lake Kossou

LIBERIA

Daloa

Sassandra

Our Lady of Peace

Yamoussoukro

This Roman Catholic basilica is one of the world's largest churches

Komoé

GHANA

These elephants live only in thick rain forests in West and Central Africa

African forest elephants

White Volta

Black Volta

Tamale

Hello!

Oti

Bondoukou

Kumasi

Lake Volta

TOGO

This is a protected area of tropical rain forest and pygmy hippopotamuses make their home here

Taï National Park

Abobo

Soccer

Ivory Coast's soccer team is one of the best in Africa

Abidjan

Sekondi-Takoradi

GULF OF GUINEA

Tuna

Large numbers of tuna are fished in the Gulf of Guinea

Kente cloth

This colorful cloth is made from cotton and silk

Kwame Nkrumah Memorial

Volta

Accra

Nkrumah led Ghana to independence in 1957

Voodoo festivals

Festivals celebrating the traditional voodoo religion take place in southern Ghana. People paint patterns on their faces using white paint.

Typical voodoo facepaint

Pygmy hippopotamus

This small hippopotamus lives in the forests and swamps of West Africa. It only ventures out at night, so is rarely seen.

43

PRODUCE
Oil palms   Cassavas
Corn   Rubber
Coffee   Rice

INDUSTRY
Copper   Cobalt
Tin   Diamonds

ACTIVITIES   **NATURAL FEATURES**
Soccer   Volcanoes

Virunga National Park

Africa's oldest national park was created in 1925, mainly to provide a safe home for mountain gorillas and other local wildlife. Years of war nearly destroyed the park, but it is now back in safe hands. Thousands of tourists visit the park every year.

Mountain gorillas

Sapeurs

The sapeurs are a group who like to wear finely tailored clothes. They live by a gentlemanly code of conduct, in keeping with their stylish dress.

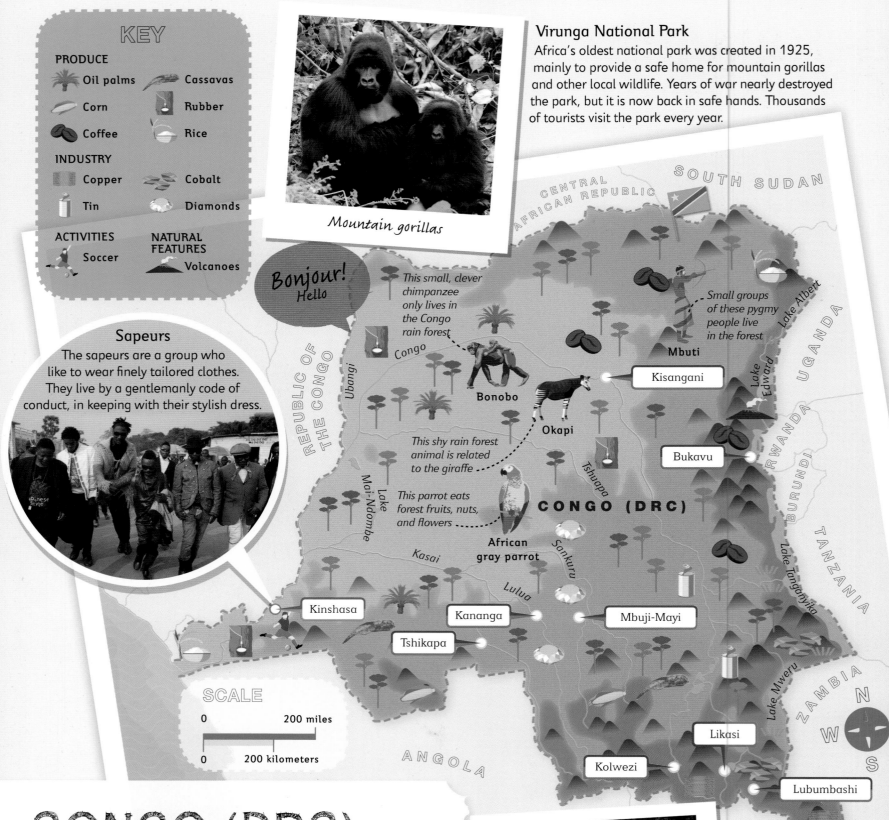

Bonjour! Hello

This small, clever chimpanzee only lives in the Congo rain forest

Small groups of these pygmy people live in the forest

Mbuti

Kisangani

Congo

Bonobo

Okapi

Bukavu

This shy rain forest animal is related to the giraffe

This parrot eats forest fruits, nuts, and flowers

Ubangi

Lake Albert

Lake Edward

Lake Kivu

RWANDA

UGANDA

BURUNDI

TANZANIA

CENTRAL AFRICAN REPUBLIC

SOUTH SUDAN

REPUBLIC OF THE CONGO

African gray parrot

CONGO (DRC)

Tshuapa

Lake Mai-Ndombe

Kasai

Sankuru

Lulua

Lake Tanganyika

Kinshasa

Kananga

Mbuji-Mayi

Tshikapa

Likasi

Lake Mweru

ZAMBIA

Kolwezi

Lubumbashi

ANGOLA

SCALE

0   200 miles

0   200 kilometers

N
W   E
S

CONGO (DRC)

The Democratic Republic of the Congo (DRC) is the largest African country south of the Sahara Desert. The world's deepest river, the Congo, runs all across the country, and some of Africa's Great Lakes lie on its eastern border. The Congo rain forest is the second largest in the world.

Cobalt mine

Mining

Many valuable minerals are mined in the Congo area, including cobalt. Cobalt has been used since ancient times to give a rich blue color to paints. It is also used in medicine, batteries, and electronic equipment.

ZAMBIA AND ZIMBABWE

Zambia and Zimbabwe are famous for their spectacular scenery and wildlife. Africa's fourth longest river, the Zambezi, flows down through Zambia, then curves along the border with Zimbabwe on its journey to the Indian Ocean.

Southern yellow-billed hornbill
This bird uses its huge beak to snatch up insects, spiders, and even scorpions from the ground. It sleeps in trees at night to avoid predators.

Nshima is a thick corn porridge that is served with vegetables or meat — Nshima

Guides take visitors on walking safaris to get closer to wildlife — Walking safari

Muli shani! Hello

Chingola

Ndola

ZAMBIA

Leopard

Leopards hunt at night and often carry their prey up into trees to eat

Kabwe

Lusaka

Mhoro! Hello

This museum has a large collection of old steam engines and carriages — Railway Museum

Livingstone

Victoria Falls

Harare

Chitungwiza

Natural rock formations like this are found in many parts of Zimbabwe

Gweru

Balancing Rocks

ZIMBABWE

These ruins are the remains of an ancient city

Bulawayo

This rhino is in danger of extinction in the wild

Great Zimbabwe

Black rhino

Victoria Falls
The world's largest waterfall is 354 ft (108 m) high and 5,604 ft (1,708 m) wide. The local name is Mosi-oa-Tunya ("the smoke that thunders").

Root vegetables
Cassavas and sweet potatoes are a main part of people's diet here. Cassava root may be cooked or made into flour that is used to make bread. Sweet potatoes are often boiled or roasted.

Cassava

Sweet potato

SCALE
0 — 200 miles
0 — 200 kilometers

KEY

PRODUCE
- Corn
- Cassavas
- Sweet potatoes
- Millet
- Peanuts
- Roses
- Soybeans
- Cotton

INDUSTRY
- Coal
- Chromium
- Copper
- Platinum
- Nickel
- Hydroelectric power

ACTIVITIES
- Soccer
- Cricket
- White-water rafting
- Safari

Lake Mweru · Lake Tanganyika · Lake Bangweulu · Luangwa · Zambezi · Kafue · Lake Kariba · Zambezi

CONGO (DRC) · TANZANIA · MALAWI · MOZAMBIQUE · ANGOLA · BOTSWANA

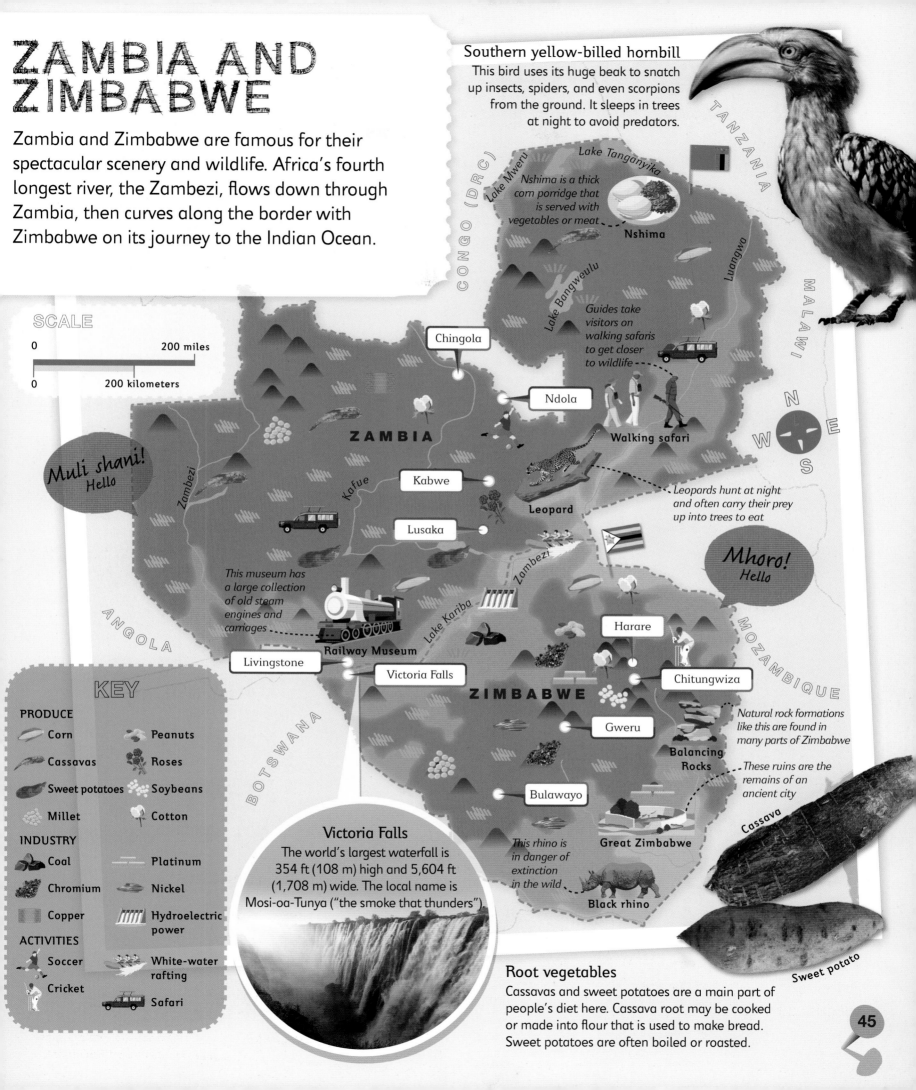

SOUTH AFRICA

South Africa is home to people from many different cultures, which is why it has 11 official languages. The landscape is equally varied, ranging from forests to deserts, and the 1,750-miles (2,800-km) coastline has many lovely beaches.

Blyde River Canyon
This is one of the world's biggest canyons. It is 16 miles (25 km) long and 2,500 ft (750 m) deep on average.

SCALE
0 — 100 miles
0 — 100 kilometers

Tourists go on safari by jeep in this large game reserve, hoping to see lions and elephants

Kruger National Park

Government and presidential offices are housed in this building

BOTSWANA

MOZAMBIQUE

KEY

PRODUCE
- Wheat
- Corn
- Vineyards
- Grapefruit
- Cattle
- Sheep

ACTIVITIES
- Rugby
- Soccer
- Hiking
- Mountain biking

INDUSTRY
- Gold
- Diamonds
- Chromium

Fossils of our human ancestors were found here

Union Building

Nelspruit

Pretoria

Slices of this spiced dried meat are a popular snack

Cradle of Humankind

Johannesburg

SWAZILAND

Herds of springbok, South Africa's national animal, live on the open plains

Biltong

Vaal

Tugela Falls

This is the world's second largest waterfall, with a total drop of 3,110 ft (948 m)

Springbok

Kimberley

Bloemfontein

LESOTHO

Durban

Orange

SOUTH AFRICA

DRAKENSBERG

Cricket
South Africa's national cricket team is one of the best in the world

Sardines
Millions of sardines are caught every year off the east coast of South Africa

Mthatha

ATLANTIC OCEAN

NAMIBIA

These large, flightless birds are bred for their meat and feathers

This type of shrubland is found only in the south

INDIAN OCEAN

This huge, flat-topped mountain overlooks the city of Cape Town

Fynbos

Ostrich

Table Mountain

Port Elizabeth

Cape Town

South African food
Food reflects the country's cultural mix. Popular dishes include bunny chow, a hollowed-out loaf filled with curry, and bobotie, minced beef with an egg topping.

Bunny chow

Bobotie

Zulus
The Zulus are the largest ethnic group in South Africa. They have a proud warrior heritage. Ritual dances are an important part of their culture.

Zulu dancer

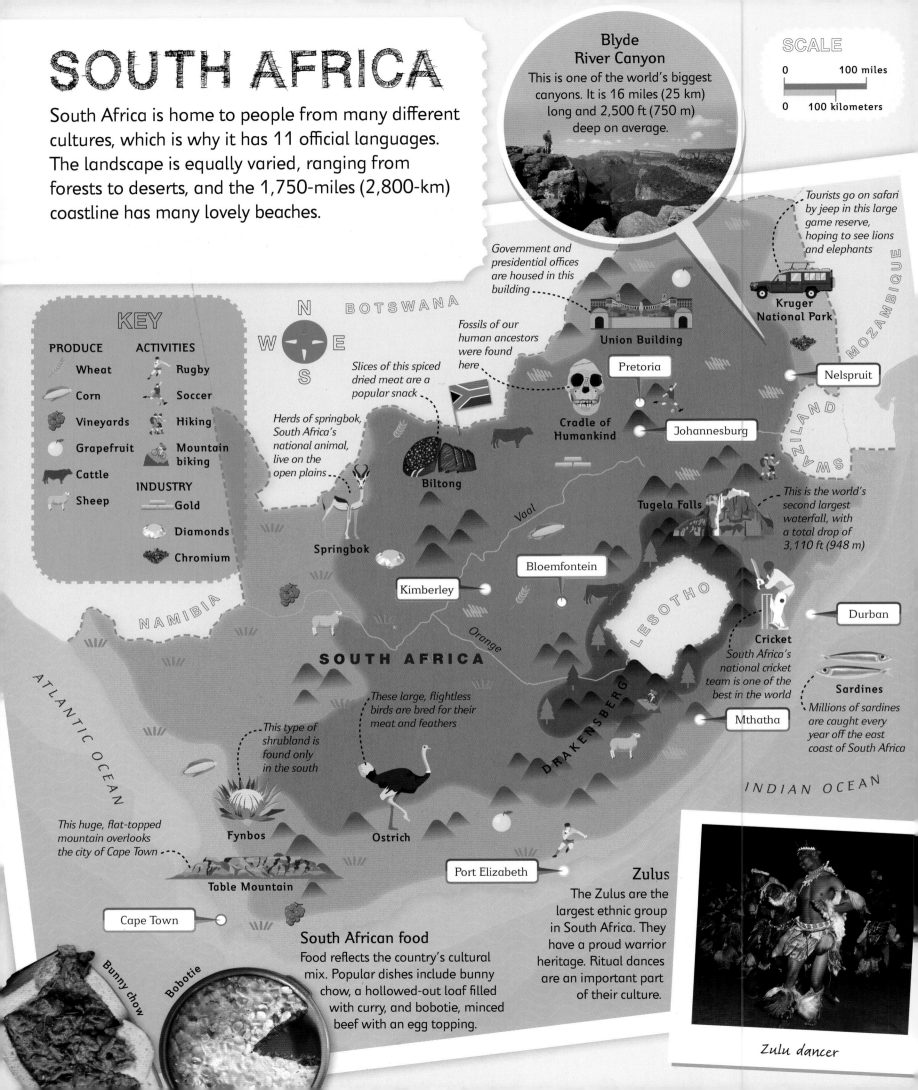

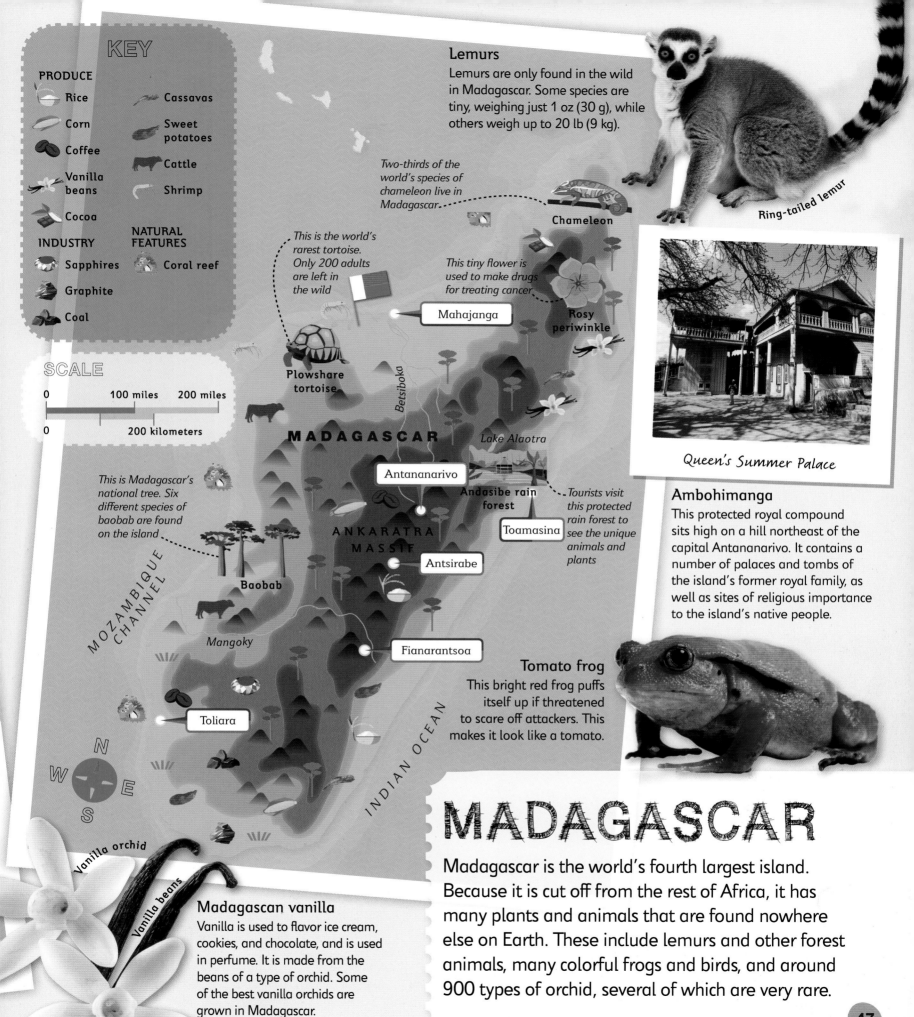

KEY

PRODUCE
- Rice
- Corn
- Coffee
- Vanilla beans
- Cocoa
- Cassavas
- Sweet potatoes
- Cattle
- Shrimp

INDUSTRY
- Sapphires
- Graphite
- Coal

NATURAL FEATURES
- Coral reef

SCALE

0   100 miles   200 miles

0   200 kilometers

Lemurs
Lemurs are only found in the wild in Madagascar. Some species are tiny, weighing just 1 oz (30 g), while others weigh up to 20 lb (9 kg).

Ring-tailed lemur

Two-thirds of the world's species of chameleon live in Madagascar

Chameleon

This is the world's rarest tortoise. Only 200 adults are left in the wild

This tiny flower is used to make drugs for treating cancer

Plowshare tortoise

Mahajanga

Rosy periwinkle

Betsiboka

MADAGASCAR

Lake Alaotra

This is Madagascar's national tree. Six different species of baobab are found on the island

Antananarivo

Andasibe rain forest

Tourists visit this protected rain forest to see the unique animals and plants

Toamasina

ANKARATRA MASSIF

Baobab

Antsirabe

MOZAMBIQUE CHANNEL

Mangoky

Fianarantsoa

Toliara

N
W   E
S

INDIAN OCEAN

Vanilla orchid

Vanilla beans

Madagascan vanilla
Vanilla is used to flavor ice cream, cookies, and chocolate, and is used in perfume. It is made from the beans of a type of orchid. Some of the best vanilla orchids are grown in Madagascar.

Queen's Summer Palace

Ambohimanga
This protected royal compound sits high on a hill northeast of the capital Antananarivo. It contains a number of palaces and tombs of the island's former royal family, as well as sites of religious importance to the island's native people.

Tomato frog
This bright red frog puffs itself up if threatened to scare off attackers. This makes it look like a tomato.

MADAGASCAR

Madagascar is the world's fourth largest island. Because it is cut off from the rest of Africa, it has many plants and animals that are found nowhere else on Earth. These include lemurs and other forest animals, many colorful frogs and birds, and around 900 types of orchid, several of which are very rare.

NATURAL WONDERS

The world is full of wonderful natural features that are part of the landscape around us. Across the world, there are lush green rain forests, colorful coral reefs, jagged mountains, smouldering volcanoes, and rushing waterfalls. While under the surface of the Earth there are dark caves, from tiny grottos to huge caverns.

Seven Natural Wonders

The Seven Natural Wonders of the World are a group of spectacular natural features. They are favorite sites for adventurous people to visit and explore.

1. NORTHERN LIGHTS

Near the Arctic Circle, amazing light effects known as the Northern Lights, or Aurora Borealis, can be seen in the night sky.

2. MOUNT EVEREST

The world's highest mountain is on the border of Nepal and China. The peak of Mount Everest is a dark pyramid shape.

4. VICTORIA FALLS

Between Zambia and Zimbabwe are the Victoria Falls. The waters of the Zambezi River thunder over these falls.

6. PARÍCUTIN VOLCANO

This volcano rose up and erupted in a farmer's cornfield in Mexico in 1943. Today, people can climb the dormant (inactive) volcano.

3. RIO DE JANEIRO HARBOR

Here, the Brazilian Highlands meet the Atlantic Ocean. Sugar Loaf Mountain marks the entrance of the bay.

5. GRAND CANYON

In Arizona, the Colorado River has formed the massive and majestic Grand Canyon. This is the largest canyon in the world.

7. GREAT BARRIER REEF

The world's largest coral reef is off the western coast of Australia. Thousands of types of fish and coral live here.

Deepest caves

Caves are underground spaces below the surface of the Earth. They form when water wears away some types of rock in the ground. This illustration shows some of the deepest caves in the world.

The longest cave is Mammoth Cave, Kentucky. It is 405 miles (651.8 km) long.

Réseau Jean Bernard, French Alps
5,256 ft (1,602 m)

Vogelshacht and Lamprechtsofen, Austria
5,354 ft (1,632 m)

Gouffre Mirolda, France
5,686 ft (1,733 m)

Illuzia-Snezhnaja-Mezhonnogo, Georgia
5,751 ft (1,753 m)

Krubera-Voronja Cave, Georgia
7,188 ft (2,191 m)

Highest waterfalls

Waterfalls are places where streams of water have a steep drop. They are formed when streams or rivers flow over different types of rock and softer rock is worn away. The five shown below are among the highest waterfalls in the world.

Angel Falls, Venezuela
3,212 ft (979 m)

Tugela Falls, South Africa
3,110 ft (948 m)

Browne Falls, New Zealand
2,743 ft (836 m)

Ramnefjellsfossen, Norway
2,684 ft (818 m)

Cataratas Gocta, Peru
2,530 ft (771 m)

Five largest deserts

Deserts are areas with very little rainfall. They are found in hot, dry regions of the world and also in cold, dry areas, such as around the North and South poles. This illustration shows the largest deserts in the world.

ANTARCTIC DESERT
5.7 million sq miles
(14.8 million sq km)

SAHARA DESERT
3.5 million sq miles
(9 million sq km)

ARABIAN DESERT
0.9 million sq miles
(2.3 million sq km)

KALAHARI DESERT
0.36 million sq miles
(0.9 million sq km)

GOBI DESERT
0.5 million sq miles
(1.3 million sq km)

49

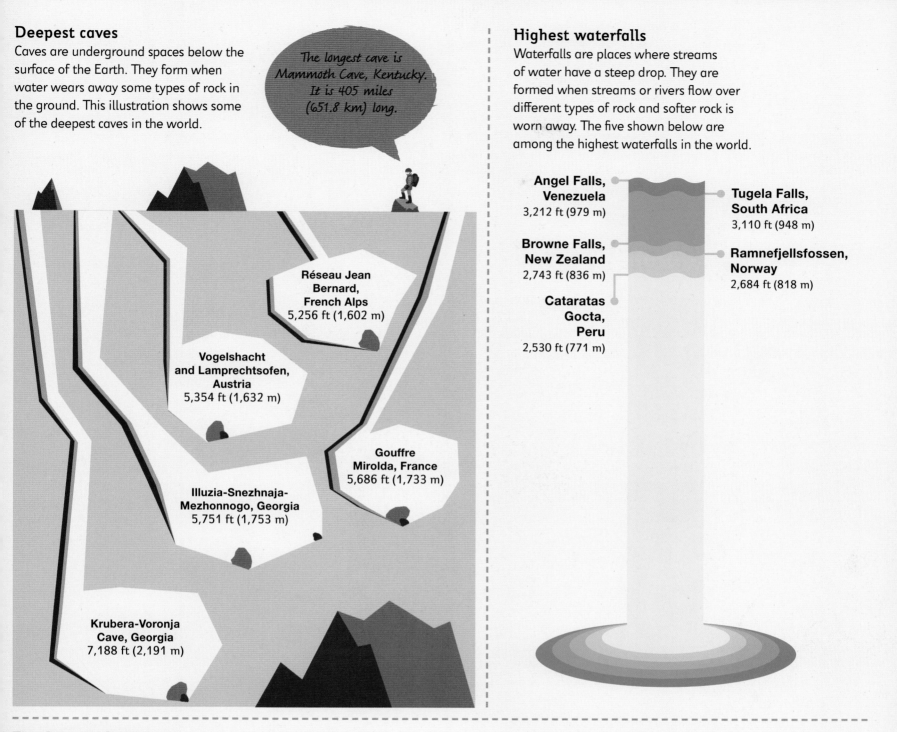

EUROPE

With many unique cultures and languages, Europe is a varied continent. It is the home of classical music, great literature, and fine art and architecture. It has medieval castles and cathedrals, as well as beautiful historic towns and cities.

8. Where would you find flamenco dancers?

7. Which river does this bridge go across?

5. Which country is the car maker Skoda based in?

6. Which country produces more than 400 kinds of cheese?

You can find all the answers and more quizzes on pages 120-121.

EUROPE

The landscape of Europe is very varied. It includes dense forests, high mountain ranges, broad plains, remote islands, and sun-soaked beaches. The continent is home to many fine historic buildings. Countries range in size from tiny Liechtenstein to Russia, the biggest country in the world.

Northern European forest

The pine forests of Nordic countries such as Norway, Sweden, and Finland are an important source of lumber.

ICELAND

ATLANTIC OCEAN

Paris

Paris, the capital of France, is an elegant city that mixes old and new styles of architecture effortlessly. At its center is the Eiffel Tower, one of the most famous structures on Earth.

Mediterranean Sea

The countries that surround the warm waters of the Mediterranean Sea enjoy hot, dry summers and mild winters. Thousands of visitors are drawn to their sunny beaches every year.

Faroe Islands

Shetland Islands

NORWEGIAN SEA

NORWAY

NORTH SEA

DENMARK

IRELAND

Isle of Man

UNITED KINGDOM

Channel Islands

NETHERLANDS

BELGIUM

LUXEMBOURG

GERMANY

CZECH REPUBLIC

LIECHTENSTEIN

SWITZERLAND

AUST

SLOVE

BAY OF BISCAY

FRANCE

Azores

PORTUGAL

SPAIN

ANDORRA

SAN MARINO

MONACO

ADRIATIC

CR

ITALY

Corsica

Majorca

Minorca

Ibiza

Sardinia

VATICAN CITY

Balearic Islands

Gibraltar

TYRRHENIAN SEA

Madeira

MEDITERRANEAN SEA

Sicily

Born

0   250 miles   500 miles

0   500 kilometers

FINLAND

GULF OF BOTHNIA

Gotland

BALTIC SEA

ESTONIA

LATVIA

LITHUANIA

RUSSIA
(KALININGRAD)

BELARUS

POLAND

OVAKIA

UNGARY

MOLDOVA

UKRAINE

RUSSIA
(European Russia)

Crimea

ROMANIA

SERBIA

EGRO

KOSOVO
(DISPUTED)

ALBANIA

MACEDONIA

BULGARIA

TURKEY

BLACK SEA

AEGEAN
SEA

GREECE

IONIAN
SEA

Crete

CASPIAN SEA

The Alps
This mountain range stretches 750 miles
(1,200 km) across the heart of Europe,
through France, Monaco, Italy, Germany,
Austria, Switzerland, Liechtenstein, and
Slovenia. The highest peak is Mont Blanc,
at 15,781 ft (4,810 m).

St. Basil's Cathedral
This spectacular building dominates
Red Square in Moscow. It was built
in the 16th century and is famous
for its unique, brightly colored,
onion-shaped domes. It has
been a museum since 1928.

NORTHERN EUROPE

The northern European countries have fairly small populations, with most people living in towns and cities. There are also large areas of unspoiled countryside. Summers are generally warm, but winters are very cold, with limited daylight in the far north.

ICELAND

Arctic fox
This fox grows a white coat in winter to blend into the snow.

Blue Lagoon
The warm waters of this spa are one of Iceland's top tourist attractions.

Reykjavik

Halló!
Hello

Eyjafjallajökull
This huge volcano in Iceland is covered by an ice cap. It erupted in 2010, producing a vast ash cloud that disrupted air travel across Europe.

Sami in traditional dress

Lapland
This large, snowy region in the far north of Norway, Sweden, and Finland is home to the Sami people. Some keep reindeer and ride around in sleighs.

Elk
The elk is the largest type of deer in the world and lives in northern forests.

Alstom Pendolino
This fast train tilts when it goes around corners.

Oulu

Lynx
This wild cat lives in forests, where it hunts deer and other animals.

Kiruna

Abisko National Park
This park contains Trollsjön lake, the clearest lake in Sweden.

Wolverine
This strong, ferocious animal can kill prey as big as deer.

Tromsø

EV plug-in electric car
These cars are very popular in Norway. They are plugged in to be recharged.

NORWEGIAN SEA

Norway's fjords
Norway's coast is lined with hundreds of narrow inlets, called fjords, with steep cliffs on each side. The cliffs of Pulpit Rock rise a spectacular 1,982 ft (604 m) above the waters of Lysefjord.

Pulpit Rock overlooking Lysefjord

Rollmop
These snacks are made from pickled herring fish fillets rolled into a cylinder shape around a tasty filling, such as olives and pickled gherkins.

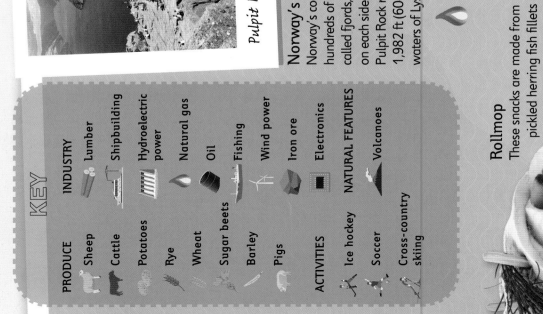

SCALE
0 — 100 miles
0 — 100 kilometers

KEY

PRODUCE
- Sheep
- Cattle
- Potatoes
- Rye
- Wheat
- Sugar beets
- Barley
- Pigs

ACTIVITIES
- Ice hockey
- Soccer
- Cross-country skiing

INDUSTRY
- Lumber
- Shipbuilding
- Hydroelectric power
- Natural gas
- Oil
- Fishing
- Wind power
- Iron ore
- Electronics

NATURAL FEATURES
- Volcanoes

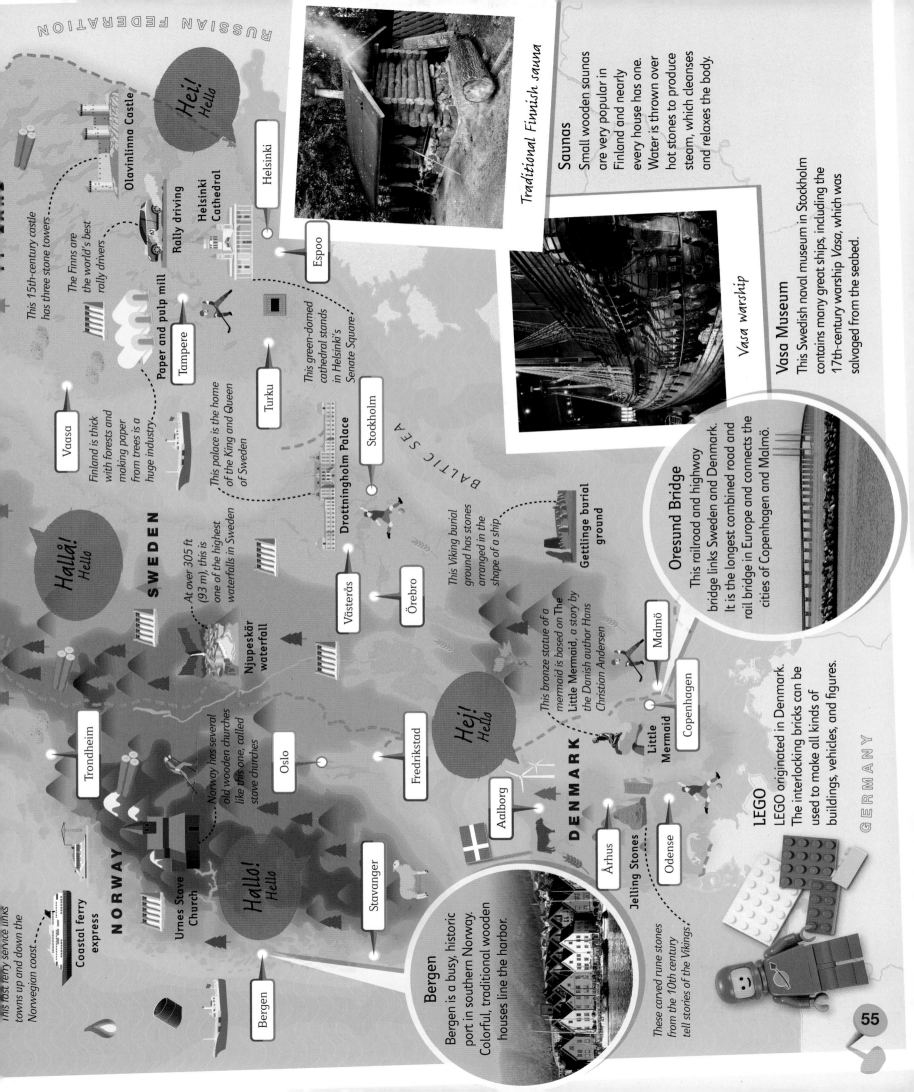

RUSSIAN FEDERATION

Hei! Hello

Olavinlinna Castle
This 15th-century castle has three stone towers

Rally driving
The Finns are the world's best rally drivers

Helsinki Cathedral
This green-domed cathedral stands in Helsinki's Senate Square

Helsinki

Espoo

Paper and pulp mill
Finland is thick with forests and making paper from trees is a huge industry.

Tampere

Vaasa

Turku

Saunas
Small wooden saunas are very popular in Finland and nearly every house has one. Water is thrown over hot stones to produce steam, which cleanses and relaxes the body.

Traditional Finnish sauna

Vasa Museum
This Swedish naval museum in Stockholm contains many great ships, including the 17th-century warship *Vasa*, which was salvaged from the seabed.

Vasa warship

Drottningholm Palace
This palace is the home of the King and Queen of Sweden

Stockholm

BALTIC SEA

Hallå! Hello

SWEDEN

Njupeskär waterfall
At over 305 ft (93 m), this is one of the highest waterfalls in Sweden

Västerås

Örebro

Gettlinge burial ground
This Viking burial ground has stones arranged in the shape of a ship

Oresund Bridge
This railroad and highway bridge links Sweden and Denmark. It is the longest combined road and rail bridge in Europe and connects the cities of Copenhagen and Malmö.

Malmö

Copenhagen

Little Mermaid
This bronze statue of a mermaid is based on The Little Mermaid, a story by the Danish author Hans Christian Andersen

Hej! Hello

Trondheim

Hallå! Hello

Oslo

Fredrikstad

NORWAY

Urnes Stave Church
Norway has several old wooden churches like this one, called stave churches

Coastal ferry express
This fast ferry service links towns up and down the Norwegian coast

Hallo! Hello

Stavanger

Bergen
Bergen is a busy, historic port in southern Norway. Colorful, traditional wooden houses line the harbor.

Bergen

DENMARK

Aalborg

Århus

Odense

Jelling Stones
These carved rune stones from the 10th century tell stories of the Vikings.

LEGO
LEGO originated in Denmark. The interlocking bricks can be used to make all kinds of buildings, vehicles, and figures.

GERMANY

55

BRITISH ISLES

The British Isles is a group of islands off the northwest coast of Europe. They consist of the United Kingdom, or UK (England, Scotland, Wales, and Northern Ireland), and Ireland. These islands are rich in history and tradition. The weather is influenced by the sea and it often rains. Ireland is known as the "Emerald Isle," because the rain makes it so green.

Scottish traditions

For special occasions, some Scots wear woollen kilts, woven from different colored threads to form a pattern called tartan. Different clans (groups) have their own design of tartan. Some Scots also play the bagpipes, a type of wind instrument.

Traditional Scottish dress

Food and drink

Fried fish and chips are a popular meal, especially by the coast. Tea is widely drunk, usually with milk and sometimes sugar.

Fish and chips

Tea

William Shakespeare

English playwright

William Shakespeare was one of the world's greatest writers. Born in Stratford-upon-Avon, England, in 1564, he wrote many poems and plays that are still performed today.

KEY

PRODUCE
- Wheat
- Fruit
- Potatoes
- Sheep
- Shellfish
- Cattle
- Vineyards
- Cheese

INDUSTRY
- Cars
- Fishing

RESOURCES
- Oil
- Gas
- Steel

ACTIVITIES
- Soccer
- Rock climbing
- Hiking
- Surfing
- Cricket

SCALE

| 0 | 50 miles | 100 miles |
| 0 | 100 kilometers | |

Shetland Islands

Orkney Islands

Outer Hebrides

Inner Hebrides

ATLANTIC OCEAN

N E S W

Aberdeen

Inverness

GRAMPIAN MOUNTAINS

Most of the UK's red squirrels live in the pine forests of Scotland

Red squirrel

This popular sport was developed in Scotland

Golf

Scotland

Clyde

Glasgow

Edinburgh

Edinburgh Castle

This ancient fortress is built on a prominent rock above the city of Edinburgh

Angel of the North

The wings of this huge steel statue are 177 ft (54 m) across

Newcastle-upon-Tyne

Giant's Causeway

This unique rock formation is made up of hexagonal (six-sided) columns formed after an ancient volcanic eruption

Belfast

Northern Ireland

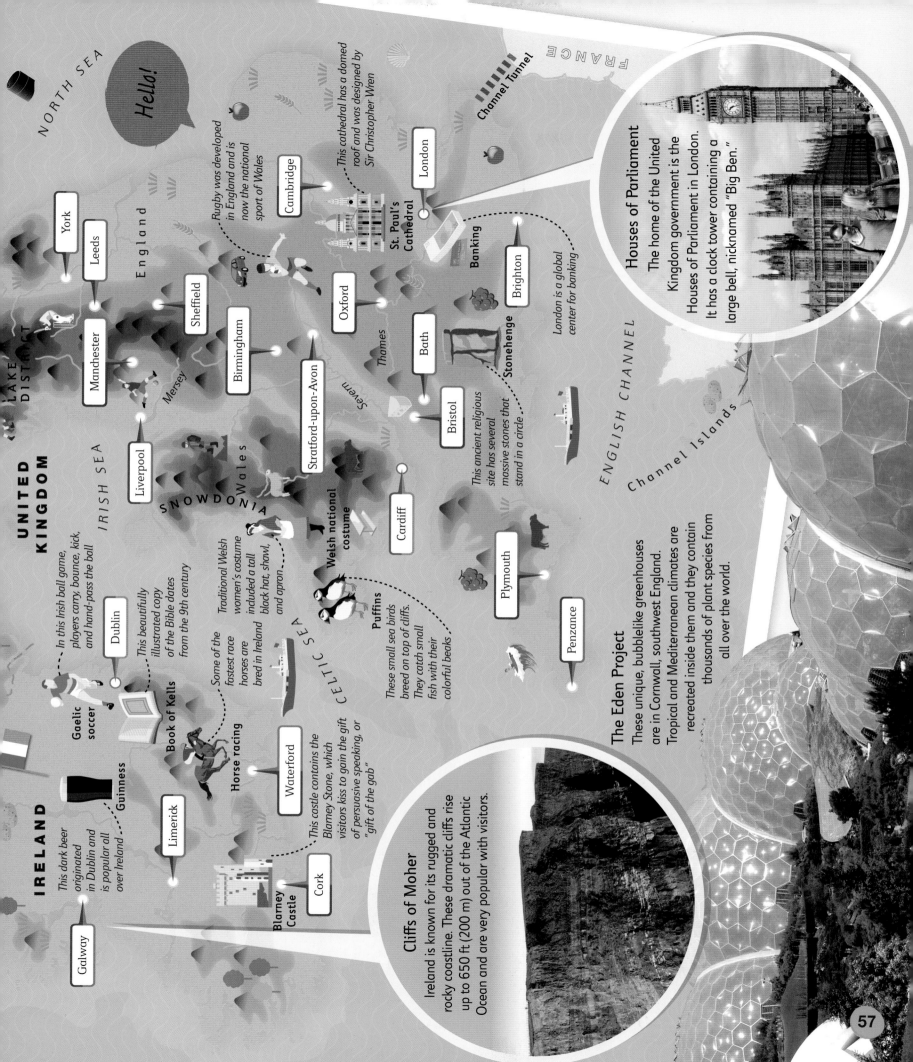

FRANCE

France is known worldwide for its food, wine, and beautiful countryside. Today, most French people live in towns and cities. France is highly industrialized and has one of the fastest train networks, the TGV. The arts, such as painting, and sports, particularly cycling, are very popular.

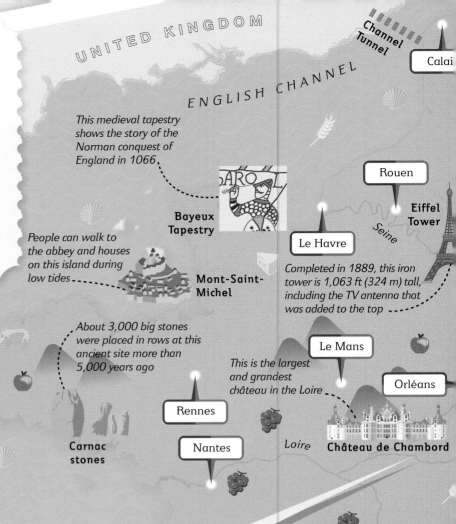

Channel Tunnel

Calai

ENGLISH CHANNEL

This medieval tapestry shows the story of the Norman conquest of England in 1066

Bayeux Tapestry

Rouen

Eiffel Tower

Le Havre

Seine

Completed in 1889, this iron tower is 1,063 ft (324 m) tall, including the TV antenna that was added to the top

People can walk to the abbey and houses on this island during low tides

Mont-Saint-Michel

About 3,000 big stones were placed in rows at this ancient site more than 5,000 years ago

Le Mans

This is the largest and grandest château in the Loire

Orléans

Rennes

Nantes

Carnac stones

Loire

Château de Chambord

Art
Millions of people visit France's museums every year to see paintings and sculptures by artists such as Claude Monet and Auguste Rodin.

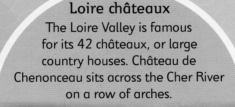

Water Lilies, by Monet

Loire châteaux
The Loire Valley is famous for its 42 châteaux, or large country houses. Château de Chenonceau sits across the Cher River on a row of arches.

ATLANTIC OCEAN

Humans painted horses and wild cattle on cave walls more than 17,000 years ago

Lascaux caves

Dordogne

Bonjour! Hello

Garonne

Périgord truffles

Bordeaux

These edible fungi sell for hundreds of dollars a pound

Cheese and wine
More than 400 different cheeses are made in France. Almost every area has its own type, ranging from soft cheeses, such as Camembert, to hard and even blue cheeses. France also produces some of the world's best wines, made from the juice of black or white grapes. Sunflowers are also grown in the south. Their seeds are pressed to make oil.

Sunflower

Bears from Slovenia were moved to the Pyrenees after the last local bear died in 2006

Brown bear

Toulouse

Camembert cheese

Grapes

SCALE

| 0 | 50 miles | 100 miles |

| 0 | 100 kilometers |

PYRENEES

SPAIN

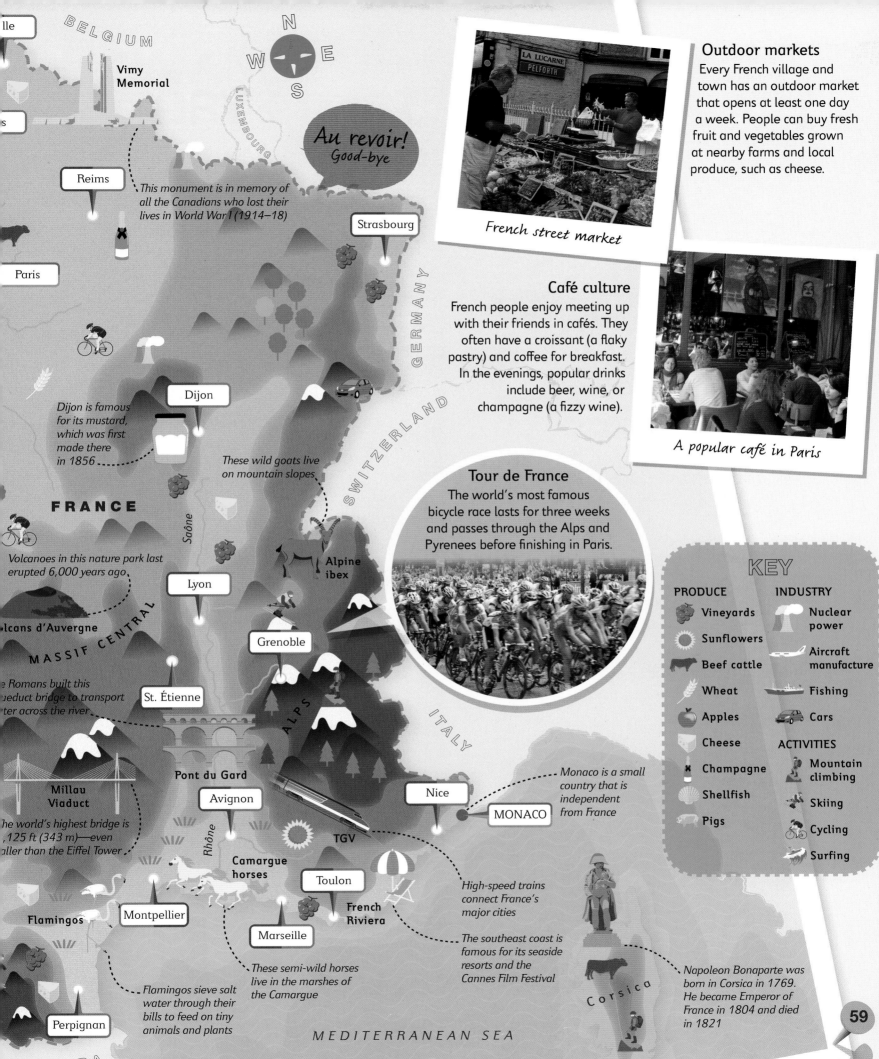

BELGIUM

Vimy Memorial

This monument is in memory of all the Canadians who lost their lives in World War I (1914–18)

Reims

LUXEMBOURG

N
W E
S

Au revoir!
Good-bye

Strasbourg

GERMANY

SWITZERLAND

Paris

Dijon

Dijon is famous for its mustard, which was first made there in 1856

These wild goats live on mountain slopes

FRANCE

Saône

Lyon

Volcanoes in this nature park last erupted 6,000 years ago

Alpine ibex

Volcans d'Auvergne

MASSIF CENTRAL

Grenoble

St. Étienne

The Romans built this aqueduct bridge to transport water across the river

ALPS

ITALY

Millau Viaduct

Pont du Gard

The world's highest bridge is 1,125 ft (343 m)—even taller than the Eiffel Tower

Rhône

Avignon

TGV

Nice

MONACO

Monaco is a small country that is independent from France

Camargue horses

Toulon

French Riviera

High-speed trains connect France's major cities

Flamingos

Montpellier

Marseille

The southeast coast is famous for its seaside resorts and the Cannes Film Festival

Flamingos sieve salt water through their bills to feed on tiny animals and plants

These semi-wild horses live in the marshes of the Camargue

Perpignan

Corsica

Napoleon Bonaparte was born in Corsica in 1769. He became Emperor of France in 1804 and died in 1821

ANDORRA

MEDITERRANEAN SEA

Outdoor markets
Every French village and town has an outdoor market that opens at least one day a week. People can buy fresh fruit and vegetables grown at nearby farms and local produce, such as cheese.

French street market

Café culture
French people enjoy meeting up with their friends in cafés. They often have a croissant (a flaky pastry) and coffee for breakfast. In the evenings, popular drinks include beer, wine, or champagne (a fizzy wine).

A popular café in Paris

Tour de France
The world's most famous bicycle race lasts for three weeks and passes through the Alps and Pyrenees before finishing in Paris.

KEY

PRODUCE
- Vineyards
- Sunflowers
- Beef cattle
- Wheat
- Apples
- Cheese
- Champagne
- Shellfish
- Pigs

INDUSTRY
- Nuclear power
- Aircraft manufacture
- Fishing
- Cars

ACTIVITIES
- Mountain climbing
- Skiing
- Cycling
- Surfing

59

NETHERLANDS AND BELGIUM

The Netherlands and Belgium are also known as the Low Countries, because most of the land is very flat, with a lot of it at or below sea level. This flat land means cycling is popular. Both countries are among the wealthiest in Europe and are heavily populated.

NORTH SEA

Wadden Islands

The Netherlands is famous for its tulip farms, most of which are in the northeast of the country

Groningen

Windmills pump water out of wet areas and help protect land from flooding

Windmill

Tulips

NETHERLANDS

This brave girl went into hiding during World War II and kept a diary of her experiences

Anne Frank

Amsterdam

There are many canals in Amsterdam and lots of people live in waterfront apartments. Amsterdam also has several important art galleries.

This building in The Hague is the home of the Dutch government

Amsterdam

The Hague

Binnenhof

Utrecht

Arnhem

Hockey is a major sport in the Netherlands

Field hockey

Rotterdam

This medieval bell tower is in the historic city of Bruges

Antwerp is a center of the diamond trade

This great artist was born in Zundert in the southern Netherlands in 1853

Vincent van Gogh

Eindhoven

Ostend

Belfry of Bruges

Diamond trade

Antwerp

Red poppy flowers grow in the fields of Belgium

Bruges

Ghent

Safe cycling

Cycling

Cycle lanes are found throughout the Netherlands and Belgium, making it safe and quick for cyclists on the move.

Field poppy

HERGÉ
TINTIN ET LES PICAROS
CASTERMAN

Brussels

Belgian lace is known for its beauty and delicacy

Belgian lace

Atomium

Belgian beer

Thousands of different types of beer are brewed across Belgium

This unique building is the symbol of Brussels

Meuse

Charleroi

Liège

Tintin

The Adventures of Tintin and his dog, Snowy, are told in the comic books written by the Belgian cartoonist Hergé.

Tintin traveled the world and solved many mysteries

BELGIUM

FRANCE

ARDENNES

LUXEMBOURG

Belgian food

Mussels and fries (called *moules* and *frites* in Belgium) is a favorite Belgian dish. Another specialty is rich and creamy Belgian chocolates.

Moules and frites

Belgian chocolates

KEY

PRODUCE	INDUSTRY
Potatoes	Steel
Cheese	Gas
Cattle	**ACTIVITIES**
Pigs	Soccer
Greenhouses	Hiking
Wheat	Cycling
Fruit	

SWITZERLAND AND AUSTRIA

Switzerland and Austria are mountainous countries in Central Europe. The Alps run through both countries, providing snow-covered slopes that are used for winter sports and beautiful alpine valleys, where hiking is popular in the summer.

Lipizzaner and rider

Spanish Riding School
The Spanish Riding School in Vienna teaches traditional horse-riding techniques and is home to the Lipizzaner, a breed of white horse.

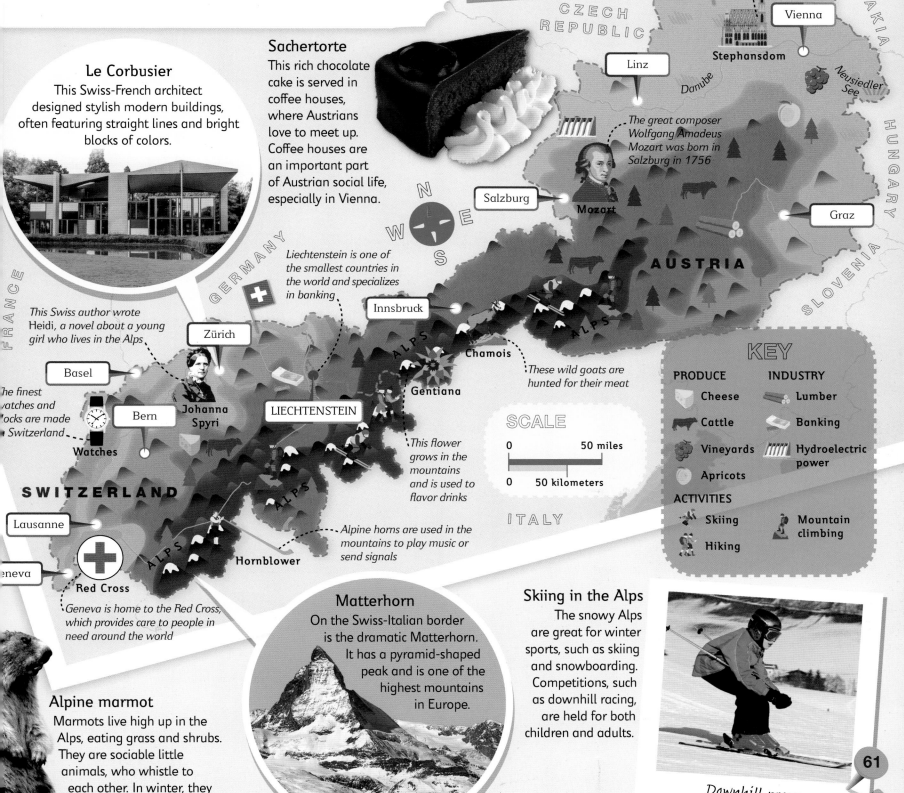

This cathedral has a multicolored roof

Le Corbusier
This Swiss-French architect designed stylish modern buildings, often featuring straight lines and bright blocks of colors.

Sachertorte
This rich chocolate cake is served in coffee houses, where Austrians love to meet up. Coffee houses are an important part of Austrian social life, especially in Vienna.

The great composer Wolfgang Amadeus Mozart was born in Salzburg in 1756

This Swiss author wrote Heidi, a novel about a young girl who lives in the Alps

Liechtenstein is one of the smallest countries in the world and specializes in banking

These wild goats are hunted for their meat

The finest watches and clocks are made in Switzerland

This flower grows in the mountains and is used to flavor drinks

Alpine horns are used in the mountains to play music or send signals

Geneva is home to the Red Cross, which provides care to people in need around the world

Map labels: CZECH REPUBLIC, SLOVAKIA, HUNGARY, SLOVENIA, ITALY, FRANCE, GERMANY, AUSTRIA, SWITZERLAND, LIECHTENSTEIN, Vienna, Stephansdom, Linz, Danube, Neusiedler See, Mozart, Salzburg, Graz, Innsbruck, Chamois, Gentiana, Zürich, Basel, Bern, Johanna Spyri, Watches, Lausanne, Geneva, Red Cross, Hornblower, ALPS, N S E W

KEY
PRODUCE	INDUSTRY
Cheese	Lumber
Cattle	Banking
Vineyards	Hydroelectric power
Apricots	

ACTIVITIES

Skiing	Mountain climbing
Hiking	

SCALE
0 — 50 miles
0 — 50 kilometers

Matterhorn
On the Swiss-Italian border is the dramatic Matterhorn. It has a pyramid-shaped peak and is one of the highest mountains in Europe.

Skiing in the Alps
The snowy Alps are great for winter sports, such as skiing and snowboarding. Competitions, such as downhill racing, are held for both children and adults.

Downhill racer

Alpine marmot
Marmots live high up in the Alps, eating grass and shrubs. They are sociable little animals, who whistle to each other. In winter, they hibernate in burrows.

61

GERMANY

Germany is one of the largest and most important countries in Europe. The Rhine River cuts through mountainous landscape and passes pretty villages in southern Germany, while farther north there are large industrial cities. Germany is a major exporter of many quality goods, including cars.

SCALE

| 0 | 50 miles | 100 miles |
| 0 | 50 kilometers | 100 kilometers |

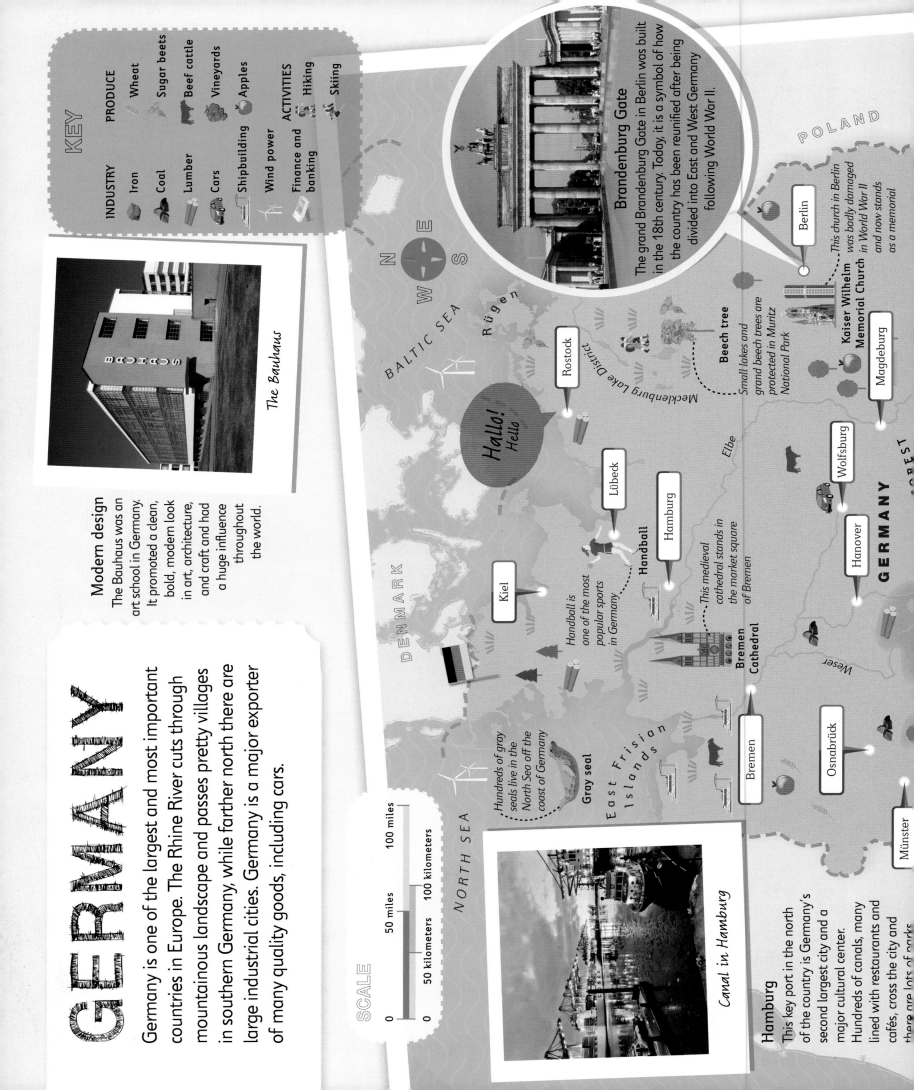

Canal in Hamburg

Hamburg
This key port in the north of the country is Germany's second largest city and a major cultural center. Hundreds of canals, many lined with restaurants and cafés, cross the city and there are lots of parks.

Modern design
The Bauhaus was an art school in Germany. It promoted a clean, bold, modern look in art, architecture, and craft and had a huge influence throughout the world.

The Bauhaus

KEY

INDUSTRY
- Iron
- Coal
- Lumber
- Cars
- Shipbuilding
- Wind power
- Finance and banking

PRODUCE
- Wheat
- Sugar beets
- Beef cattle
- Vineyards
- Apples

ACTIVITIES
- Hiking
- Skiing

Brandenburg Gate
The grand Brandenburg Gate in Berlin was built in the 18th century. Today, it is a symbol of how the country has been reunified after being divided into East and West Germany following World War II.

NORTH SEA

BALTIC SEA

Rügen

Hallo!
Hello

DENMARK

POLAND

N E S W

Kiel

Rostock

Mecklenburg Lake District

Beech tree
Small lakes and grand beech trees are protected in Müritz National Park

Lübeck

Handball
Handball is one of the most popular sports in Germany

Hamburg

Berlin

This church in Berlin was badly damaged in World War II and now stands as a memorial

Kaiser Wilhelm Memorial Church

Magdeburg

Wolfsburg

Hanover

Bremen Cathedral
This medieval cathedral stands in the market square of Bremen

Elbe

Weser

Bremen

Osnabrück

GERMANY

FOREST

Münster

Gray seal
Hundreds of gray seals live in the North Sea off the coast of Germany

East Frisian Islands

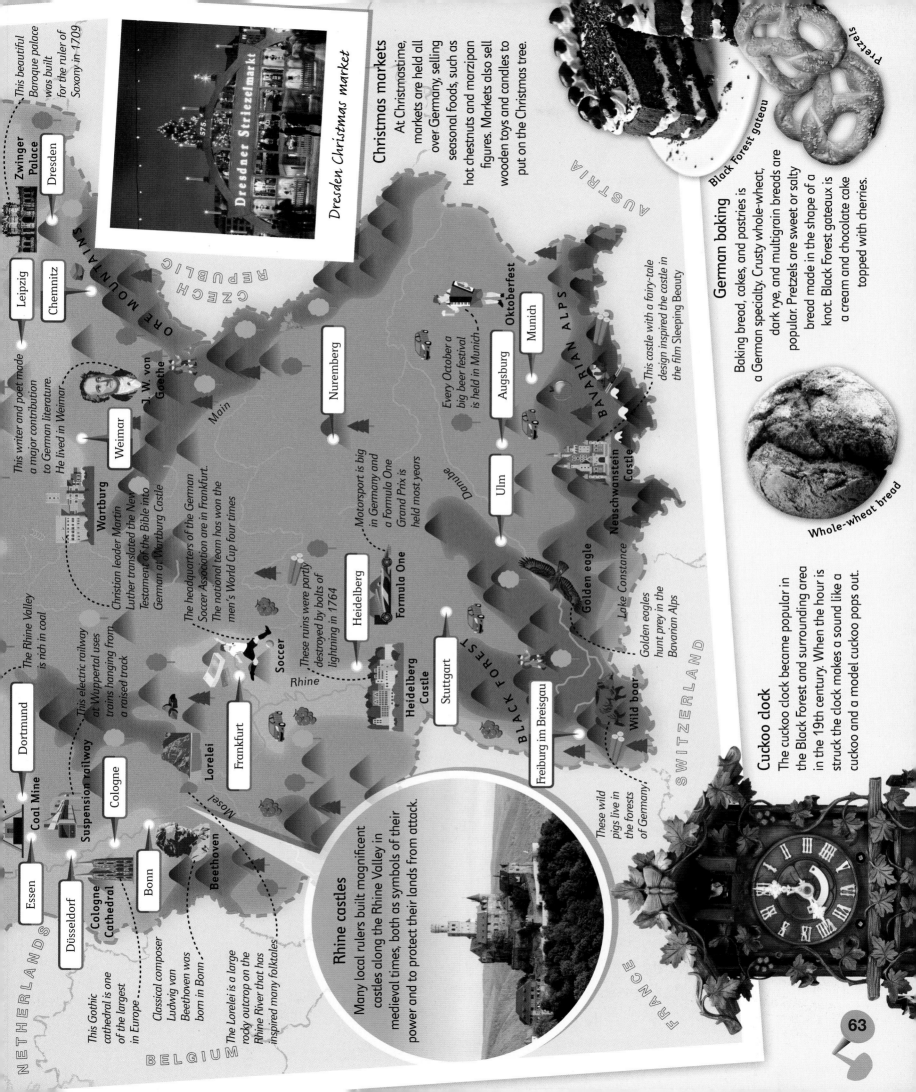

Zwinger Palace
Dresden

This beautiful Baroque palace was built for the ruler of Saxony in 1709.

Dresdner Striezelmarkt

Dresden Christmas market

Christmas markets

At Christmastime, markets are held all over Germany, selling seasonal foods, such as hot chestnuts and marzipan figures. Markets also sell wooden toys and candles to put on the Christmas tree.

Leipzig

Chemnitz

ORE MOUNTAINS

CZECH REPUBLIC

Pretzels

Black Forest gateau

German baking

Baking bread, cakes, and pastries is a German specialty. Crusty whole-wheat, dark rye, and multigrain breads are popular. Pretzels are sweet or salty bread made in the shape of a knot. Black Forest gateaux is a cream and chocolate cake topped with cherries.

Whole-wheat bread

AUSTRIA

J. W. von Goethe

Weimar

This writer and poet made a major contribution to German literature. He lived in Weimar.

Wartburg

Christian leader Martin Luther translated the New Testament of the Bible into German at Wartburg Castle

Nuremberg

Main

Oktoberfest

Every October a big beer festival is held in Munich

Munich

Augsburg

BAVARIAN ALPS

Neuschwanstein Castle

This castle with a fairy-tale design inspired the castle in the film Sleeping Beauty

Danube

Ulm

Lake Constance

Golden eagle

Golden eagles hunt prey in the Bavarian Alps

Cuckoo clock

The cuckoo clock became popular in the Black Forest and surrounding area in the 19th century. When the hour is struck the clock makes a sound like a cuckoo and a model cuckoo pops out.

Soccer

The headquarters of the German Soccer Association are in Frankfurt. The national team has won the men's World Cup four times

Formula One

Motorsport is big in Germany and a Formula One Grand Prix is held most years

Heidelberg

These ruins were partly destroyed by bolts of lightning in 1764

Heidelberg Castle

Stuttgart

BLACK FOREST

Freiburg im Breisgau

Wild boar

These wild pigs live in the forests of Germany,

SWITZERLAND

Dortmund

NETHERLANDS

Essen

Coal Mine

The Rhine Valley is rich in coal

Suspension railway

This electric railway at Wuppertal uses trains hanging from a raised track

Düsseldorf

Cologne Cathedral

Cologne

This Gothic cathedral is one of the largest in Europe

Bonn

Beethoven

Classical composer Ludwig van Beethoven was born in Bonn

Lorelei

The Lorelei is a large rocky outcrop on the Rhine River that has inspired many folktales

Frankfurt

Rhine

Mosel

Rhine castles

Many local rulers built magnificent castles along the Rhine Valley in medieval times, both as symbols of their power and to protect their lands from attack.

BELGIUM

FRANCE

SPAIN AND PORTUGAL

Spain and Portugal are part of sunny southern Europe. Both countries have long coastlines and spectacular scenery, making them popular with vacationers. The sea is a major source of food, and fishing is an important industry in both countries.

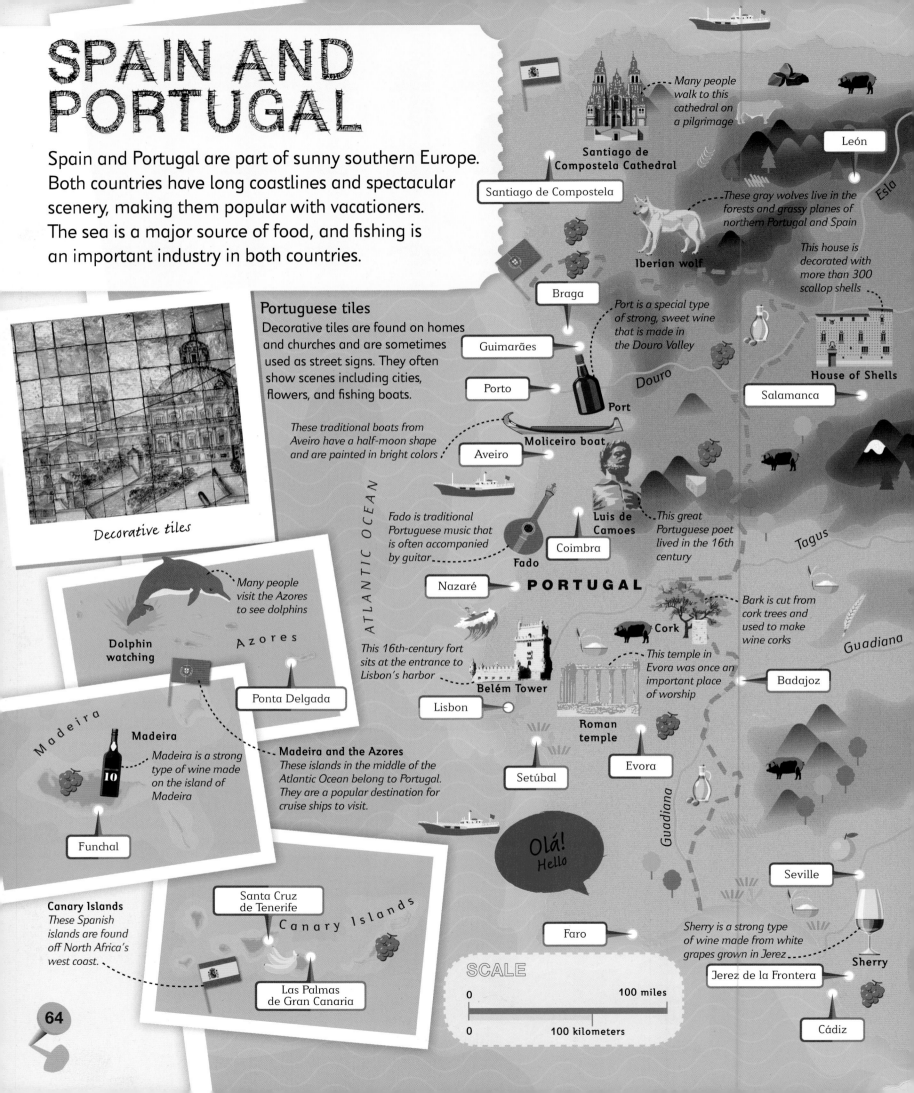

Many people walk to this cathedral on a pilgrimage

Santiago de Compostela Cathedral

Santiago de Compostela

León

These gray wolves live in the forests and grassy planes of northern Portugal and Spain

Iberian wolf

This house is decorated with more than 300 scallop shells

House of Shells

Salamanca

Portuguese tiles
Decorative tiles are found on homes and churches and are sometimes used as street signs. They often show scenes including cities, flowers, and fishing boats.

Braga

Port is a special type of strong, sweet wine that is made in the Douro Valley

Guimarães

Douro

Porto

Port

Decorative tiles

These traditional boats from Aveiro have a half-moon shape and are painted in bright colors

Moliceiro boat

Aveiro

Tagus

Fado is traditional Portuguese music that is often accompanied by guitar

Fado

Coimbra

Nazaré

Luis de Camoes

This great Portuguese poet lived in the 16th century

PORTUGAL

Many people visit the Azores to see dolphins

Dolphin watching

A z o r e s

Bark is cut from cork trees and used to make wine corks

Cork

Guadiana

This 16th-century fort sits at the entrance to Lisbon's harbor

Belém Tower

This temple in Evora was once an important place of worship

Badajoz

ATLANTIC OCEAN

Ponta Delgada

Lisbon

Roman temple

M a d e i r a

Madeira

Madeira is a strong type of wine made on the island of Madeira

Madeira and the Azores
These islands in the middle of the Atlantic Ocean belong to Portugal. They are a popular destination for cruise ships to visit.

Setúbal

Evora

Olá!
Hello

Guadiana

Funchal

Seville

Canary Islands
These Spanish islands are found off North Africa's west coast.

Santa Cruz de Tenerife

C a n a r y   I s l a n d s

Faro

Sherry is a strong type of wine made from white grapes grown in Jerez

Sherry

Las Palmas de Gran Canaria

SCALE

0   100 miles

0   100 kilometers

Jerez de la Frontera

Cádiz

Esla

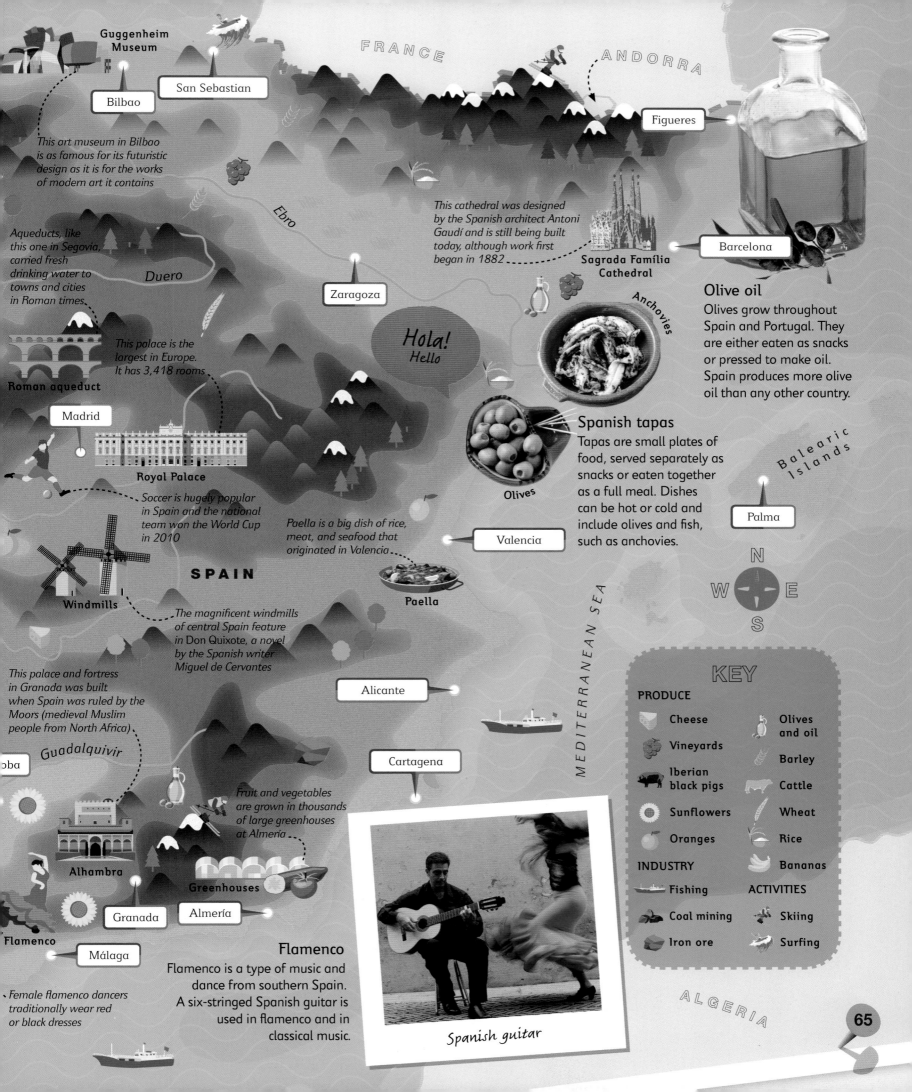

Guggenheim Museum

Bilbao

San Sebastian

FRANCE

ANDORRA

Figueres

This art museum in Bilbao is as famous for its futuristic design as it is for the works of modern art it contains

Ebro

This cathedral was designed by the Spanish architect Antoni Gaudí and is still being built today, although work first began in 1882

Barcelona

Aqueducts, like this one in Segovia, carried fresh drinking water to towns and cities in Roman times

Duero

Sagrada Família Cathedral

Zaragoza

Anchovies

Olive oil
Olives grow throughout Spain and Portugal. They are either eaten as snacks or pressed to make oil. Spain produces more olive oil than any other country.

Roman aqueduct

This palace is the largest in Europe. It has 3,418 rooms

Hola!
Hello

Madrid

Olives

*B a l e a r i c
I s l a n d s*

Spanish tapas
Tapas are small plates of food, served separately as snacks or eaten together as a full meal. Dishes can be hot or cold and include olives and fish, such as anchovies.

Royal Palace

Soccer is hugely popular in Spain and the national team won the World Cup in 2010

Palma

Paella is a big dish of rice, meat, and seafood that originated in Valencia

Valencia

SPAIN

Windmills

The magnificent windmills of central Spain feature in Don Quixote, a novel by the Spanish writer Miguel de Cervantes

Paella

N
W · E
S

M E D I T E R R A N E A N   S E A

This palace and fortress in Granada was built when Spain was ruled by the Moors (medieval Muslim people from North Africa)

Alicante

Guadalquivir

oba

Cartagena

KEY

PRODUCE

Fruit and vegetables are grown in thousands of large greenhouses at Almería

Cheese		Olives and oil	
Vineyards		Barley	
Iberian black pigs		Cattle	
Sunflowers		Wheat	
Oranges		Rice	

INDUSTRY

Bananas

Alhambra

Greenhouses

Granada

Almería

		ACTIVITIES	
Fishing			
Coal mining		Skiing	
Iron ore		Surfing	

Flamenco

Málaga

Flamenco
Flamenco is a type of music and dance from southern Spain. A six-stringed Spanish guitar is used in flamenco and in classical music.

Female flamenco dancers traditionally wear red or black dresses

Spanish guitar

ALGERIA

ITALY

Italy stretches down from the Alps in the north to the Mediterranean island of Sicily in the south. The country is shaped like a boot, with its toe almost touching Sicily. In ancient times, the Romans built a great empire that was ruled from Rome. Italy is also famous for its art and architecture.

Scooters

There are lots of twisting little lanes and streets in Italy, so many people use small scooters to get around towns and cities.

The Last Supper

Leonardo da Vinci

Leonardo da Vinci was one of the world's greatest artists and inventors. In the late 15th century he painted *The Last Supper*, an oil painting showing Jesus Christ's last meal with his apostles (followers).

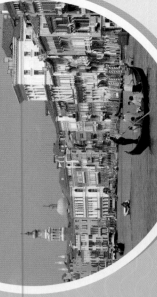

Venice

Venice is a city of canals instead of streets. It is built on 118 small islands linked together by bridges. People travel around the city on boats called gondolas.

CROATIA

SLOVENIA

AUSTRIA

SWITZERLAND

FRANCE

Ciao! Hello

The play Romeo and Juliet by William Shakespeare is set in Verona, and "Juliet's balcony," where Romeo was said to woo Juliet, attracts many visitors

Juliet's balcony

Ferrari make sports and formula One race cars in Maranello, northwest of Bologna

Venice

Adige

Po

SAN MARINO

This tiny independent republic has an area of just over 24 sq miles (61 sq km)

This famous statue in Florence, of the biblical character David, was created by the Italian artist Michelangelo

Michelangelo's sculpture of David

Bologna

Verona

Ferrari

Some of the finest violins are made in northern Italy

Violin

Leaning Tower of Pisa

Florence

Siena

Tiber

This bell tower tilts to one side because it was built on soft ground

La Scala opera house

Milan

Pisa

Arno

This magnificent opera house in Milan hosts many classical performances

Genoa

White marble quarry

Italian marble is a hard, smooth stone used to make bright, white sculptures

Po

Turin

LIGURIAN SEA

Corsica

Gelato

Italian ice cream is called gelato and is soft and creamy. It comes in lots of delicious flavors, such as vanilla, strawberry, chocolate, and pistachio.

Gelato

ADRIATIC SEA

These dry stone huts with cone roofs are called trulli and are found in the Italian region of Apulia

Bari

Trulli

Arrivederci!
Good-bye

KEY

PRODUCE
Vineyards · Lemons
Olives and oil · Almonds
Figs · Goats
Wheat · Cheese
Rice · Shellfish
Tomatoes

ACTIVITIES
Soccer · Scuba diving
Skiing · Hiking

INDUSTRY
Fishing

This large dormouse is so named because the ancient Romans ate it as a delicacy
Edible dormouse

Ofanto

The Vatican City in Rome is the home of the Pope, the head of the Roman Catholic Church. It is the world's smallest sovereign state

VATICAN CITY

Biferno

ITALY

Rome

Mount Vesuvius

Mount Vesuvius is a volcano near Naples that erupted in Ancient Roman times, destroying the city of Pompeii. It is still erupting today

Naples

Sicily

Sicily is the largest island in the Mediterranean Sea. Its historic towns and cities, rugged coastline, ancient ruins, and natural wonders, such as the volcano Mount Etna, make it popular with tourists.

Reggio di Calabria

IONIAN SEA

At 10,991 ft (3,350 m), Etna on the island of Sicily is Europe's highest active volcano

Mount Etna

Catania

Colosseum

This large open-air amphitheater (circular theater) was built by the Ancient Romans as an arena for gladiator fights. It is the largest amphitheater ever built.

Food and drink

Italian food and drink is enjoyed around the world. Italy is the home of the pizza and one of its most popular flavors is the simple margherita pizza, made with mozzarella cheese, tomato, and basil.

Sicily

Palermo

Margherita pizza

MEDITERRANEAN SEA

SCALE
0 — 50 miles — 100 miles
0 — 100 kilometers

To start the day, Italians drink strong espresso coffee, often made in stovetop coffee pots

Spaghetti

Spaghetti is one of hundreds of types of pasta made in Italy, and spaghetti with tomato sauce is a classic dish.

Cagliari

Sardinia

Stovetop coffee pot

CENTRAL EUROPE

Central Europe is a region of historic cities and ancient castles. Farming is important in Poland, as are industries such as coal mining and steel. To the south, people enjoy hiking and skiing in the rugged mountains of the Czech Republic and Slovakia.

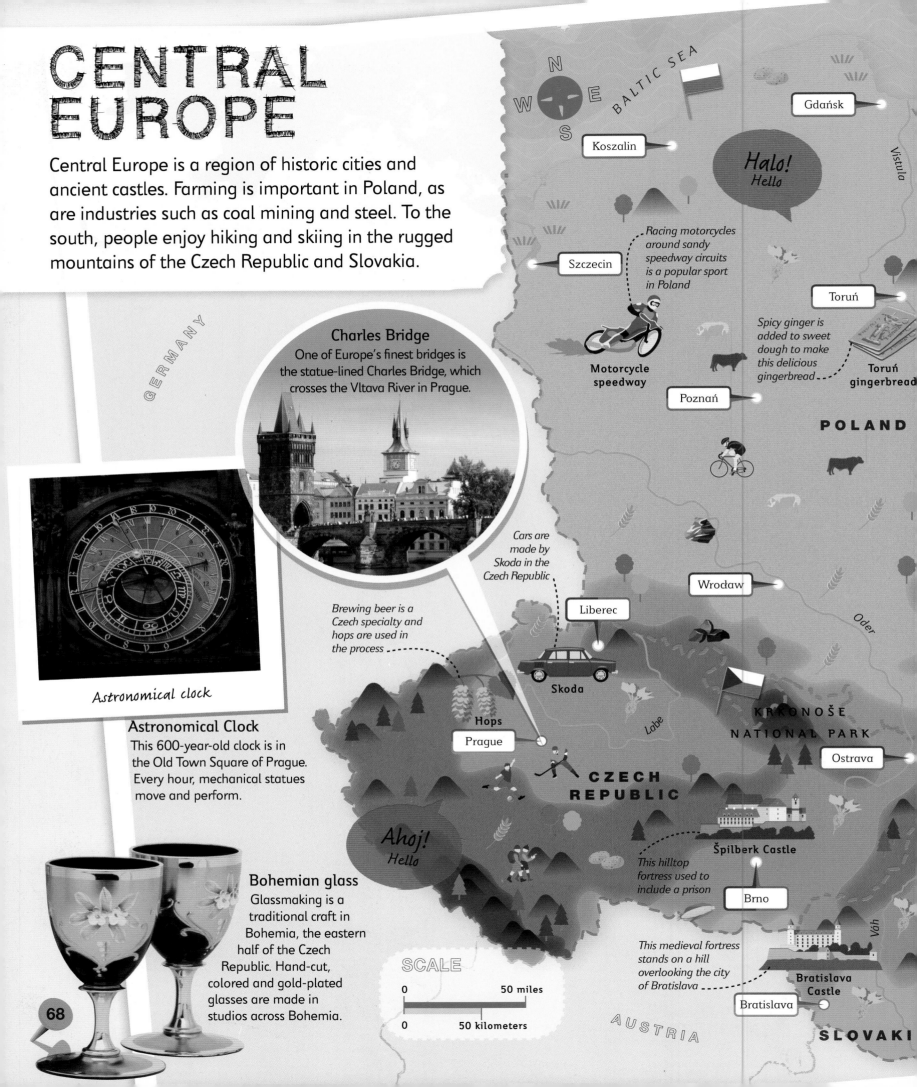

BALTIC SEA

Halo!
Hello

Koszalin

Gdańsk

Szczecin

Racing motorcycles around sandy speedway circuits is a popular sport in Poland

Toruń

Spicy ginger is added to sweet dough to make this delicious gingerbread

Motorcycle speedway

Poznań

Toruń gingerbread

POLAND

Vistula

Charles Bridge
One of Europe's finest bridges is the statue-lined Charles Bridge, which crosses the Vltava River in Prague.

GERMANY

Cars are made by Skoda in the Czech Republic

Wrocław

Oder

Brewing beer is a Czech specialty and hops are used in the process

Liberec

Skoda

Astronomical clock

Astronomical Clock
This 600-year-old clock is in the Old Town Square of Prague. Every hour, mechanical statues move and perform.

Hops

Prague

Labe

KRKONOŠE NATIONAL PARK

Ostrava

CZECH REPUBLIC

Ahoj!
Hello

Špilberk Castle

This hilltop fortress used to include a prison

Bohemian glass
Glassmaking is a traditional craft in Bohemia, the eastern half of the Czech Republic. Hand-cut, colored and gold-plated glasses are made in studios across Bohemia.

Brno

Váh

SCALE

0 — 50 miles

0 — 50 kilometers

This medieval fortress stands on a hill overlooking the city of Bratislava

Bratislava Castle

Bratislava

AUSTRIA

SLOVAKIA

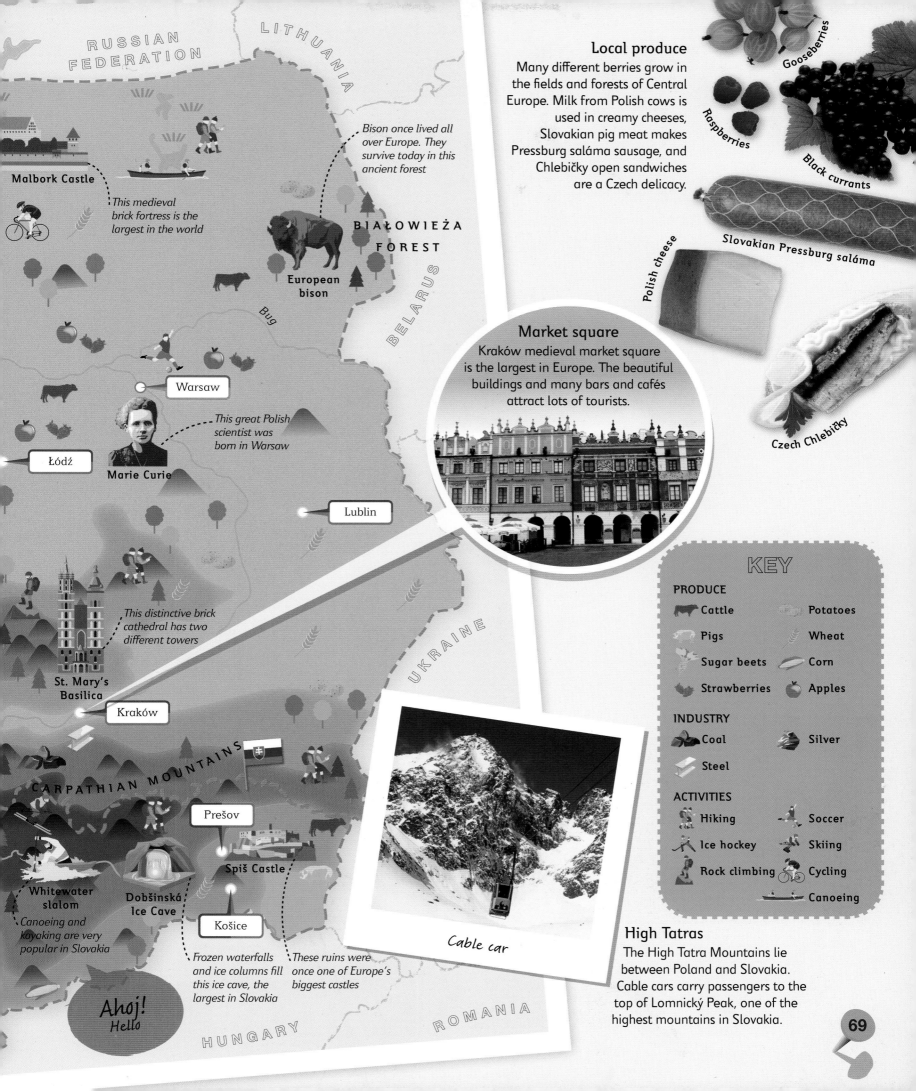

RUSSIAN FEDERATION

LITHUANIA

BELARUS

Malbork Castle

This medieval brick fortress is the largest in the world

Bison once lived all over Europe. They survive today in this ancient forest

BIAŁOWIEŻA FOREST

European bison

Bug

Warsaw

Marie Curie

This great Polish scientist was born in Warsaw

Łódź

Lublin

St. Mary's Basilica

This distinctive brick cathedral has two different towers

Kraków

UKRAINE

CARPATHIAN MOUNTAINS

Prešov

Spiš Castle

Whitewater slalom

Canoeing and kayaking are very popular in Slovakia

Dobšinská Ice Cave

Košice

Frozen waterfalls and ice columns fill this ice cave, the largest in Slovakia

These ruins were once one of Europe's biggest castles

Ahoj!
Hello

HUNGARY

ROMANIA

Cable car

Local produce

Many different berries grow in the fields and forests of Central Europe. Milk from Polish cows is used in creamy cheeses, Slovakian pig meat makes Pressburg saláma sausage, and Chlebíčky open sandwiches are a Czech delicacy.

Gooseberries

Raspberries

Black currants

Slovakian Pressburg saláma

Polish cheese

Czech Chlebíčky

Market square

Kraków medieval market square is the largest in Europe. The beautiful buildings and many bars and cafés attract lots of tourists.

KEY

PRODUCE

Cattle
Potatoes

Pigs
Wheat

Sugar beets
Corn

Strawberries
Apples

INDUSTRY

Coal
Silver

Steel

ACTIVITIES

Hiking
Soccer

Ice hockey
Skiing

Rock climbing
Cycling

Canoeing

High Tatras

The High Tatra Mountains lie between Poland and Slovakia. Cable cars carry passengers to the top of Lomnický Peak, one of the highest mountains in Slovakia.

69

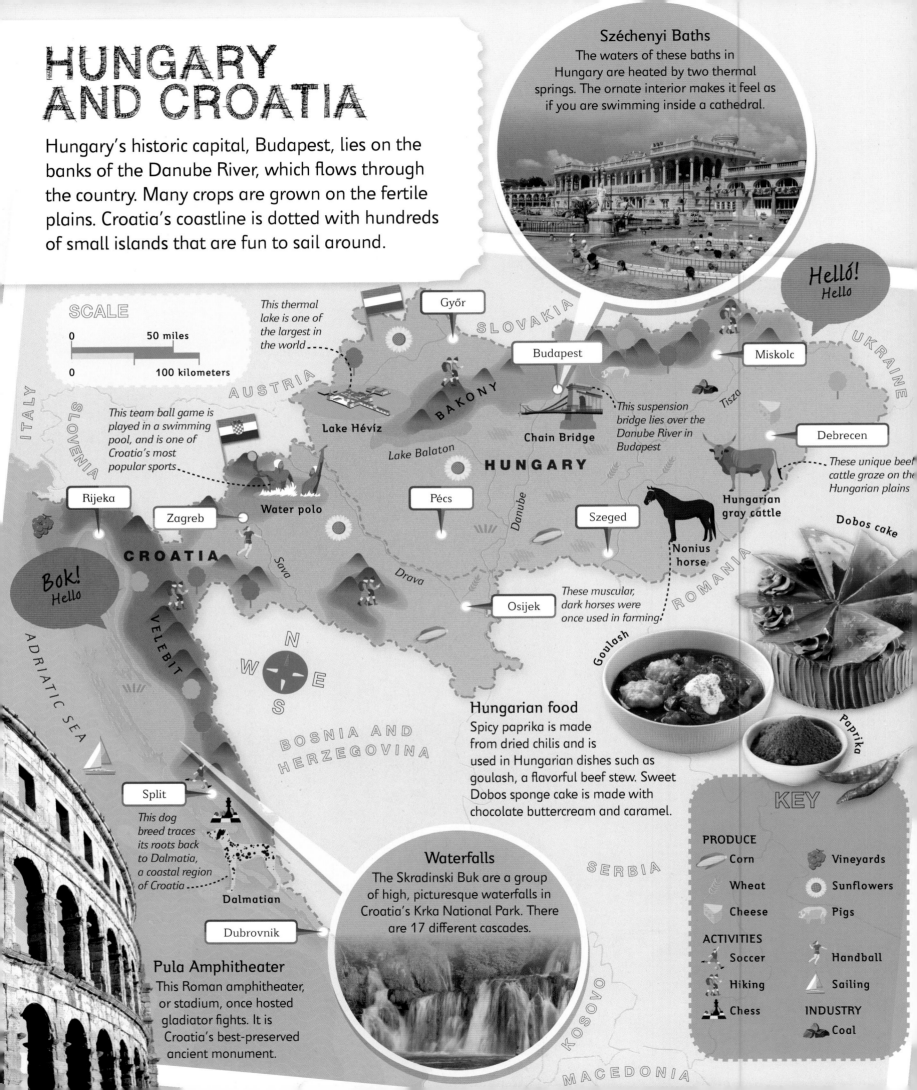

HUNGARY AND CROATIA

Hungary's historic capital, Budapest, lies on the banks of the Danube River, which flows through the country. Many crops are grown on the fertile plains. Croatia's coastline is dotted with hundreds of small islands that are fun to sail around.

Széchenyi Baths
The waters of these baths in Hungary are heated by two thermal springs. The ornate interior makes it feel as if you are swimming inside a cathedral.

Helló! Hello

Bok! Hello

SCALE
0   50 miles
0   100 kilometers

SLOVAKIA

UKRAINE

AUSTRIA

ITALY

SLOVENIA

This thermal lake is one of the largest in the world

Győr

Budapest

Miskolc

This team ball game is played in a swimming pool, and is one of Croatia's most popular sports

BAKONY

Tisza

This suspension bridge lies over the Danube River in Budapest

Chain Bridge

Debrecen

Lake Hévíz

Lake Balaton

HUNGARY

These unique beef cattle graze on the Hungarian plains

Rijeka

Zagreb

Water polo

Pécs

Szeged

Hungarian gray cattle

Dobos cake

CROATIA

Nonius horse

Sava

Drava

Danube

These muscular, dark horses were once used in farming

Osijek

ROMANIA

VELEBIT

Goulash

Paprika

ADRIATIC SEA

N W E S

BOSNIA AND HERZEGOVINA

Hungarian food
Spicy paprika is made from dried chilis and is used in Hungarian dishes such as goulash, a flavorful beef stew. Sweet Dobos sponge cake is made with chocolate buttercream and caramel.

Split

This dog breed traces its roots back to Dalmatia, a coastal region of Croatia

Dalmatian

Dubrovnik

SERBIA

Waterfalls
The Skradinski Buk are a group of high, picturesque waterfalls in Croatia's Krka National Park. There are 17 different cascades.

Pula Amphitheater
This Roman amphitheater, or stadium, once hosted gladiator fights. It is Croatia's best-preserved ancient monument.

KOSOVO

MACEDONIA

KEY

PRODUCE
- Corn
- Wheat
- Cheese
- Vineyards
- Sunflowers
- Pigs

ACTIVITIES
- Soccer
- Hiking
- Chess
- Handball
- Sailing

INDUSTRY
- Coal

UKRAINE

Ukraine is the second largest country in Europe after Russia, and is home to people from a variety of different ethnic groups. Fields of wheat and bright sunflowers cover large areas of the landscape. Industry is also important, with Ukraine being a major producer of hydroelectric power, steel, and coal.

Children's Parade

Children's Day
Children's Day is a special day that honors all children around the world. It is celebrated by a parade on June 1 every year in Kiev, the capital of Ukraine.

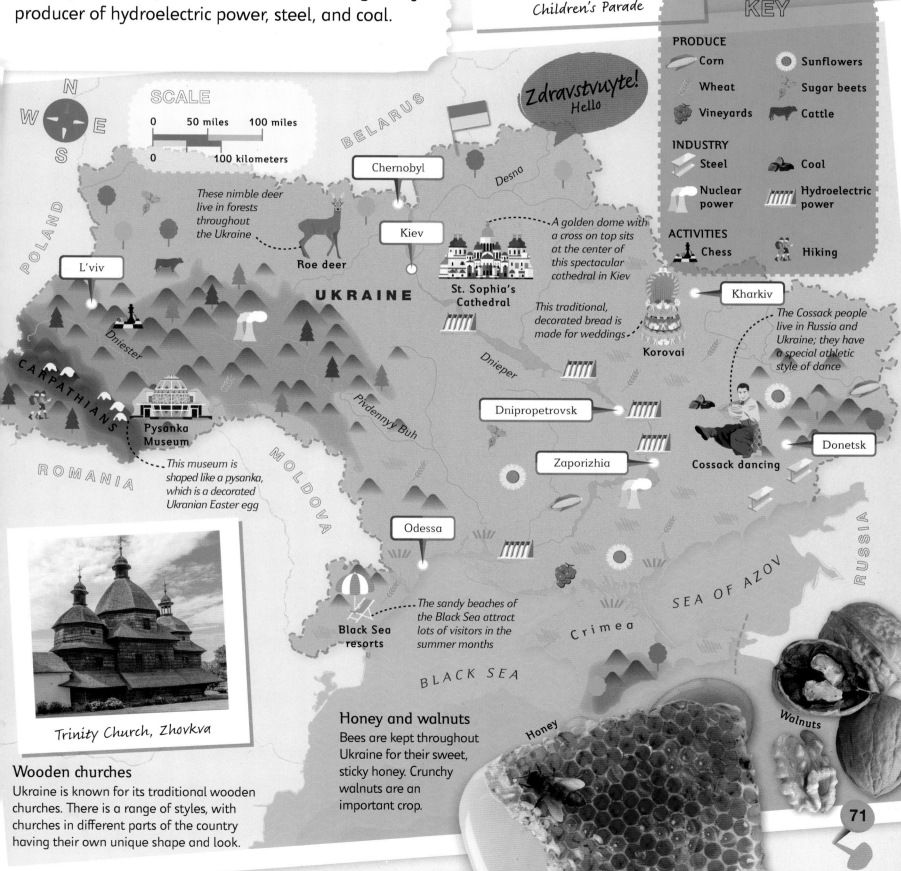

Zdravstvuyte! Hello

KEY

PRODUCE
- Corn
- Sunflowers
- Wheat
- Sugar beets
- Vineyards
- Cattle

INDUSTRY
- Steel
- Coal
- Nuclear power
- Hydroelectric power

ACTIVITIES
- Chess
- Hiking

SCALE

0　50 miles　100 miles

0　100 kilometers

BELARUS

Desna

Chernobyl

Kiev

These nimble deer live in forests throughout the Ukraine ... **Roe deer**

POLAND

L'viv

Dniester

UKRAINE

St. Sophia's Cathedral

A golden dome with a cross on top sits at the center of this spectacular cathedral in Kiev

This traditional, decorated bread is made for weddings — **Korovai**

Kharkiv

The Cossack people live in Russia and Ukraine; they have a special athletic style of dance

CARPATHIANS

Pysanka Museum

This museum is shaped like a pysanka, which is a decorated Ukranian Easter egg

Pydennyy Buh

Dnieper

Dnipropetrovsk

Zaporizhia

Cossack dancing

Donetsk

ROMANIA

MOLDOVA

Odessa

Black Sea resorts

The sandy beaches of the Black Sea attract lots of visitors in the summer months

Crimea

SEA OF AZOV

RUSSIA

BLACK SEA

Trinity Church, Zhovkva

Wooden churches
Ukraine is known for its traditional wooden churches. There is a range of styles, with churches in different parts of the country having their own unique shape and look.

Honey and walnuts
Bees are kept throughout Ukraine for their sweet, sticky honey. Crunchy walnuts are an important crop.

Honey

Walnuts

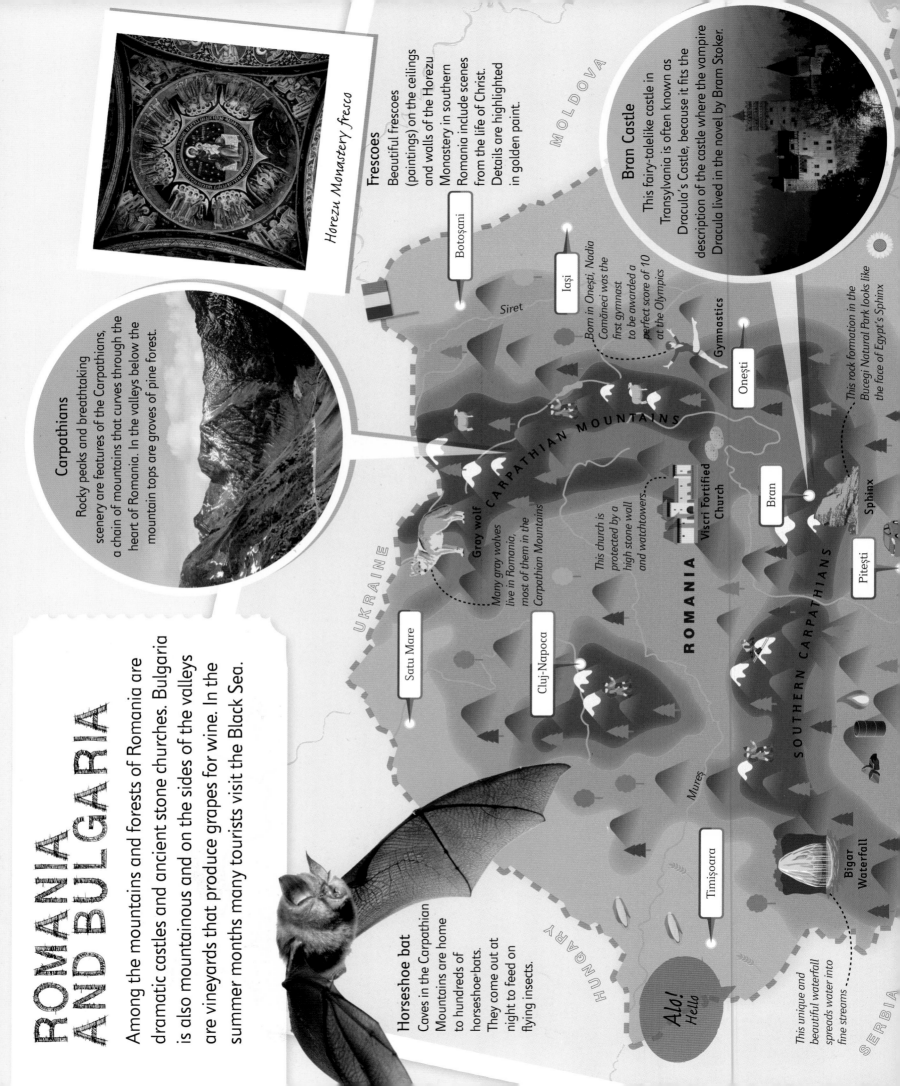

ROMANIA AND BULGARIA

Among the mountains and forests of Romania are dramatic castles and ancient stone churches. Bulgaria is also mountainous and on the sides of the valleys are vineyards that produce grapes for wine. In the summer months many tourists visit the Black Sea.

Horezu Monastery fresco

Carpathians
Rocky peaks and breathtaking scenery are features of the Carpathians, a chain of mountains that curves through the heart of Romania. In the valleys below the mountain tops are groves of pine forest.

Horseshoe bat
Caves in the Carpathian Mountains are home to hundreds of horseshoe bats. They come out at night to feed on flying insects.

Frescoes
Beautiful frescoes (paintings) on the ceilings and walls of the Horezu Monastery in southern Romania include scenes from the life of Christ. Details are highlighted in golden paint.

Bran Castle
This fairy-talelike castle in Transylvania is often known as Dracula's Castle, because it fits the description of the castle where the vampire Dracula lived in the novel by Bram Stoker.

Born in Onești, Nadia Comăneci was the first gymnast to be awarded a perfect score of 10 at the Olympics

Gymnastics

This rock formation in the Bucegi Natural Park looks like the face of Egypt's Sphinx

Sphinx

This church is protected by a high stone wall and watchtowers

Vișcri Fortified Church

This unique and beautiful waterfall spreads water into fine streams

Bigar Waterfall

Alo! *Hello*

Many gray wolves live in Romania, most of them in the Carpathian Mountains

Gray wolf

MOLDOVA

UKRAINE

HUNGARY

SERBIA

CARPATHIAN MOUNTAINS

SOUTHERN CARPATHIANS

ROMANIA

Botoșani

Iași

Onești

Bran

Pitești

Satu Mare

Cluj-Napoca

Timișoara

Siret

Mureș

Damask rose

Rose oil

Alexander Nevsky Cathedral
This cathedral in Sofia, Bulgaria's capital, is named after a Russian prince and saint. Bulgaria's main religion is Eastern Orthodox.

Valley of the Roses
Pink Damask roses are grown in the center of Bulgaria. The petals are used to make rose oil, which is used in perfumes, and rosewater, which can be used to flavor food.

Hiking
Mountainous landscapes, such as the Carpathians of Romania and the Pirin Mountains in southwest Bulgaria, are popular places for hiking and exploring. The Pirin Mountains are known for their many beautiful, crystal-clear lakes.

Pirin Mountains, Bulgaria

N E S W

SCALE
50 miles
0
50 kilometers
0

Constanța

Varna

BLACK SEA

Burgas

Dalmatian pelican
These large birds live on the lower part of the Danube River and on the Black Sea coast

Bucharest

Palace of Parliament
This is one of the biggest civic buildings in the world

Danube

Olt

Iskur

Rock-hewn churches of Ivanovo
These churches and chapels were carved into the rocks and decorated with murals

Zdravey!
Hello

BULGARIA

BALKAN MOUNTAINS

Maritsa

Plovdiv

RHODOPE MOUNTAINS

PIRIN MOUNTAINS

Sofia

Rila Monastery
This monastery is an important holy site in the Eastern Orthodox Church

MACEDONIA

GREECE

TURKEY

KEY

PRODUCE
🌾 Wheat
🌻 Sunflowers
🌽 Corn

🍇 Vineyards
🐑 Sheep
🥔 Potatoes

INDUSTRY
Wind power
Coal
Oil

Natural gas
Cars
Hydroelectric power

Nuclear power

ACTIVITIES
Hiking
Skiing

Wrestling

73

GREECE

Greece is the home of one of the world's first great civilizations and has a long and fascinating history. Today, it is a major tourist destination. There are ancient ruins, magnificent mountains, and hundreds of islands with glorious beaches to explore, as well as delicious traditional food to enjoy.

Monasteries

Medieval monks built more than 20 monasteries at Metéora, each perched at the top of one of the tall rock pillars found at this spectacular site. Today, only six of them remain.

Dancing

Traditional dancing plays an important role in many Greek celebrations. These are happy, sociable occasions with lots of lively music.

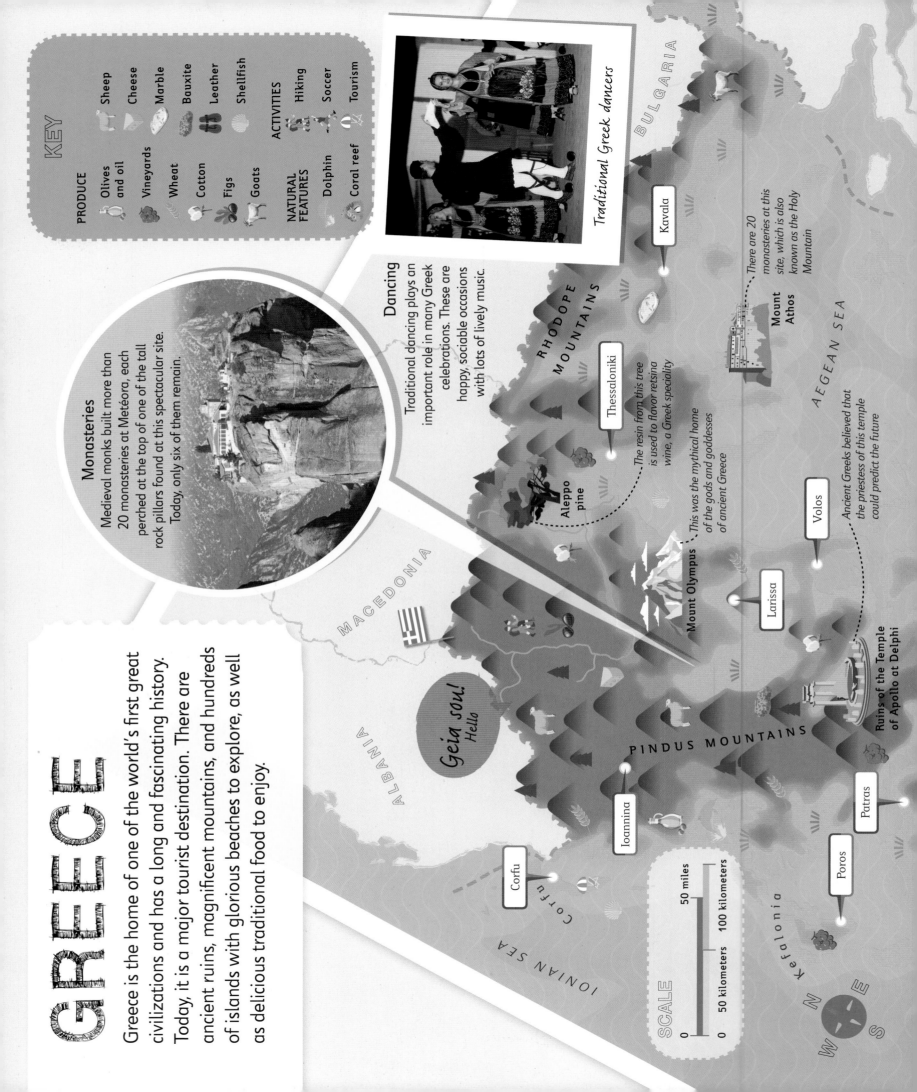

Traditional Greek dancers

KEY

PRODUCE
- Olives and oil
- Sheep
- Cheese
- Vineyards
- Marble
- Wheat
- Bauxite
- Cotton
- Leather
- Figs
- Shellfish
- Goats

NATURAL FEATURES
- Dolphin
- Coral reef

ACTIVITIES
- Hiking
- Soccer
- Tourism

Geia sou! Hello

BULGARIA

MACEDONIA

ALBANIA

RHODOPE MOUNTAINS

PINDUS MOUNTAINS

AEGEAN SEA

IONIAN SEA

Kavala

Thessaloniki

Aleppo pine — *The resin from this tree is used to flavor retsina wine, a Greek speciality.*

Mount Olympus — *This was the mythical home of the gods and goddesses of ancient Greece*

Mount Athos — *There are 20 monasteries at this site, which is also known as the Holy Mountain*

Volos

Larissa

Ruins of the Temple of Apollo at Delphi — *Ancient Greeks believed that the priestess of this temple could predict the future*

Ioannina

Patras

Poros

Corfu

Corfu

Kefalonia

SCALE

0   50 miles

0   100 kilometers

0 — 50 kilometers — 50 kilometers

N W E S

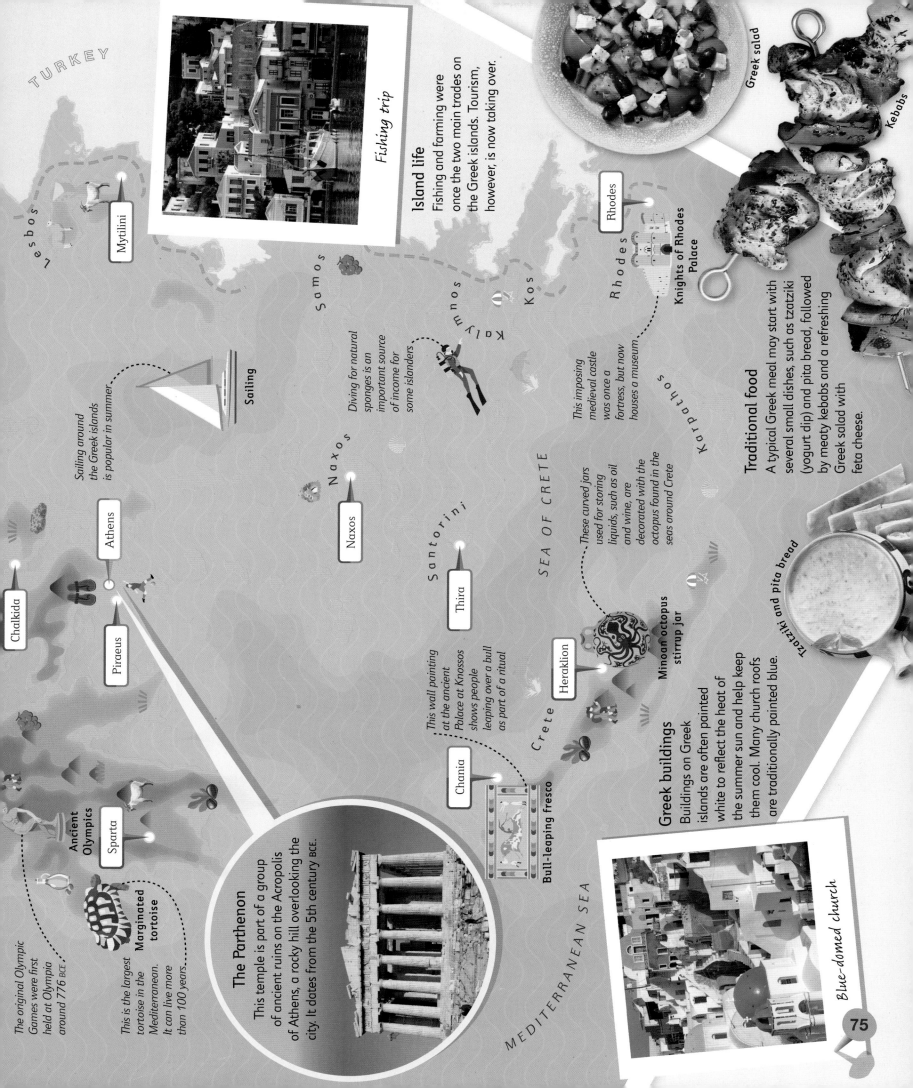

TURKEY

L e s b o s

Mytilini

Fishing trip

Island life
Fishing and farming were once the two main trades on the Greek islands. Tourism, however, is now taking over.

Greek salad

Kebabs

S a m o s

K a l y m n o s

Kos

Diving for natural sponges is an important source of income for some islanders

R h o d e s

Rhodes

Knights of Rhodes Palace

This imposing medieval castle was once a fortress, but now houses a museum

K a r p a t h o s

Sailing around the Greek islands is popular in summer

Sailing

Athens

N a x o s

Naxos

Traditional food
A typical Greek meal may start with several small dishes, such as tzatziki (yogurt dip) and pita bread, followed by meaty kebabs and a refreshing Greek salad with feta cheese.

Chalkida

Piraeus

S a n t o r i n i

Thira

SEA OF CRETE

These curved jars used for storing liquids, such as oil and wine, are decorated with the octopus found in the seas around Crete

Tzatziki and pita bread

Ancient Olympics

Sparta

This wall painting at the ancient Palace at Knossos shows people leaping over a bull as part of a ritual

Chania

C r e t e

Heraklion

Minoan octopus stirrup jar

Greek buildings
Buildings on Greek islands are often painted white to reflect the heat of the summer sun and help keep them cool. Many church roofs are traditionally painted blue.

The original Olympic Games were first held at Olympia around 776 BCE.

This is the largest tortoise in the Mediterranean. It can live more than 100 years.

Marginated tortoise

The Parthenon
This temple is part of a group of ancient ruins on the Acropolis of Athens, a rocky hill overlooking the city. It dates from the 5th century BCE.

Bull-leaping fresco

MEDITERRANEAN SEA

Blue-domed church

75

EUROPEAN RUSSIA

Russia is the largest country in the world and stretches across two continents: Europe and Asia. European Russia lies to the west of the Ural Mountains. The people of St. Petersburg and Moscow are proud of their history and culture.

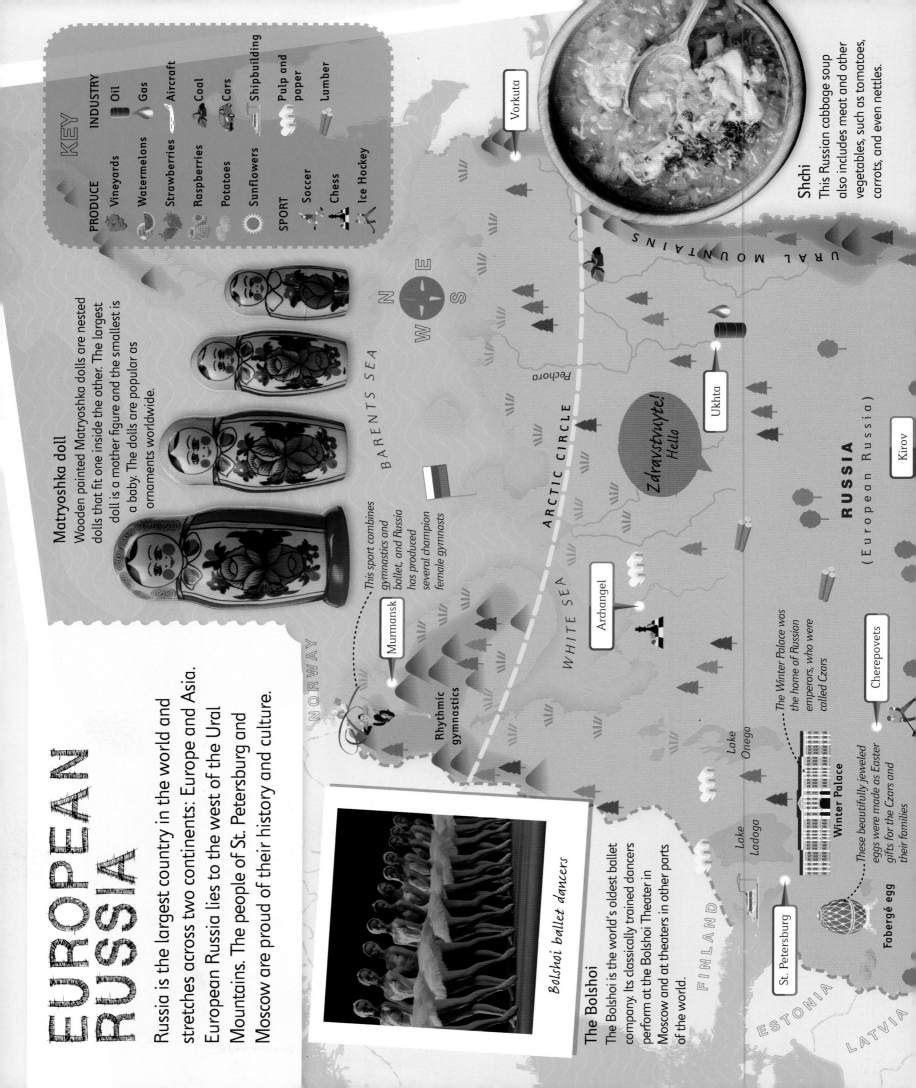

Bolshoi ballet dancers

The Bolshoi

The Bolshoi is the world's oldest ballet company. Its classically trained dancers perform at the Bolshoi Theater in Moscow and at theaters in other parts of the world.

Matryoshka doll

Wooden painted Matryoshka dolls are nested dolls that fit one inside the other. The largest doll is a mother figure and the smallest is a baby. The dolls are popular as ornaments worldwide.

This sport combines gymnastics and ballet, and Russia has produced several champion female gymnasts

Rhythmic gymnastics

Shchi

This Russian cabbage soup also includes meat and other vegetables, such as tomatoes, carrots, and even nettles.

Vorkuta

URAL MOUNTAINS

BARENTS SEA

N E S W

ARCTIC CIRCLE

Pechora

Zdravstvuyte! Hello

Ukhta

RUSSIA

(European Russia)

Kirov

WHITE SEA

Archangel

Murmansk

NORWAY

Cherepovets

Lake Onega

The Winter Palace was the home of Russian emperors, who were called Czars

Winter Palace

Lake Ladoga

FINLAND

St. Petersburg

These beautifully jeweled eggs were made as Easter gifts for the Czars and their families

Fabergé egg

ESTONIA

LATVIA

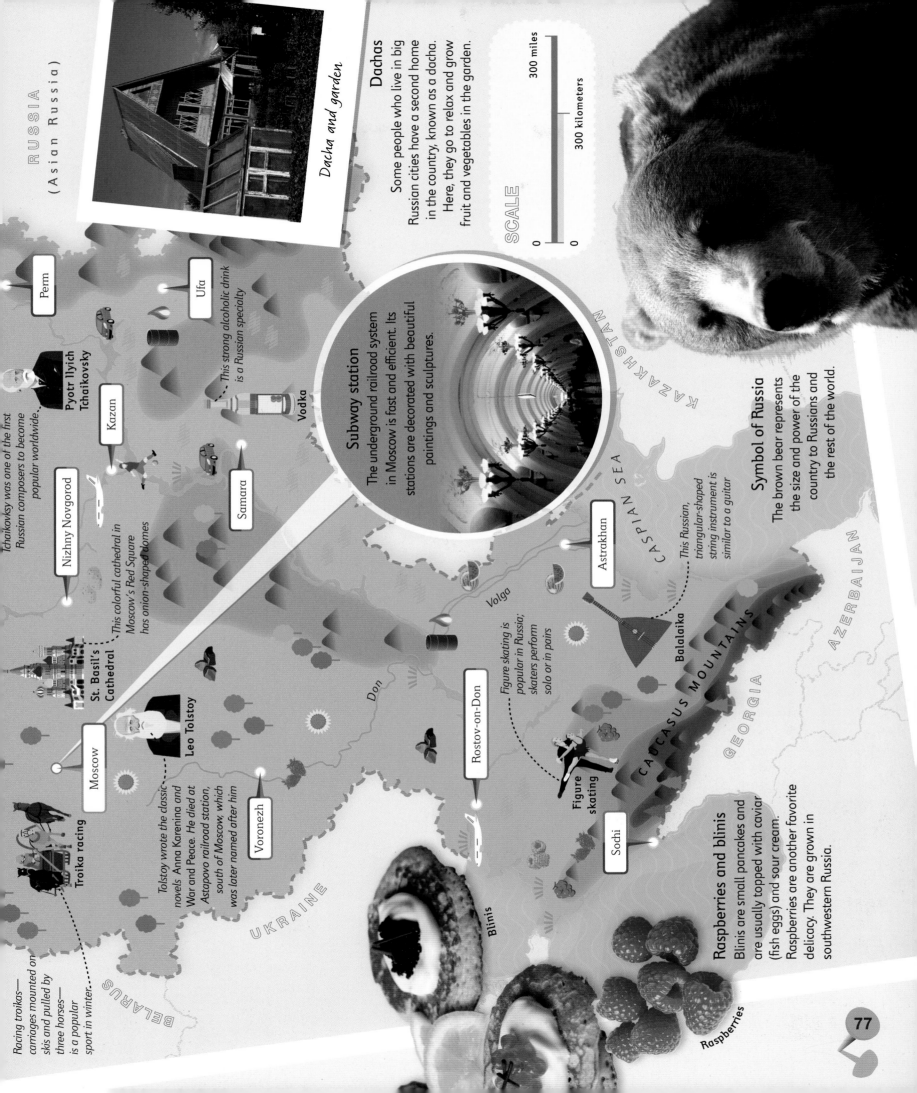

RUSSIA (Asian Russia)

Dacha and garden

Dachas

Some people who live in big Russian cities have a second home in the country, known as a dacha. Here, they go to relax and grow fruit and vegetables in the garden.

SCALE

0   300 miles
0   300 kilometers

Perm

Ufa

This strong alcoholic drink is a Russian specialty

Vodka

Pyotr Ilyich Tchaikovsky

Tchaikovsky was one of the first Russian composers to become popular worldwide.

Kazan

Nizhny Novgorod

Samara

Subway station

The underground railroad system in Moscow is fast and efficient. Its stations are decorated with beautiful paintings and sculptures.

KAZAKHSTAN

This colorful cathedral in Moscow's Red Square has onion-shaped domes

St. Basil's Cathedral

Moscow

Leo Tolstoy

Tolstoy wrote the classic novels Anna Karenina and War and Peace. He died at Astapovo railroad station, south of Moscow, which was later named after him

Voronezh

Astrakhan

This Russian, triangular-shaped string instrument is similar to a guitar

Balalaika

CASPIAN SEA

Volga

Don

Figure skating is popular in Russia; skaters perform solo or in pairs

Rostov-on-Don

Figure skating

CAUCASUS MOUNTAINS

GEORGIA

AZERBAIJAN

Symbol of Russia

The brown bear represents the size and power of the country to Russians and the rest of the world.

Raspberries and blinis

Blinis are small pancakes and are usually topped with caviar (fish eggs) and sour cream. Raspberries are another favorite delicacy. They are grown in southwestern Russia.

Blinis

Sochi

Raspberries

Racing troikas—carriages mounted on skis and pulled by three horses—is a popular sport in winter.

Troika racing

BELARUS

UKRAINE

RIVERS, LAKES, AND MOUNTAINS

Earth's surface is crisscrossed with streams and rivers, lakes, and high mountains. Many rivers begin as streams high up in the mountains, flow downhill through valleys to low-lying areas, and then pour out into seas. Lakes are large pools of water surrounded by land. Mountains are formed over millions of years, as huge areas of land push into each other, forcing the ground upward.

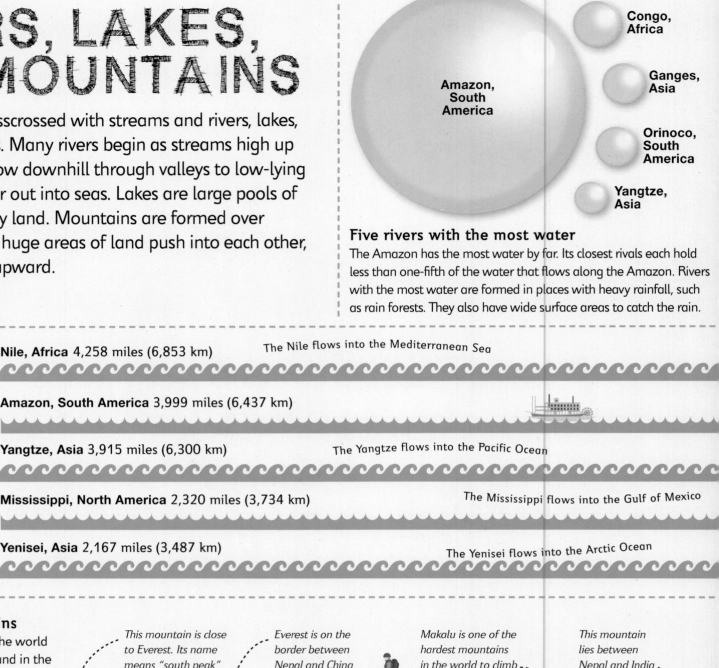

Congo, Africa

Ganges, Asia

Orinoco, South America

Yangtze, Asia

Amazon, South America

Five rivers with the most water

The Amazon has the most water by far. Its closest rivals each hold less than one-fifth of the water that flows along the Amazon. Rivers with the most water are formed in places with heavy rainfall, such as rain forests. They also have wide surface areas to catch the rain.

Five longest rivers

The longest rivers in the world flow across large continents. They begin in the mountains and flow all the way to the open sea.

Nile, Africa 4,258 miles (6,853 km)

The Nile flows into the Mediterranean Sea

Amazon, South America 3,999 miles (6,437 km)

Yangtze, Asia 3,915 miles (6,300 km)

The Yangtze flows into the Pacific Ocean

Mississippi, North America 2,320 miles (3,734 km)

The Mississippi flows into the Gulf of Mexico

Yenisei, Asia 2,167 miles (3,487 km)

The Yenisei flows into the Arctic Ocean

Five highest mountains

The highest mountains in the world are all in Asia. They are found in the borderlands between China, India, Nepal, and Pakistan. There is little difference in height between them, but there is no doubt that Mount Everest has the highest peak.

This mountain is close to Everest. Its name means "south peak"

Everest is on the border between Nepal and China

Makalu is one of the hardest mountains in the world to climb

This mountain lies between Nepal and India

K2 lies between China and Pakistan

1. Mount Everest 29,029 ft (8,848 m)

2. K2 28,251 ft (8,611 m)

3. Kangchenjunga 28,169 ft (8,586 m)

4. Lhotse 27,940 ft (8,516 m)

5. Makalu 27,838 ft (8,485 m)

Three largest lakes

The three biggest lakes are spread across four different continents. The largest is the Caspian Sea, which borders Asia and Europe. It has salty water and is both a sea and a lake. Lake Superior is the world's largest freshwater lake.

Victoria is the largest tropical lake and is the source of the Nile River.

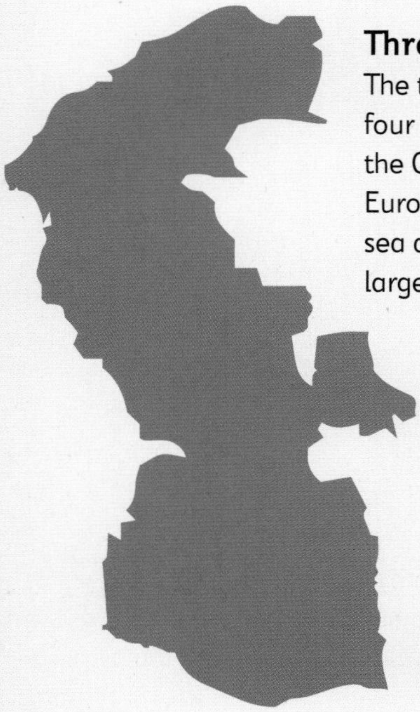

LAND OF LAKES

There are more than 187,000 lakes in Finland, which gives the country the nickname "The Land of the Thousand Lakes."

1. Caspian Sea, Asia and Europe
143,000 sq miles
(371,000 sq km)

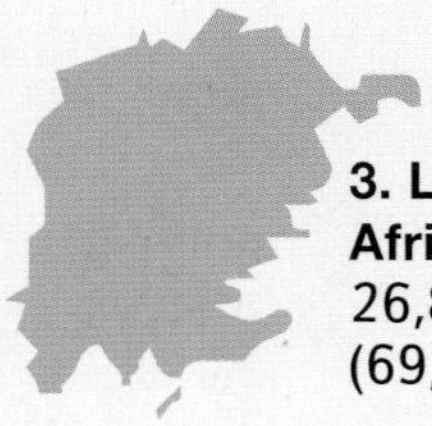

3. Lake Victoria, Africa
26,828 sq miles
(69,485 sq km)

2. Lake Superior, North America
31,820 sq miles
(82, 414 sq km)

The Amazon flows into the Atlantic Ocean

FASTEST-FLOWING RIVER

The Amazon is the fastest-flowing river in the world. Its waves are so strong that it is possible to surf down the river!

Mountains make up about one-fifth of the world's landscape.

1. Mount Tambora, Indonesia 1815 CE

2. Changbaishan Volcano, China 969 CE

3. Mount Thera, Santorini, Greece 1610 BCE

Three powerful volcanic eruptions

Many volcanoes are also mountains. These are three of the most powerful volcanic eruptions in history. When they erupt, volcanoes can cause great damage and change the landscape.

ASIA

Asia is the world's largest, most crowded continent. China and India are big, bustling countries, where industry is growing rapidly. The main world religions all began in Asia. Many early civilizations flourished here, and the continent has many ancient sites.

8. Rose mallow is the national flower of which country?

7. What is Japan's tallest structure called?

6. Which country is the home of table tennis?

You can find all the answers and more quizzes on pages 120-121.

5. On which island would you find the Taipei 101 tower?

ASIA

Asia is the world's largest continent and home to over half the world's population. Countries range from big, powerful nations, such as China, to the tiny state of Qatar. The landscape includes dry deserts, green forests, snowy mountains, and vast expanses of wild, open countryside.

SCALE

	500 miles	1,000 miles
0		
0	1,000 kilometers	

Dead Sea

The Dead Sea, on the borders of Israel, Jordan, and the West Bank, is a large salt lake. It gets its name because the water is too salty for any animal to live there. The salt, however, makes floating in the water easy, and is used in health and skin care products.

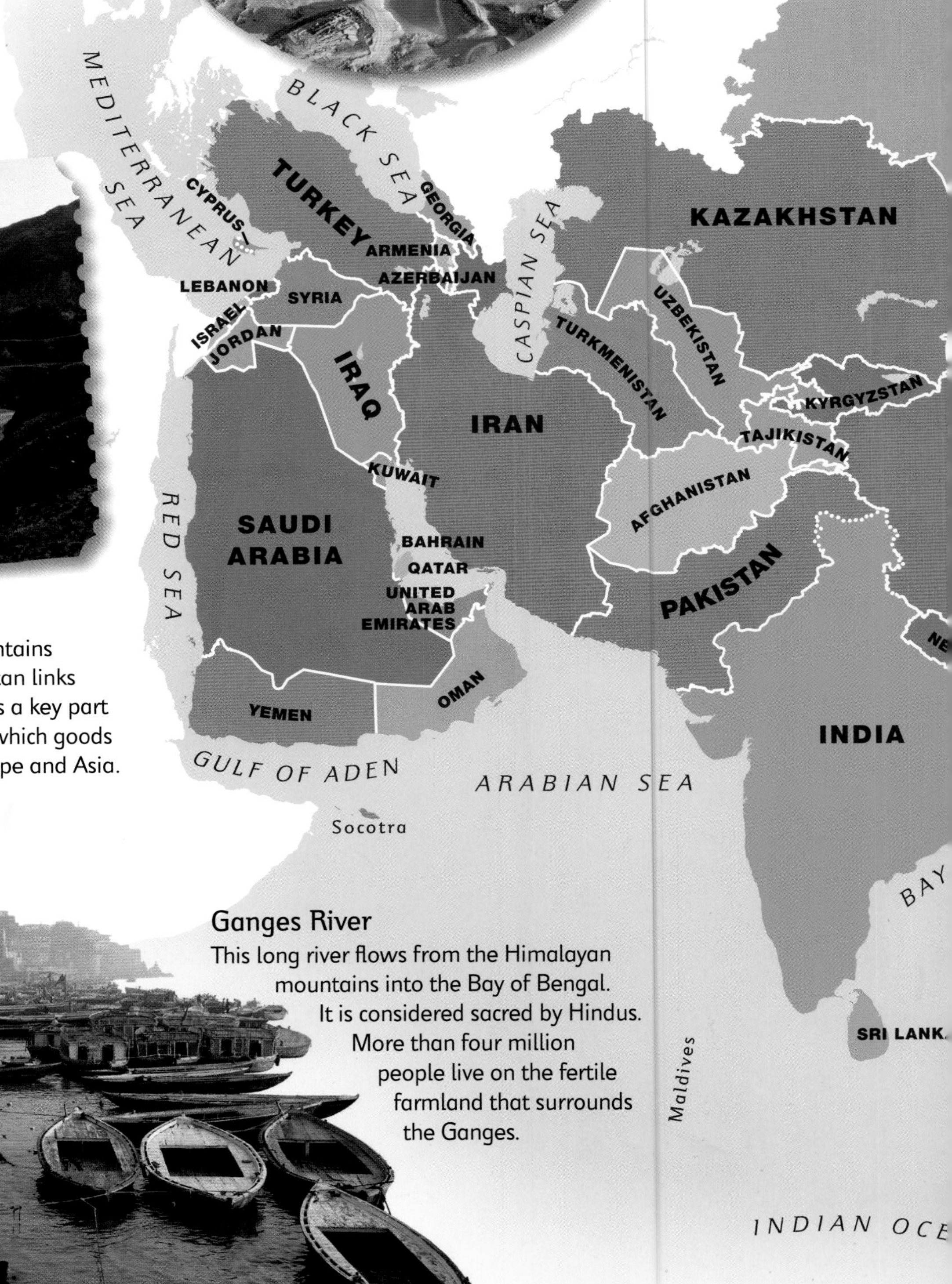

Khyber Pass

This high pass through the mountains between Afghanistan and Pakistan links central and southern Asia. It was a key part of the ancient Silk Road, along which goods were once traded between Europe and Asia.

Ganges River

This long river flows from the Himalayan mountains into the Bay of Bengal. It is considered sacred by Hindus. More than four million people live on the fertile farmland that surrounds the Ganges.

MEDITERRANEAN SEA

BLACK SEA

CYPRUS

TURKEY

GEORGIA

ARMENIA

AZERBAIJAN

LEBANON

SYRIA

ISRAEL

JORDAN

IRAQ

CASPIAN SEA

KAZAKHSTAN

UZBEKISTAN

TURKMENISTAN

KYRGYZSTAN

TAJIKISTAN

IRAN

KUWAIT

AFGHANISTAN

RED SEA

SAUDI ARABIA

BAHRAIN

QATAR

UNITED ARAB EMIRATES

PAKISTAN

NE

YEMEN

OMAN

INDIA

GULF OF ADEN

ARABIAN SEA

Socotra

Maldives

BAY

SRI LANK

INDIAN OCE

ARCTIC
OCEAN

EAST
SIBERIAN
SEA

BERING SEA

RUSSIAN
FEDERATION

SEA OF OKHOTSK

Kurile Islands

MONGOLIA

SEA OF JAPAN

JAPAN

NORTH
KOREA

SOUTH
KOREA

CHINA

EAST
CHINA
SEA

PACIFIC
OCEAN

TAIWAN

PHILIPPINE SEA

PHILIPPINES

HUTAN

MYANMAR
(BURMA)

Hainan
Dao

LAOS

VIETNAM

SOUTH
CHINA
SEA

ADESH

THAILAND

CAMBODIA

NGAL

Andaman
Islands

ANDAMAN
SEA

GULF OF
THAILAND

Nicobar
Islands

BRUNEI

MALAYSIA

Borneo

Sumatra

INDONESIA

JAVA SEA

EAST TIMOR

Java

TIMOR SEA

Mongolian plains
Most of Mongolia is made up of wild, grassy plains. Around a third of the country's people live a nomadic life, roaming the plains on horseback and living in large tents called ghers.

Seoul
This crowded city is the capital of South Korea. It is an exciting mix of the old and the new, with traditional street markets and ancient Buddhist temples next to modern high-rise buildings and shops selling all the latest high-tech gadgets.

Rice fields
Rice is grown in many parts of Asia, including China, India, and Southeast Asia. Farmers grow the rice in fields that are flooded with water, called paddy fields.

ASIAN RUSSIA AND KAZAKHSTAN

Asian Russia stretches from Europe's border to the Pacific Ocean. Much of the landscape is rugged, with few people living there. Kazakhstan lies to the southwest. This country also has large open spaces, including the vast plains of the Kazakh Steppe.

Presidential Palace
The Akorda Presidential Palace in Astana is the official workplace of the president of Kazakhstan and his staff. This impressive building opened in 2004.

Hunting with golden eagles
Kazakhs are skilled horse riders. They hunt on horseback on the wide, open plains, using golden eagles to catch prey, such as foxes and hares.

Kazakhs hunting

ARCTIC OCEAN

KARA SEA

RUSSIA (European Russia)

Noril'sk

Cross-country skiing
This sport is a popular form of exercise during the long winter months

RUSSIA (Asian Russia)

Yekaterinburg

Ural

Sälem!
Hello

Aktobe

These thin, white and silver trees are covered in paperlike bark

Aktau

CASPIAN SEA

KAZAKH STEPPE

Irtysh

Ob'

Yenisei

Omsk

Novosibirsk

Krasnoyarsk

KEY

PRODUCE
- 🌾 Wheat
- Sugar beets
- 🐄 Cattle
- 🐟 Salmon
- 🐑 Sheep
- 🐪 Bactrian camel

INDUSTRY
- Natural gas
- Oil
- Coal
- Diamonds
- Gold
- Lumber
- Aluminum
- Steel
- Iron
- Uranium
- Chromium

SPORT
- Ice hockey

NATURAL FEATURES
- Volcanoes
- Earthquakes

Weightlifting is popular in Kazakhstan, with competitions for both men and women

Weightlifting

KAZAKHSTAN

This 318-ft (97-m) tower is the symbol of Astana

Bayterek Monument

Astana

Pavlodar

Silver birch

This antelope has an unusually shaped nose that filters out the dust blowing across the plains in summer

ARAL SEA

Karaganda

UZBEKISTAN

Shymkent

Lake Balkhash

Saiga antelope

Taraz

This Russian Orthodox cathedral is the second tallest wooden building in the world

Almaty

Zenkov Cathedral

KYRGYZSTAN

CHINA

Hazrat Sultan Mosque
This huge mosque in Kazakhstan's capital, Astana, can hold more than 10,000 worshipers.

SCALE

0 — 600 miles

0 — 600 kilometers

International Space Station

The space station orbits the Earth and was built using Russian technology. Russia's Soyuz spacecraft carries people and supplies to the space station.

Soyuz spacecraft

USA

BERING SEA

LAPTEV SEA

This small squirrel can glide from tree to tree using the skin stretched between its legs as a parachute

Siberian flying squirrel

Lena

Do svidaniya! Good-bye

At 15,580 ft (4,750 m), this is the highest, active volcano in Europe and Asia

Klyuchevskaya Sopka

Magadan

Pacific salmon

Yakutsk

Yakuts

Yakut people live in the east of Russia. Those near the coast catch fish and breed reindeer, while Yakuts in the south raise cattle and horses

These hot thermal springs naturally heat water to a warming temperature of 104–140°F (40–60°C)

Kamchatka hot springs

Salmon farming

Pacific salmon are farmed off the eastern coast of Russia. They are kept in netted areas of the sea and fed on fishfood pellets and small fish.

This small seal lives only in Lake Baikal

Baikal seal

Irkutsk

Lake Baikal

YABLONOI MOUNTAINS

This is the longest railroad in the world, stretching 5,780 miles (9,300 km) from Moscow in Europe to the far east of Russia

Amur

Khabarovsk

Siberian tiger

The Siberian, or Amur, tiger lives in forests in the far east of Russia. These tigers are rare, and many live in protected conservation areas.

Lake Baikal

Lake Baikal is the world's oldest and deepest freshwater lake. The lake is home to more than 1,500 unique species of plants and animals.

MONGOLIA

N
W E
S

Trans-Siberian Railroad

CHINA

Vladivostok

TURKEY

Turkey lies partly in Asia and partly in Europe and is influenced by both Eastern and Western culture. Istanbul, the historic city on the Bosphorus River, links the two continents. This huge country has a varied landscape, and its mountains, lakes, beaches, and ancient sites make it attractive to tourists.

Sultan Ahmed Mosque

This mosque in Istanbul is also called the Blue Mosque, because the walls of the interior are covered in light blue tiles. It has six tall minarets, or towers.

Tiles panel, Topkapi Palace

Iznik tiles

These beautiful painted tiles are named after the town where they were made. They decorate the walls of the Topkapi Palace in Istanbul.

Cotton Palace

This unique geological formation is called Pamukkale, or Cotton Palace. It has white limestone terraces, thermal pools, and hot springs, as well as Roman ruins.

BULGARIA

GREECE

Volleyball is a popular sport with both men and women

Volleyball

Bosphorus

SEA OF MARMARA

Istanbul

Hagia Sophia

Built as a Christian church, the Hagia Sophia became a mosque and is now a museum

Bursa

Eskişehir

These pine trees are important in the Turkish lumber industry

Turkish pine

Mustafa Kemal Atatürk

Atatürk was the first president of Turkey; he set up his government in Ankara, which replaced Istanbul as the capital in 1923

Ankara

Balıkesir

Merhaba! Hello

TURKEY

İzmir

This ancient Roman building in Ephesus was partly destroyed by an earthquake in 262 CE.

Library of Celsus

This ancient city was built on hot springs and so had Roman baths as well as an amphitheater

Denizli

Hierapolis

Lake Tuz

Konya

This group of waterfalls flows into the Mediterranean Sea

This stone castle once protected the port of Bodrum

Bodrum Castle

Düden waterfalls

TAURUS MOUNTAINS

Antalya

Mersin

MEDITERRANEAN SEA

CYPRUS

KEY

PRODUCE
- Wheat
- Sunflowers
- Barley
- Cotton
- Potatoes
- Vineyards
- Sheep
- Goats

INDUSTRY
- Cars
- Shipbuilding
- Electronics
- Natural gas

SPORT
- Basketball
- Soccer
- Scuba diving
- Hiking

NATURAL FEATURES
- Green turtle
- Earthquakes

Black Sea folk dancers

Traditional dance
Folk dancing is popular throughout Turkey. In the Black Sea region, men and women dress in black and red outfits trimmed with gold and silver. They dance using short, quick steps accompanied by violins.

Turkish coffee is very strong ----

Turkish coffee

Dondurma

Kabab b'il karaz

Turkish food
The food of Turkey has rich flavors and aromas. Kabab b'il karaz (sour cherry kebab) is made from minced lamb and sour cherry. Dondurma is a thick, sweet ice cream.

GEORGIA

ARMENIA

AZERBAIJAN

IRAN

This bird nests in Turkish mountains

Alpine chough

BLACK SEA

Trabzon

Samsun

Cherries

Turkey is the world's largest producer of cherries ----

PONTIC MOUNTAINS

Güle güle!
Good-bye

Euphrates

Lake Van

Van

Kayseri

Malatya

The remains of large statues and a royal tomb are found on this mountain ----

Mount Nemrut

Diyarbakır

Batman

Tigris

Gaziantep

Adana

SYRIA

IRAQ

N E S W

Green lizard
Large green lizards live among rocks and bushes. They like to bask in the Sun and eat insects.

SCALE

| 0 | 50 miles | 100 miles |

| 0 | 100 kilometers |

87

SYRIA AND LEBANON

Syria is largely hot desert, but most people live in the cooler, fertile coastal areas by the Mediterranean Sea. Lebanon lies to the southwest of Syria and has a varied cultural history. The land covered by Syria and Lebanon was once part of the Roman Empire.

Carpet weaving
Beautiful, handwoven carpets are produced in Syria. Their highly detailed, traditional patterns come in a mix of colors, with red and black being particularly popular.

Woman weaving on a loom

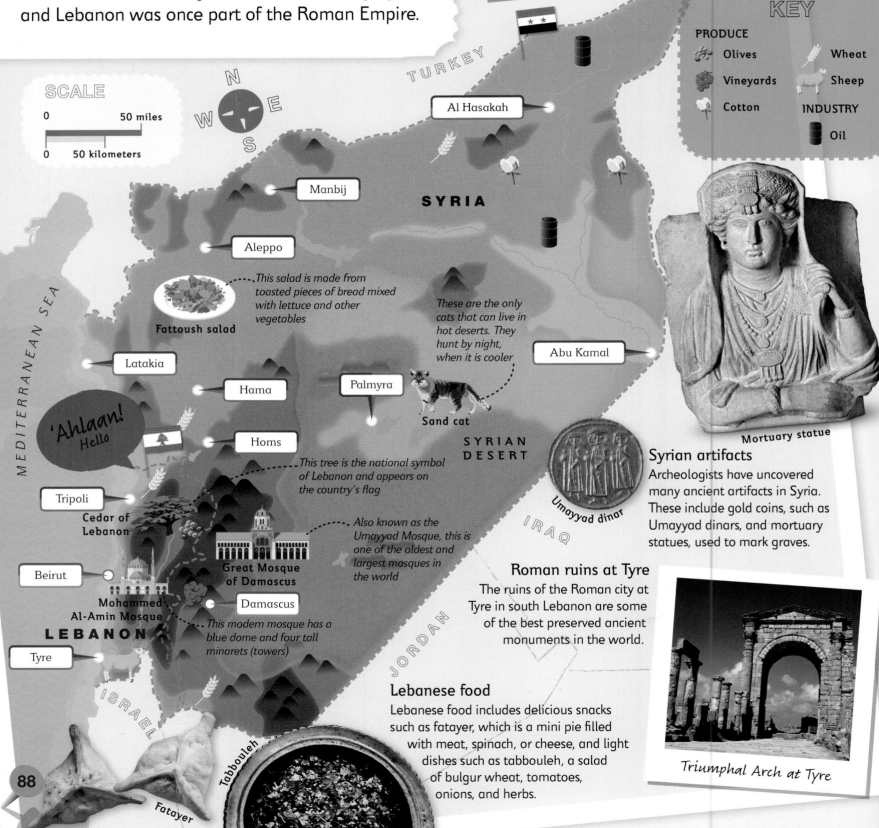

KEY

PRODUCE
- Olives
- Wheat
- Vineyards
- Sheep
- Cotton

INDUSTRY
- Oil

SCALE
0   50 miles

0   50 kilometers

TURKEY

SYRIA

Al Hasakah

Manbij

Aleppo

This salad is made from toasted pieces of bread mixed with lettuce and other vegetables

Fattoush salad

These are the only cats that can live in hot deserts. They hunt by night, when it is cooler

Abu Kamal

Latakia

Hama

Palmyra

Sand cat

Homs

S Y R I A N   D E S E R T

'Ahlaan!
Hello

This tree is the national symbol of Lebanon and appears on the country's flag

Tripoli

Cedar of Lebanon

IRAQ

Also known as the Umayyad Mosque, this is one of the oldest and largest mosques in the world

Great Mosque of Damascus

Beirut

Mohammed Al-Amin Mosque

Damascus

This modern mosque has a blue dome and four tall minarets (towers)

LEBANON

Tyre

JORDAN

ISRAEL

MEDITERRANEAN SEA

Tabbouleh

Fatayer

Mortuary statue

Syrian artifacts
Archeologists have uncovered many ancient artifacts in Syria. These include gold coins, such as Umayyad dinars, and mortuary statues, used to mark graves.

Umayyad dinar

Roman ruins at Tyre
The ruins of the Roman city at Tyre in south Lebanon are some of the best preserved ancient monuments in the world.

Lebanese food
Lebanese food includes delicious snacks such as fatayer, which is a mini pie filled with meat, spinach, or cheese, and light dishes such as tabbouleh, a salad of bulgur wheat, tomatoes, onions, and herbs.

Triumphal Arch at Tyre

Bedouin hospitality

The Bedouin tribes that roam the desert are known for their hospitality. Guests are welcomed and served food and drink, including freshly brewed coffee and spiced tea.

Bedouin brewing coffee

SCALE

0   50 miles

0   50 kilometers

Mae alssama! *Good-bye*

Traditional crafts of the region include pottery and colorful, handwoven carpets

IRAQ

SYRIA

JORDAN

LEBANON

Muqat

Irbid

Haifa

Crafts

This gallery contains a major collection of early 20th-century art

Nazareth

Jericho

Tel Aviv

Tel Aviv Museum of Art

Jerusalem

Temple of Artemis

This Greek temple was dedicated to Artemis, the goddess of the Moon and of hunting

Zarqa

Amman

This church in Bethlehem was built on what is believed to be the birthplace of Jesus

Bethlehem

Gaza

Church of the Nativity

Dead Sea scrolls

Be'er Sheva

This sculpture is on Mount Nebo, where the Bible says Moses died and was buried

Brazen serpent sculpture

These ancient scrolls were found in the Qumran caves, and are some of the oldest texts of the Hebrew Bible

Jordan's national flower blooms briefly in spring and is a symbol of renewal

Black iris

ISRAEL

Shalom! *Hello*

Petra

Copper has been mined in this valley for centuries, and many ancient remains have been found here

Timna Valley

Elat

Oryx, a type of antelope, live in the desert. Their long horns can be up to 30 in (70 cm) long

Arabian Oryx

EGYPT

Aqaba

SAUDI ARABIA

KEY

PRODUCE

- Wheat
- Olives and oil
- Vineyards
- Grapefruit
- Goats
- Oranges

- Figs
- Almonds
- Avocados
- Cattle
- Sheep

INDUSTRY
- Natural Gas
- Fishing

ACTIVITIES
- Scuba diving

NATURAL FEATURES
- Coral reef

Petra

The ruins of Petra are famous for their temples and tombs, carved directly out of pink sandstone cliffs. Petra is also called the Rose City, because of the stone's color.

Jerusalem

The ancient city of Jerusalem has been a place of pilgrimage for Christians, Jews, and Muslims since biblical times.

ISRAEL AND JORDAN

Israel and Jordan are part of an area often known as the Holy Land, and many sites are important to different faiths. There are vast areas of open desert, but also fertile farming land, where crops such as citrus fruit, grapes, dates, nuts, and olives are grown.

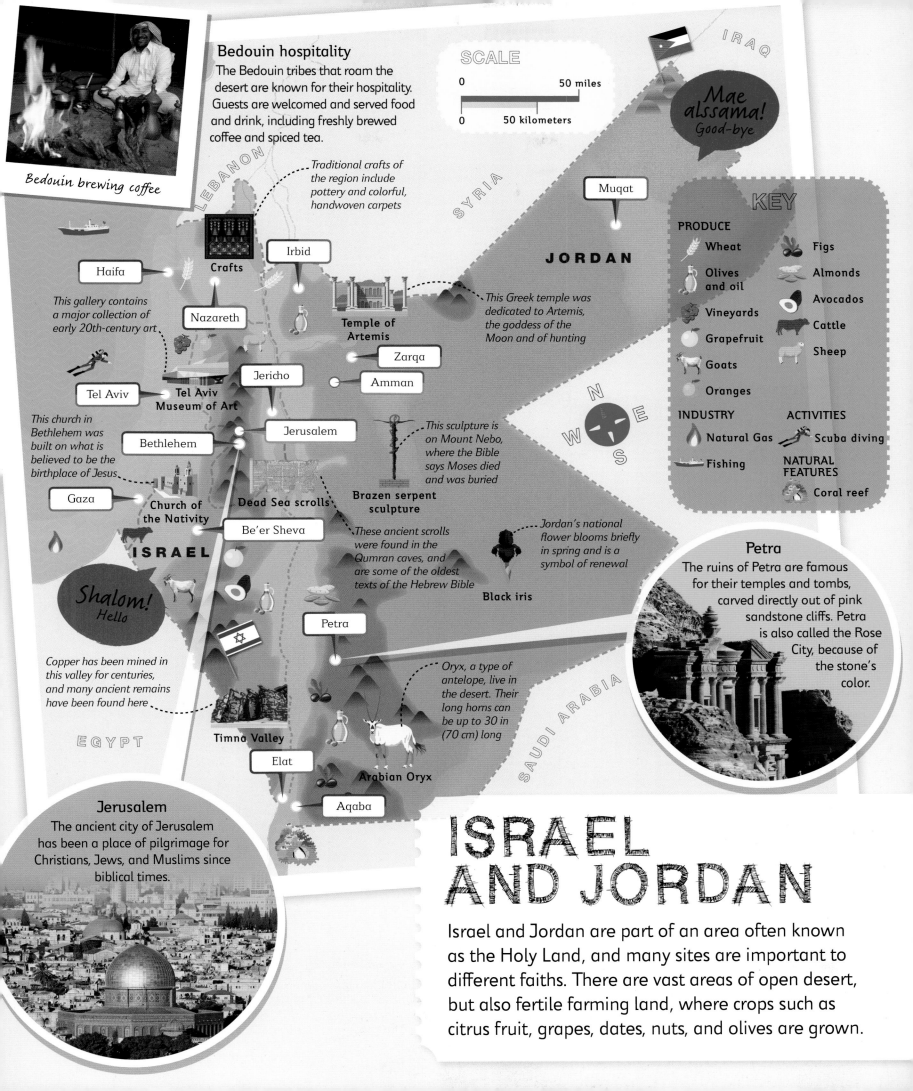

IRAN, IRAQ, AND SAUDI ARABIA

Iran, Iraq, and Saudi Arabia all contain large areas of hot, sandy desert, with huge reserves of oil and natural gas. Some of the world's earliest civilizations flourished in these lands, and all three countries have many ancient ruins and other treasures.

Dates

Saffron

Caviar

Fine foods
This region is noted for producing some of the world's most prized delicacies. These include high-quality dates, the delicate spice saffron, and the best and most expensive caviar (fish eggs).

Isfahan tile

Colorful tiles
The Safavid Empire ruled Persia (modern-day Iran) from the 14th to the 18th century. The capital of this empire was Isfahan, which was known for its fine art, including colorful tiles.

Ur treasure
Ur was an important ancient city in what is now Iraq. Many treasures were found in tombs there. These include intricate gold jewelry and a lyre (type of harp) decorated with a golden bull's head.

Bull's head lyre

Gold wreath

Queen's jewelry

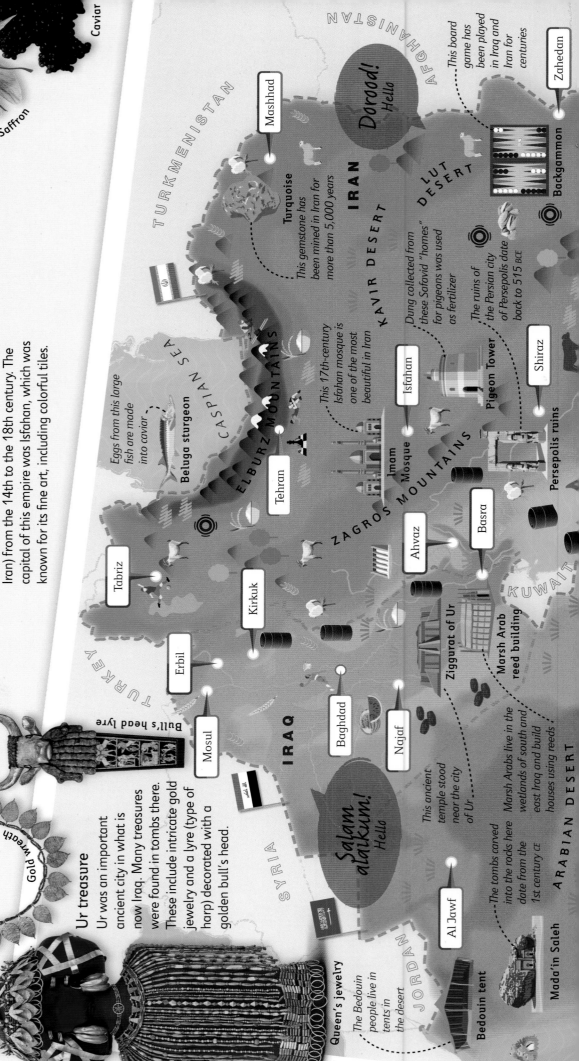

TURKMENISTAN

AFGHANISTAN

Mashhad

Dorood!
Hello

IRAN

Turquoise
This gemstone has been mined in Iran for more than 5,000 years

LUT DESERT

This board game has been played in Iraq and Iran for centuries

Backgammon

Zahedan

KAVIR DESERT

Dung collected from these Safavid "homes" for pigeons was used as fertilizer

This 17th-century Isfahan mosque is one of the most beautiful in Iran

Isfahan

Pigeon Tower

The ruins of the Persian city of Persepolis date back to 515 BCE

Shiraz

Persepolis ruins

CASPIAN SEA

Eggs from this large fish are made into caviar

Beluga sturgeon

ELBURZ MOUNTAINS

Imam Mosque

Tehran

ZAGROS MOUNTAINS

Ahvaz

Basra

Tabriz

Kirkuk

KUWAIT

Erbil

Mosul

TURKEY

Baghdad

Najaf

IRAQ

Salam alaikum!
Hello

Ziggurat of Ur

This ancient temple stood near the city of Ur

Marsh Arab reed building

Marsh Arabs live in the wetlands of south and east Iraq and build houses using reeds

SYRIA

JORDAN

Al Jawf

The Bedouin people live in tents in the desert

Bedouin tent

The tombs carved into the rocks here date from the 1st century CE

Mada'in Saleh

ARABIAN DESERT

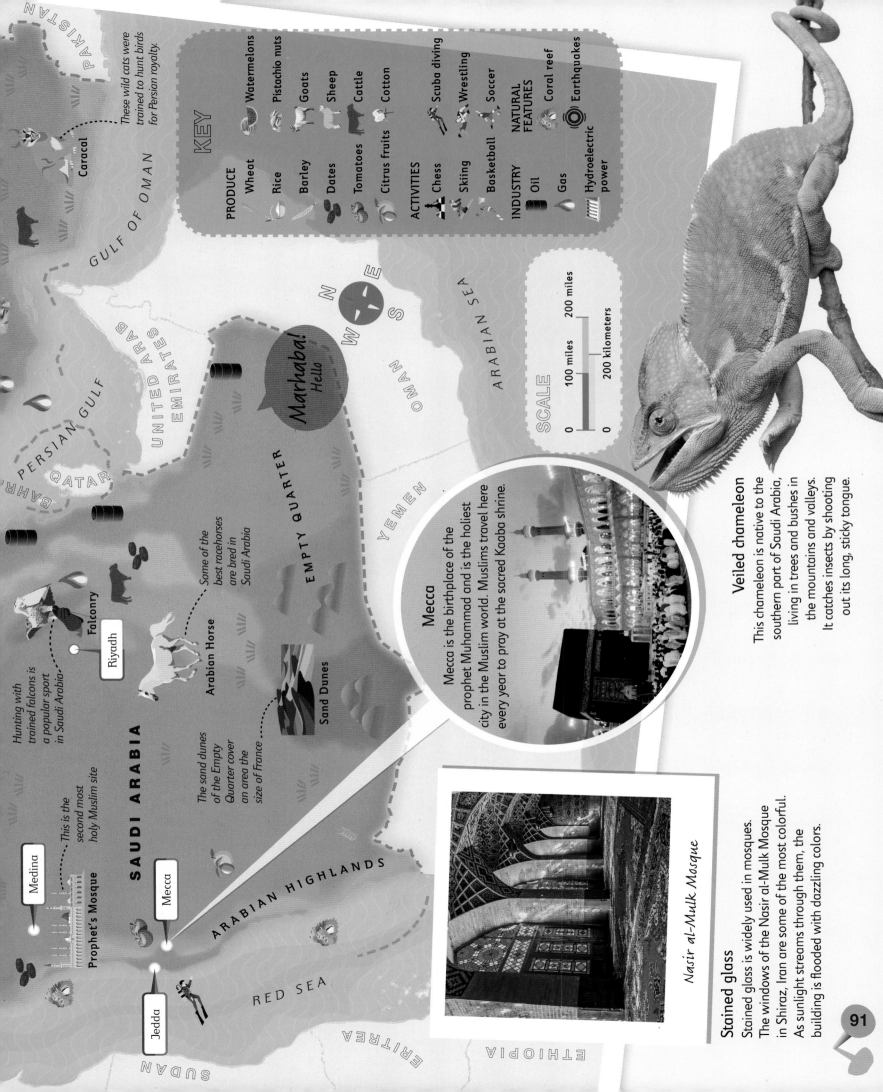

KEY

PRODUCE
Wheat
Rice
Barley
Dates
Tomatoes
Citrus fruits

Watermelons
Pistachio nuts
Goats
Sheep
Cattle
Cotton

ACTIVITIES
Chess
Skiing
Basketball

Scuba diving
Wrestling
Soccer

INDUSTRY
Oil
Gas
Hydroelectric power

NATURAL FEATURES
Coral reef
Earthquakes

PAKISTAN

Caracal

These wild cats were trained to hunt birds for Persian royalty.

GULF OF OMAN

UNITED ARAB EMIRATES

PERSIAN GULF

QATAR

BAHRAIN

OMAN

ARABIAN SEA

Marhaba!
Hello

N W E S

SCALE

0   100 miles   200 miles
0   200 kilometers

YEMEN

EMPTY QUARTER

Some of the best racehorses are bred in Saudi Arabia

Arabian Horse

The sand dunes of the Empty Quarter cover an area the size of France

Sand Dunes

SAUDI ARABIA

Falconry

Hunting with trained falcons is a popular sport in Saudi Arabia

Riyadh

Medina

This is the second most holy Muslim site

Prophet's Mosque

Mecca

Jedda

RED SEA

ARABIAN HIGHLANDS

SUDAN

ERITREA

ETHIOPIA

Mecca
Mecca is the birthplace of the prophet Muhammad and is the holiest city in the Muslim world. Muslims travel here every year to pray at the sacred Kaaba shrine.

Veiled chameleon
This chameleon is native to the southern part of Saudi Arabia, living in trees and bushes in the mountains and valleys. It catches insects by shooting out its long, sticky tongue.

Nasir al-Mulk Mosque

Stained glass
Stained glass is widely used in mosques. The windows of the Nasir al-Mulk Mosque in Shiraz, Iran are some of the most colorful. As sunlight streams through them, the building is flooded with dazzling colors.

91

AFGHANISTAN

Afghanistan lies between Central Asia and China. In ancient times, Chinese silk and other goods were traded along the Silk Road that passed through the Hindu Kush mountains. Temperatures in the deserts and mountains of Afghanistan vary from very hot in summer to freezing cold in winter.

Band-e Amir lakes
Six deep lakes lie side by side at Band-e Amir, in the Hindu Kush mountains. They are part of Afghanistan's first national park.

N W S E
CHINA

These unusual sheep have huge, spiraling horns, which can be up to 27 in (70 cm) long

Marco Polo sheep

This highly prized gemstone has been mined in Afghanistan for over 5,000 years

Citadel of Herat
This huge castle has 18 towers and 6½-ft (2-m) thick brick walls. It stands on the site of a fort built by Alexander the Great in 330 BCE.

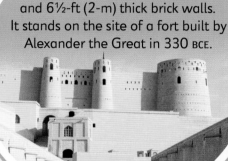

TURKMENISTAN

UZBEKISTAN

TAJIKISTAN

Mazar-i-Sharif

Ancient Buddhist statues and manuscripts were discovered in these caves

Pistachio trees grow wild in many parts of Afghanistan

Bamiyan

Bamiyan caves

HINDU KUSH

Lapis lazuli

Jalalabad

Apricots

Pistachios

Khyber Pass
This mountain pass links Afghanistan with Pakistan

Kabul

Pomegranates

IRAN

Hari Rud

Herat

Pistachio tree

Jama Masjid
This large mosque in Herat is covered in beautiful glazed tiles

Afghan rug

Afghan rugs are prized all over the world

Farah Rud

Fruit and nuts
Afghanistan's farms produce some of the tastiest nuts and fruit in the world. These include large quantities of pistachio nuts, apricots, and pomegranates.

PAKISTAN

Bactrian gold
This hoard of gold artifacts was discovered in ancient burial mounds in northern Afghanistan in 1978. It includes jewelry, coins, and figures.

Kandahar

REGISTAN DESERT

Helmand

Embroidered hat
Traditional clothes in Afghanistan have colorful, detailed embroidery, such as on this child's hat.

Salaam!
Hello

SCALE

0   100 miles

0   100 kilometers

KEY

PRODUCE

Wheat	Apricots
Corn	Cotton
Barley	Sheep
Rice	Goats
Potatoes	Pomegranates
Raisins	

ACTIVITIES
- Basketball
- Soccer
- Cricket

NATURAL FEATURES
- Sapphires
- Earthquakes

PAKISTAN

Pakistan has the world's sixth largest population. Many people live along the Indus River and its tributaries (streams), which flow down through the middle of the country, providing water to irrigate the fertile farmland along the riverbanks. Farming is Pakistan's main source of income.

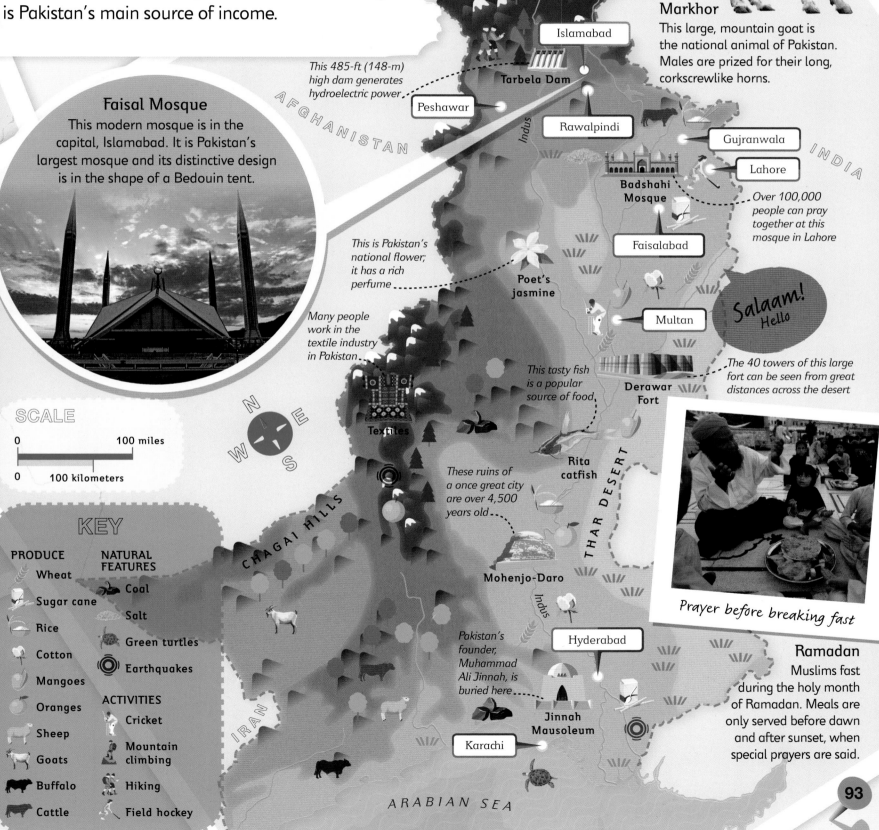

Snow leopards live in Pakistan's northern mountains, which include K2, the world's second highest mountain

Markhor
This large, mountain goat is the national animal of Pakistan. Males are prized for their long, corkscrewlike horns.

This 485-ft (148-m) high dam generates hydroelectric power

Faisal Mosque
This modern mosque is in the capital, Islamabad. It is Pakistan's largest mosque and its distinctive design is in the shape of a Bedouin tent.

Over 100,000 people can pray together at this mosque in Lahore

This is Pakistan's national flower; it has a rich perfume

Salaam! Hello

Many people work in the textile industry in Pakistan

The 40 towers of this large fort can be seen from great distances across the desert

This tasty fish is a popular source of food

These ruins of a once great city are over 4,500 years old

Prayer before breaking fast

Ramadan
Muslims fast during the holy month of Ramadan. Meals are only served before dawn and after sunset, when special prayers are said.

Pakistan's founder, Muhammad Ali Jinnah, is buried here

Map labels
Islamabad · Tarbela Dam · Peshawar · Rawalpindi · Gujranwala · Lahore · Badshahi Mosque · Faisalabad · Poet's jasmine · Multan · Derawar Fort · Textiles · Rita catfish · Mohenjo-Daro · Hyderabad · Jinnah Mausoleum · Karachi · K 2

CHINA · HINDU KUSH · KARAKORUM RANGE · AFGHANISTAN · INDIA · Indus · IRAN · CHAGAI HILLS · THAR DESERT · ARABIAN SEA

Snow Leopard

SCALE
| 0 | 100 miles |
| 0 | 100 kilometers |

N W E S

KEY

PRODUCE
- Wheat
- Sugar cane
- Rice
- Cotton
- Mangoes
- Oranges
- Sheep
- Goats
- Buffalo
- Cattle

NATURAL FEATURES
- Coal
- Salt
- Green turtles
- Earthquakes

ACTIVITIES
- Cricket
- Mountain climbing
- Hiking
- Field hockey

INDIA AND SRI LANKA

India is a colorful and crowded country. It stretches from the snowy Himalayan mountains to the warm waters of the Indian Ocean. Sri Lanka is a tropical island that is known for its tea plantations.

Land of spices

Rich and fragrant spices are grown in India and Sri Lanka. The ginger root adds warmth to sweet and savory dishes and several different spices are used in curries.

Selection of spices

Ginger

Cricket

Cricket is the most popular sport in India. It is played across the country on grass cricket grounds like this one in the city of Mumbai.

Cricketers in Mumbai

Holi Festival

The Hindu spring festival celebrates color and love. People throw paint powder and get covered in bright colors.

Throwing colored paint

Peacock

The peacock is the national bird of India. The males have amazing tail feathers with swirled patterns that look like eyes.

CHINA

MYANMAR (BURMA)

Brahmaputra

BHUTAN

BANGLADESH

Indian rhinoceros

India has passed special laws to protect this rare rhino

Kolkata's largest cricket ground is a venue for international matches

Kolkata

Eden Gardens

NEPAL

Ganges

The Varanasi ghats are stone steps that lead down to the Ganges River and are used in bathing and religious ceremonies

Ghats

Mahabodhi Temple

This red sandstone tower was built in 1200 CE and is 243 ft (74 m) tall

This holy Buddhist site is built entirely from brick

Varanasi

Ganges

Yamuna

Namastē! Hello

New Delhi

Qutub Minar

Narmada

HIMALAYAS

Srinagar

Golden Temple

The Harmandir Sahib is a golden Sikh temple, which contains a holy text

The beautiful palace is made of white marble.

Taj Mahal

About 2,000 of these tigers live in the wild in India

Bengal Tiger

Jaipur

Bhopal

PAKISTAN

THAR DESERT

City Palace

This huge, picturesque palace is in Udaipur.

Ahmedabad

Mandvi

Nicobar Islands

Andaman Islands

KEY

PRODUCE
- Rice
- Cotton
- Tea
- Mangoes
- Black pepper
- Wheat

INDUSTRY
- Coal
- Silk
- Technology
- Nuclear power
- Fishing

NATURAL FEATURES
- Green turtles

ACTIVITIES
- Cricket
- Field hockey

Kathakali

In Kerala state, South India, Kathakali performers wear face paint and costumes and perform dances that act out traditional stories.

Kathakali performers

The classical Indian dance Odissi features delicate hand and head movements

Odissi dancer

BAY OF BENGAL

Cave temple

The Golden Temple of Dambulla is a sacred site that includes many golden Buddha statues and a monastery carved into the rock.

Hampi was once a rich and large city and is home to several important monuments

This snake is extremely dangerous, thanks to its venomous bite

EASTERN GHATS

Godavari

Indian cobra

INDIA

Hyderabad

Krishna

Hampi

These Buddhist cave monuments contain rock carvings and paintings

Ajanta and Ellora Caves

Daman

Goa

Bangalore

WESTERN GHATS

Chennai

Asian elephants used to roam across most of India but are now endangered

Asian elephant

Kovalam

SRI LANKA

Kuhomadu!
Hello

Colombo

INDIAN OCEAN

N E S W

Sri Jayawardenepura Kotte

Gemstones

Precious gemstones are mined in Sri Lanka, including unique blue sapphires. The island has some of the richest gem fields in the world.

This lion is only found in the Gir Forest region of northwest India

Asiatic lion

Diu

Mumbai

ARABIAN SEA

Jodhaa Akbar

Poster for a Bollywood film

Bollywood

Bollywood is one of the world's biggest film industries. It is based in Mumbai, India, and is popular at home and internationally. The films feature songs, dancing, romance, and adventure. They are shot in bright, bold colors, like the posters that advertise them.

SCALE

0 — 200 miles

0 — 200 kilometers

95

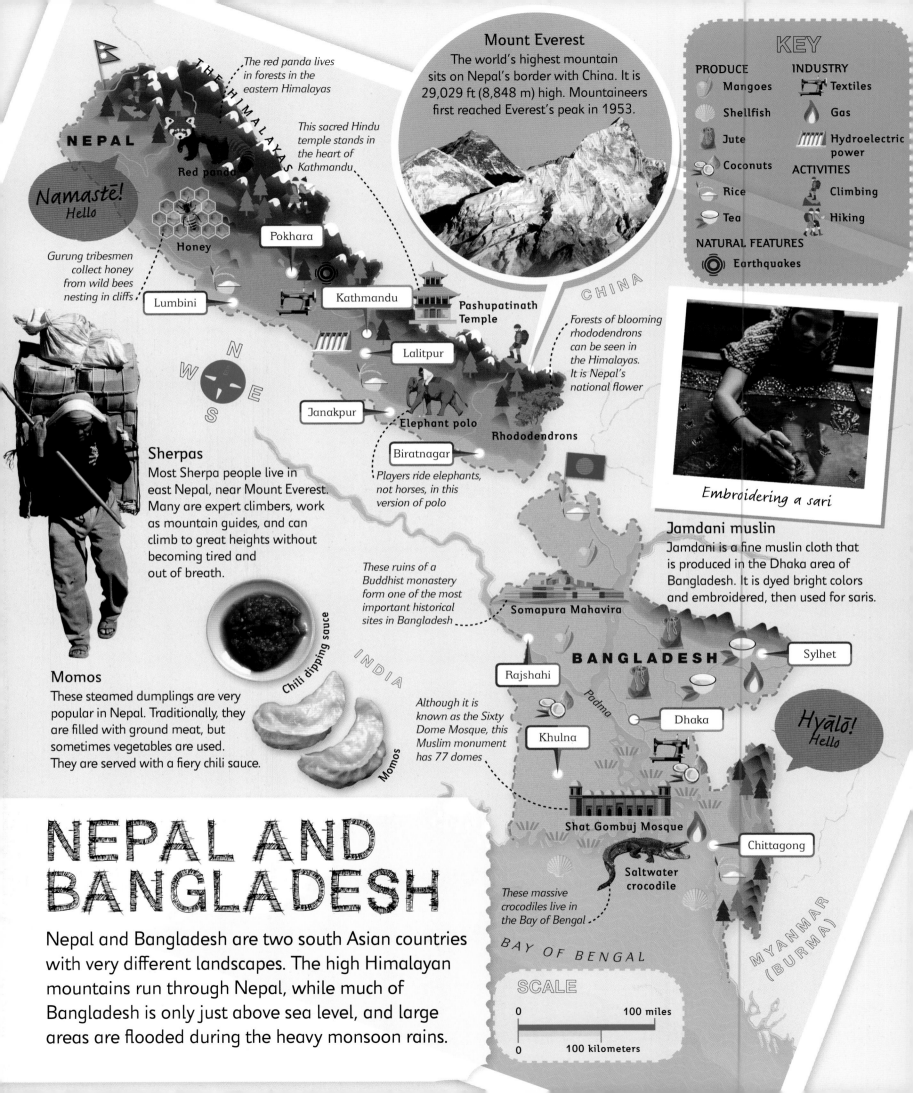

The red panda lives in forests in the eastern Himalayas

THE HIMALAYAS

NEPAL

Red panda

Namasté!
Hello

This sacred Hindu temple stands in the heart of Kathmandu

Honey

Gurung tribesmen collect honey from wild bees nesting in cliffs

Lumbini

Pokhara

Kathmandu

Pashupatinath Temple

Lalitpur

CHINA

Mount Everest
The world's highest mountain sits on Nepal's border with China. It is 29,029 ft (8,848 m) high. Mountaineers first reached Everest's peak in 1953.

Forests of blooming rhododendrons can be seen in the Himalayas. It is Nepal's national flower

Janakpur

Elephant polo

Rhododendrons

Biratnagar

Players ride elephants, not horses, in this version of polo

Embroidering a sari

Sherpas
Most Sherpa people live in east Nepal, near Mount Everest. Many are expert climbers, work as mountain guides, and can climb to great heights without becoming tired and out of breath.

Jamdani muslin
Jamdani is a fine muslin cloth that is produced in the Dhaka area of Bangladesh. It is dyed bright colors and embroidered, then used for saris.

These ruins of a Buddhist monastery form one of the most important historical sites in Bangladesh

Somapura Mahavira

INDIA

Chili dipping sauce

Momos
These steamed dumplings are very popular in Nepal. Traditionally, they are filled with ground meat, but sometimes vegetables are used. They are served with a fiery chili sauce.

Momos

Although it is known as the Sixty Dome Mosque, this Muslim monument has 77 domes

BANGLADESH

Rajshahi

Padma

Sylhet

Dhaka

Khulna

Hyālō!
Hello

Shat Gombuj Mosque

Chittagong

Saltwater crocodile

These massive crocodiles live in the Bay of Bengal

BAY OF BENGAL

MYANMAR (BURMA)

NEPAL AND BANGLADESH

Nepal and Bangladesh are two south Asian countries with very different landscapes. The high Himalayan mountains run through Nepal, while much of Bangladesh is only just above sea level, and large areas are flooded during the heavy monsoon rains.

SCALE
0 — 100 miles
0 — 100 kilometers

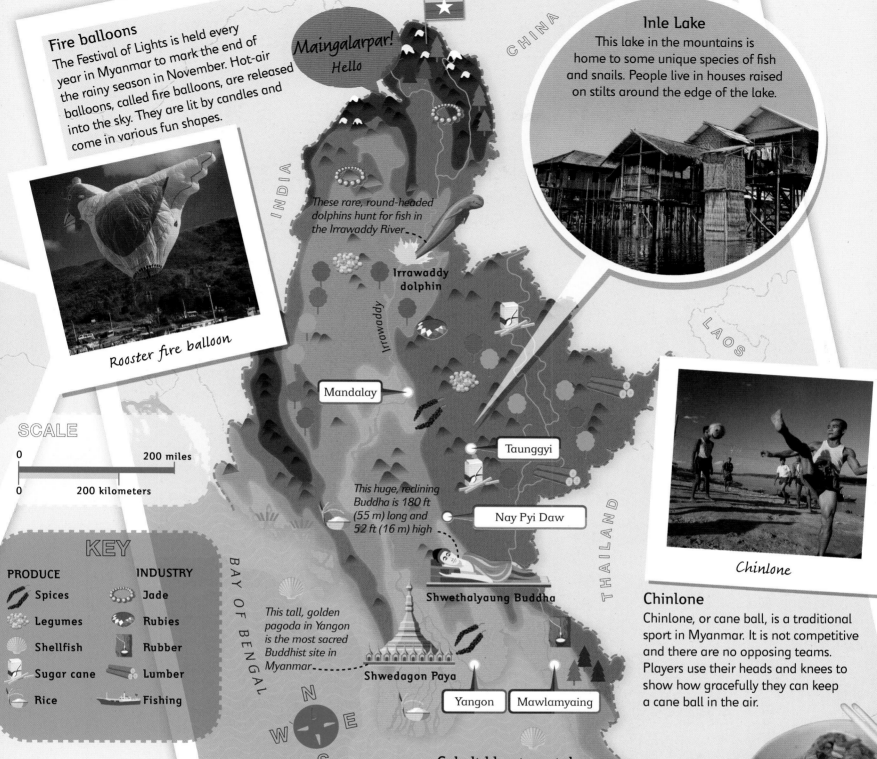

Fire balloons
The Festival of Lights is held every year in Myanmar to mark the end of the rainy season in November. Hot-air balloons, called fire balloons, are released into the sky. They are lit by candles and come in various fun shapes.

Rooster fire balloon

Maingalarpar!
Hello

CHINA

INDIA

LAOS

These rare, round-headed dolphins hunt for fish in the Irrawaddy River

Irrawaddy dolphin

Irrawaddy

Inle Lake
This lake in the mountains is home to some unique species of fish and snails. People live in houses raised on stilts around the edge of the lake.

Mandalay

Taunggyi

This huge, reclining Buddha is 180 ft (55 m) long and 52 ft (16 m) high

Nay Pyi Daw

Shwethalyaung Buddha

Chinlone

SCALE
0 — 200 miles
0 — 200 kilometers

KEY

PRODUCE	INDUSTRY
Spices	Jade
Legumes	Rubies
Shellfish	Rubber
Sugar cane	Lumber
Rice	Fishing

BAY OF BENGAL

This tall, golden pagoda in Yangon is the most sacred Buddhist site in Myanmar

Shwedagon Paya

THAILAND

Yangon   **Mawlamyaing**

N W E S

Chinlone
Chinlone, or cane ball, is a traditional sport in Myanmar. It is not competitive and there are no opposing teams. Players use their heads and knees to show how gracefully they can keep a cane ball in the air.

Cobalt blue tarantula
This blue-legged spider lives in Myanmar's tropical forests. It uses deadly venom to catch its prey, including mice and frogs.

Shan noodles
This popular dish uses flat rice noodles, which are served in a spicy broth with chicken or pork. It is served topped with mustard greens and chopped peanuts.

MYANMAR

Myanmar (formerly Burma) is a long, thin country that follows the Irrawaddy River and the coast of the Bay of Bengal. In the hills and forests of Myanmar, there are mines containing precious gemstones, such as jade and rubies. Its forests produce some of the world's finest teak wood, which is very strong and is used in shipbuilding and to make furniture.

CHINA AND MONGOLIA

More than 1 billion people live in China. Most people live in the industrialized east of this vast and ancient land, which was once the home of a great empire. Mongolia has far fewer people and much of the country is desert or grassland, called steppe.

Baby dinosaur fossils

Dinosaurs in the Gobi
Dinosaurs lived in Mongolia and China millions of years ago. Many well preserved dinosaur fossils have been found in the Gobi desert.

MONGOLIA
People use this two-humped camel to carry goods in the Gobi desert

KAZAKHSTAN

KYRGYZSTAN

Ni hǎo!
Hello

TAJIKISTAN

PAKISTAN

TAKLAMAKAN DESERT

Sain uu!
Hello

Bactrian camel

Tibetan monk

Buddhism
Buddhism is a religion and a philosophy based on the teachings of the Buddha. In Tibet, Buddhist monks wear red robes.

Tai Chi in the park

Tai Chi
This popular group exercise involves a series of slow, controlled movements. People practice Tai Chi for defensive training and to keep healthy.

Yak are kept for their milk, meat, and wool, and for transportation

Yak

PLATEAU OF TIBET

HIMALAYAS

Lhasa

NEPAL

Potala Palace

BHUTAN

INDIA

This Tibetan palace was the home of the Dalai Lama, the spiritual head of Tibetan Buddhism

MYANMAR (BURMA)

Giant panda
The giant panda lives in the mountainous forests of south-central China. It feeds on bamboo and is one of the rarest animals in the world.

Chinese New Year
This is China's most important festival, when people celebrate the coming of spring. People hold parades led by a huge dancing dragon, a symbol of China that is believed to bring good luck.

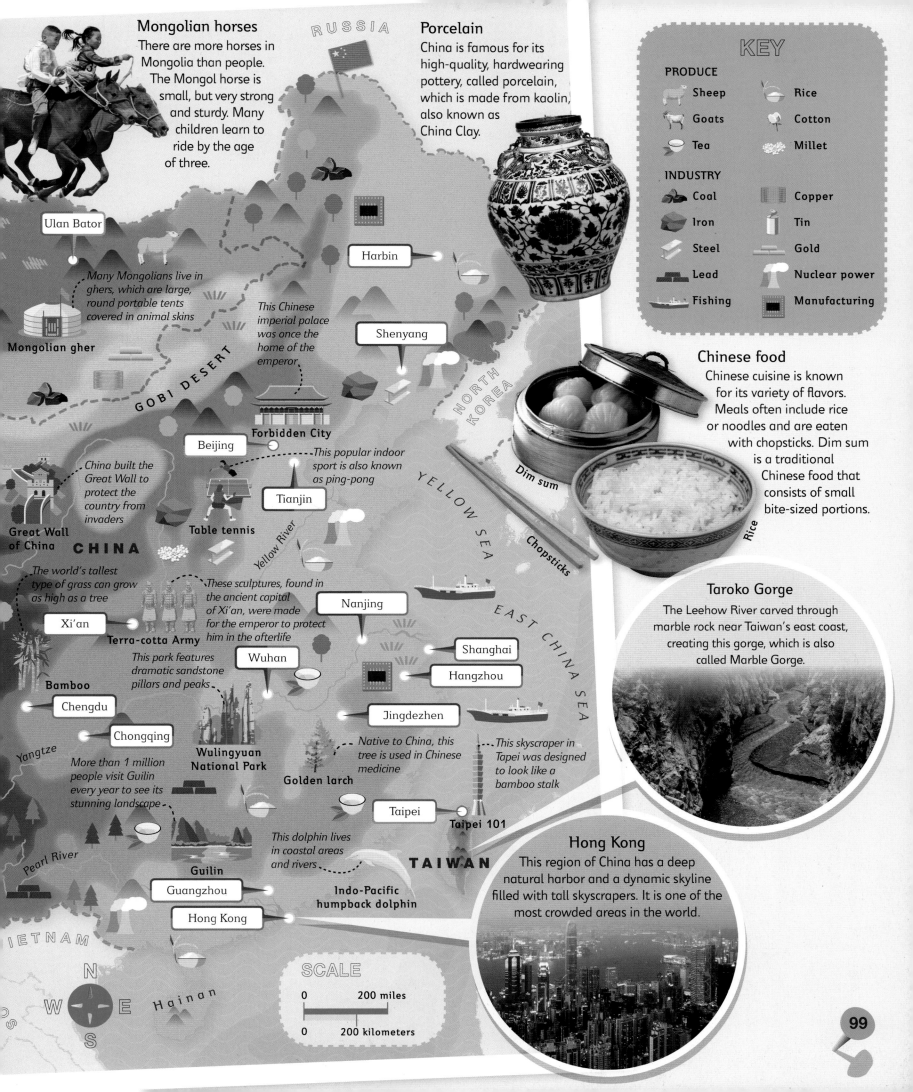

Mongolian horses
There are more horses in Mongolia than people. The Mongol horse is small, but very strong and sturdy. Many children learn to ride by the age of three.

Porcelain
China is famous for its high-quality, hardwearing pottery, called porcelain, which is made from kaolin, also known as China Clay.

RUSSIA

KEY

PRODUCE
- Sheep
- Goats
- Tea
- Rice
- Cotton
- Millet

INDUSTRY
- Coal
- Iron
- Steel
- Lead
- Fishing
- Copper
- Tin
- Gold
- Nuclear power
- Manufacturing

Ulan Bator

Many Mongolians live in ghers, which are large, round portable tents covered in animal skins

Mongolian gher

Harbin

This Chinese imperial palace was once the home of the emperor

GOBI DESERT

Shenyang

NORTH KOREA

Forbidden City

Beijing

This popular indoor sport is also known as ping-pong

China built the Great Wall to protect the country from invaders

Tianjin

Great Wall of China

CHINA

Table tennis

Yellow River

YELLOW SEA

Chinese food
Chinese cuisine is known for its variety of flavors. Meals often include rice or noodles and are eaten with chopsticks. Dim sum is a traditional Chinese food that consists of small bite-sized portions.

Dim sum

Chopsticks

Rice

The world's tallest type of grass can grow as high as a tree

These sculptures, found in the ancient capital of Xi'an, were made for the emperor to protect him in the afterlife

Nanjing

EAST CHINA SEA

Xi'an

Terra-cotta Army

This park features dramatic sandstone pillars and peaks

Wuhan

Shanghai

Hangzhou

Bamboo

Chengdu

Jingdezhen

Chongqing

Wulingyuan National Park

Native to China, this tree is used in Chinese medicine

This skyscraper in Tapei was designed to look like a bamboo stalk

Taroko Gorge
The Leehow River carved through marble rock near Taiwan's east coast, creating this gorge, which is also called Marble Gorge.

Yangtze

More than 1 million people visit Guilin every year to see its stunning landscape

Golden larch

Taipei

Taipei 101

Pearl River

This dolphin lives in coastal areas and rivers

TAIWAN

Guilin

Guangzhou

Indo-Pacific humpback dolphin

Hong Kong

Hong Kong
This region of China has a deep natural harbor and a dynamic skyline filled with tall skyscrapers. It is one of the most crowded areas in the world.

VIETNAM

Hainan

SCALE
0   200 miles

0   200 kilometers

N W E S

KOREA

Korea is a long peninsula that is divided into two countries: North Korea and South Korea, which are very different from each other. North Korea is mountainous and rural. Its society is ordered and closed off from the world. South Korea is more modern and has a thriving electronics industry.

Fruit and vegetables

The Asian pear is native to Korea and is commonly found in gardens. The pear has a yellow skin and a crisp texture. Chinese cabbage, a green-leaf vegetable, is grown in Korea.

Asian pear

Chinese cabbage

Sacred mountain

Mount Paektu is Korea's highest mountain and is sacred to the Korean people. It is also an active volcano and has a large lake at the top.

Chongjin

RUSSIA

Annyeonghi gaseyo! Good-bye

Raccoon dog

This animal fattens up for the cold Korean winter by eating birds, frogs, and fru...

CHINA

Kumsusan Palace of the Sun

This palace in Pyongyang is a mausoleum (burial chamber) that contains the body of Kim Il-sung, the founding president of North Korea.

Sinuiju

KOREA BAY

Pyongyang

...dong

Juche Tower

This 492-ft (150-m) high monument has a metal torch at the top, which is lit up at night

Myohyang-san

This mountain is a sacred site and major tourist attraction

Hamhung

NORTH KOREA

Wonsan

Mount Kumgang

This beautiful mountain features in many Korean works of art.

SEA OF JAPAN / EAST SEA

The internet

South Korea has the fastest internet connection rate in the world. Everyone uses the internet for work, school, and play. Many Korean teenagers enjoy playing games online.

Using the internet

SCALE

| 0 | 50 miles |
| 0 | 50 kilometers |

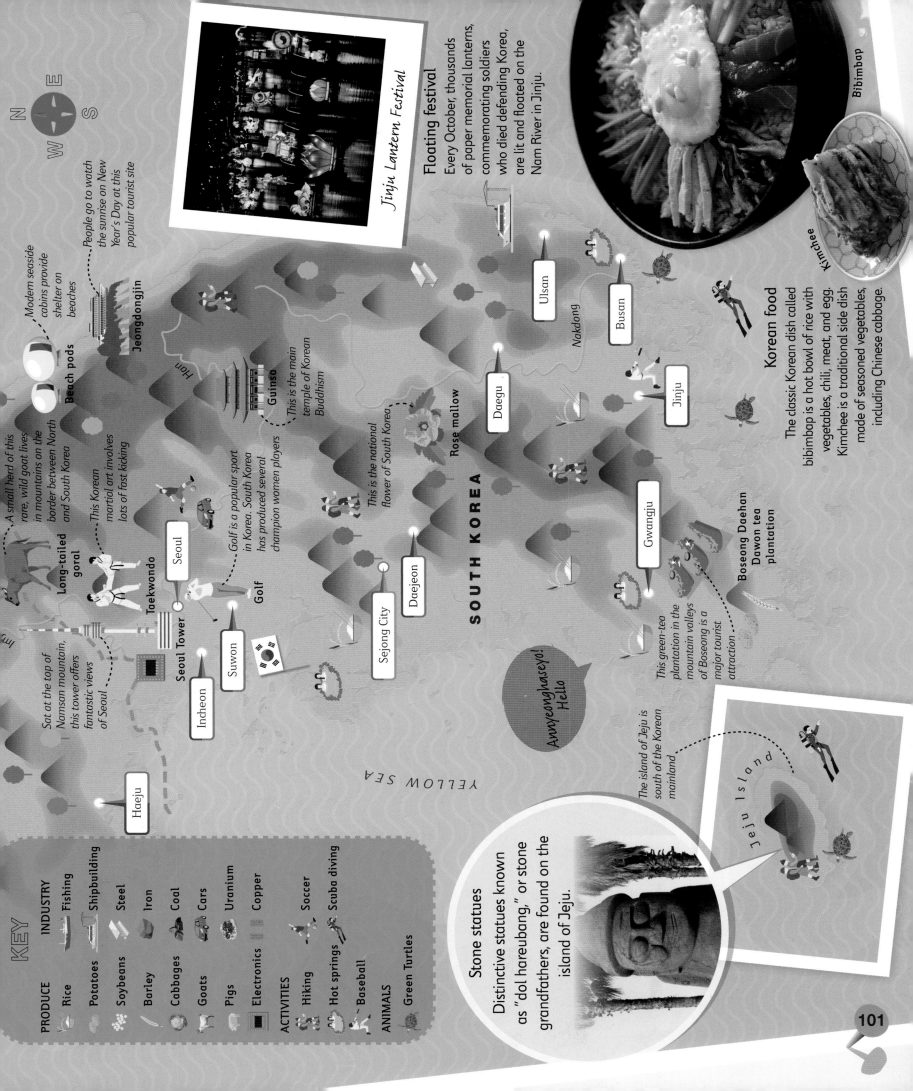

KEY

PRODUCE
- Rice
- Potatoes
- Soybeans
- Barley
- Cabbages
- Goats
- Pigs
- Electronics

INDUSTRY
- Fishing
- Shipbuilding
- Steel
- Iron
- Coal
- Cars
- Uranium
- Copper

ACTIVITIES
- Hiking
- Hot springs
- Baseball
- Soccer
- Scuba diving

ANIMALS
- Green Turtles

Stone statues
Distinctive statues known as "dol hareubang," or stone grandfathers, are found on the island of Jeju.

The island of Jeju is south of the Korean mainland

Jeju Island

Annyeonghaseyo! Hello

YELLOW SEA

Haeju

Jeongdongjin

People go to watch the sunrise on New Year's Day at this popular tourist site

Modern seaside cabins provide shelter on beaches

Beach pods

A small herd of this rare, wild goat lives in mountains on the border between North and South Korea

Long-tailed goral

This Korean martial art involves lots of fast kicking

Taekwondo

Seoul

Sat at the top of Namsan mountain, this tower offers fantastic views of Seoul

Seoul Tower

Incheon

Suwon

Golf is a popular sport in Korea. South Korea has produced several champion women players

Golf

Han

Guinsa

This is the main temple of Korean Buddhism

Sejong City

Daejeon

This is the national flower of South Korea

Rose mallow

SOUTH KOREA

Daegu

Nakdong

Ulsan

Busan

Jinju

Gwangju

Boseong Daehan Dawon tea plantation

This green-tea plantation in the mountain valleys of Boseong is a major tourist attraction

Jinju Lantern Festival

Floating festival
Every October, thousands of paper memorial lanterns, commemorating soldiers who died defending Korea, are lit and floated on the Nam River in Jinju.

Korean food
The classic Korean dish called bibimbap is a hot bowl of rice with vegetables, chili, meat, and egg. Kimchee is a traditional side dish made of seasoned vegetables, including Chinese cabbage.

Kimchee

Bibimbap

JAPAN

Japan is a modern, industrial country, but ancient traditions are still an important part of Japanese culture. Most people live in cities on one of the four main islands. Much of the country is mountainous, with many active volcanoes.

Aomori Nebuta festival

Festivals are held throughout Japan. Every summer, the city of Aomori holds a festival where huge paper lantern floats (nebutas), painted with pictures of mythical beasts and warriors, are carried through the streets.

Lantern float

Bento

On special occasions, Japanese parents send their children to school with a lunch box, or bento, containing decorated food.

Pandas made from rice balls and pieces of seaweed

Kuril Islands

Tokyo

The crosswalk near Shibuya Station is one of the busiest places in this crowded city. Often over 1,000 people, coming from all directions, will be on it at the same time.

This rare wetland bird is a symbol of long life in Japan

Red-crowned crane

Kushiro

Two million people visit Sapporo every winter to see the snow and ice sculptures

Hokkaidō

Asahikawa

Sapporo

Tomakomai

Snow sculptures

Hakodate

Aomori

Hirosaki

Earthquakes are common in Japan and this earthquake was the most powerful ever recorded in Japan

Honshū

JAPAN

Sendai

Tōhoku earthquake

Tea ceremony

Matcha green tea is served in a chawan (special tea bowl) in a traditional ceremony that symbolizes friendship and respect between host and guest. Tea is placed in a small container (natsume). It is then added to hot water with a scoop (chashaku) and stirred with a bamboo whisk (chasen).

Natsume

Chasen

Chashaku

Chawan

Martial arts

Kendo is one of the most popular martial arts in Japan. Fighters use bamboo swords and wear protective armor.

Anime

Kendo

Comics and cartoons

Cartoon drawings are very popular in Japan. Comics in the distinctive hand-drawn style are called manga, while moving cartoons are known as anime.

RUSSIA

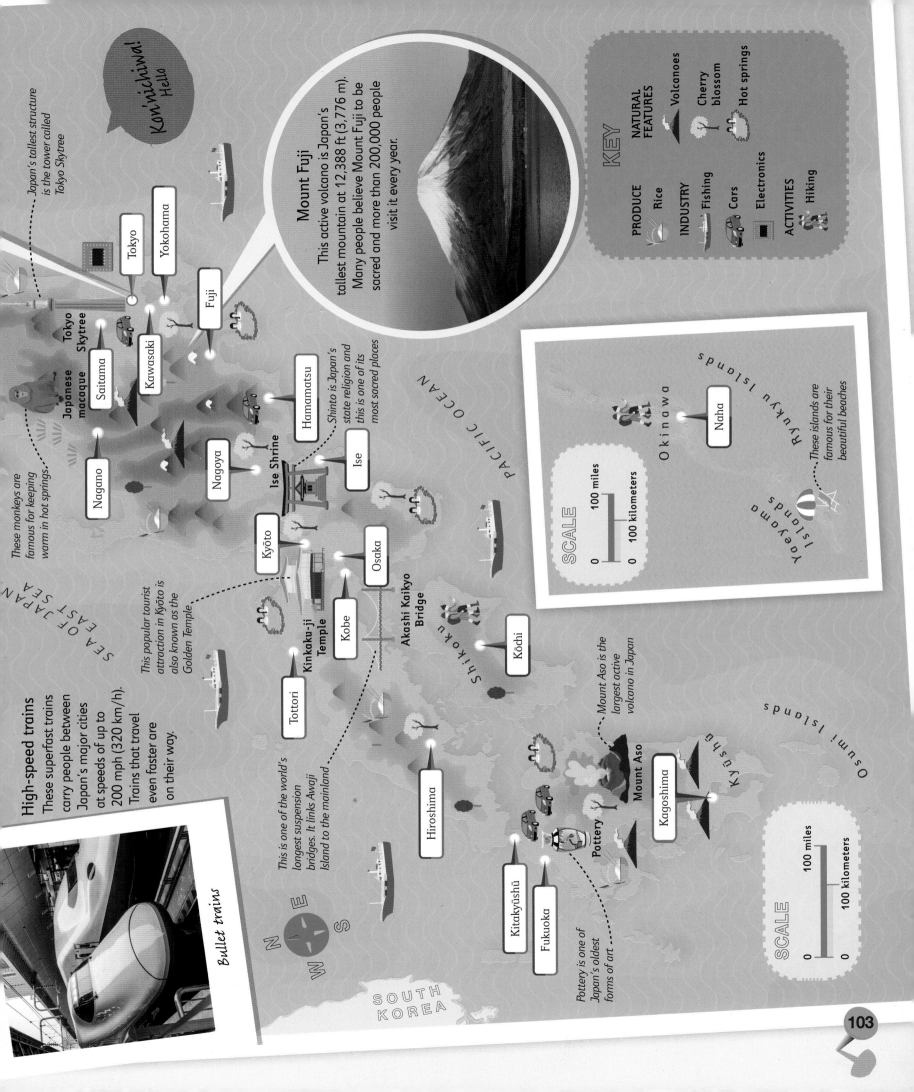

Kon'nichiwa!
Hello

Japan's tallest structure is the tower called Tokyo Skytree

Mount Fuji
This active volcano is Japan's tallest mountain at 12,388 ft (3,776 m). Many people believe Mount Fuji to be sacred and more than 200,000 people visit it every year.

Tokyo

Yokohama

Fuji

Tokyo Skytree

Japanese macaque

Saitama

Kawasaki

Nagano

Nagoya

Hamamatsu

These monkeys are famous for keeping warm in hot springs.

Ise Shrine
Ise

Shinto is Japan's state religion and this is one of its most sacred places

Kyōto

Osaka

Kobe

Kinkaku-ji Temple

This popular tourist attraction in Kyōto is also known as the Golden Temple

Tottori

Akashi Kaikyo Bridge

This is one of the world's longest suspension bridges. It links Awaji Island to the mainland

Kōchi

Shikoku

Hiroshima

Kitakyūshū

Fukuoka

Pottery

Pottery is one of Japan's oldest forms of art

Mount Aso
Mount Aso is the largest active volcano in Japan

Kagoshima

Kyūshū

Osumi Islands

Naha

Okinawa

Ryūkyū Islands

Yaeyama Islands

These islands are famous for their beautiful beaches

PACIFIC OCEAN

SEA OF JAPAN
EAST SEA

SOUTH KOREA

N
W   E
S

High-speed trains
These superfast trains carry people between Japan's major cities at speeds of up to 200 mph (320 km/h). Trains that travel even faster are on their way.

Bullet trains

KEY

NATURAL FEATURES
Volcanoes
Cherry blossom
Hot springs

PRODUCE
Rice

INDUSTRY
Fishing
Cars
Electronics

ACTIVITIES
Hiking

SCALE
0 — 100 miles
0 — 100 kilometers

SCALE
0 — 100 miles
0 — 100 kilometers

103

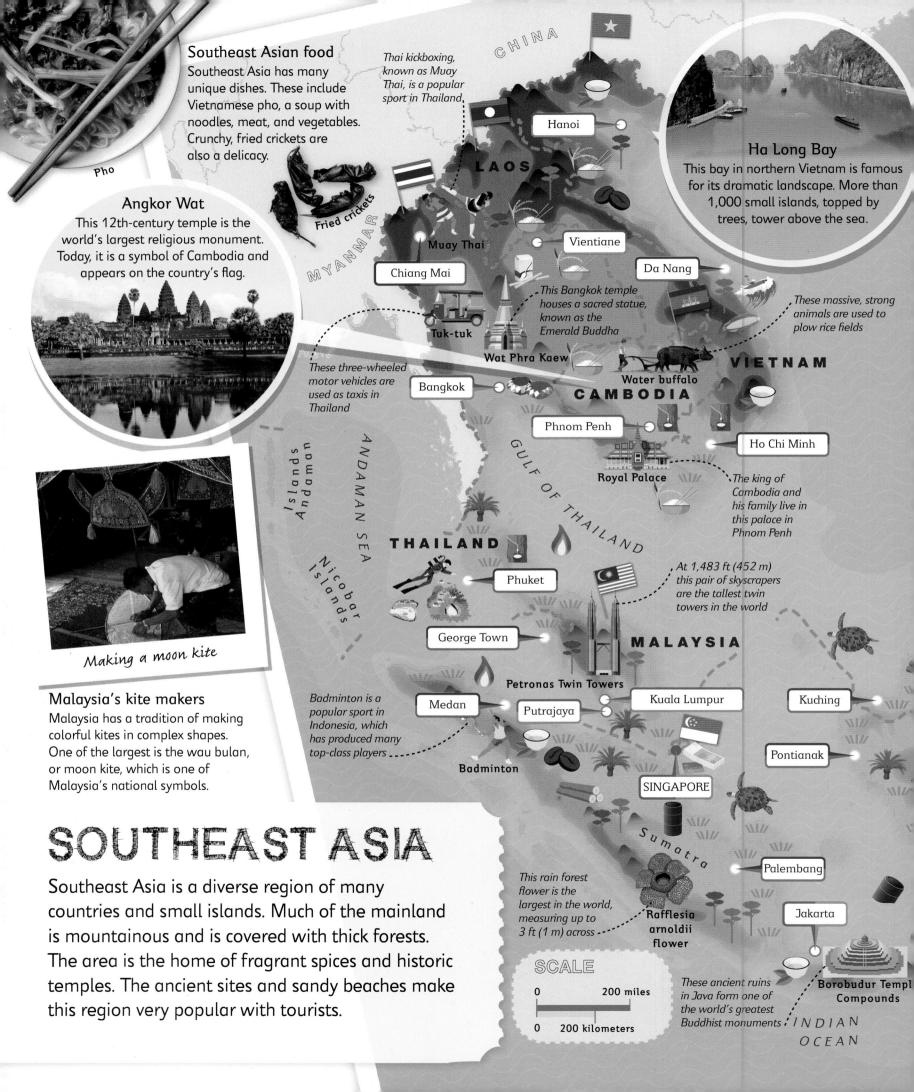

Southeast Asian food

Southeast Asia has many unique dishes. These include Vietnamese pho, a soup with noodles, meat, and vegetables. Crunchy, fried crickets are also a delicacy.

Pho

Fried crickets

Angkor Wat

This 12th-century temple is the world's largest religious monument. Today, it is a symbol of Cambodia and appears on the country's flag.

Making a moon kite

Malaysia's kite makers

Malaysia has a tradition of making colorful kites in complex shapes. One of the largest is the wau bulan, or moon kite, which is one of Malaysia's national symbols.

Thai kickboxing, known as Muay Thai, is a popular sport in Thailand.

CHINA

Hanoi

LAOS

Muay Thai

Vientiane

Chiang Mai

Da Nang

M Y A N M A R

This Bangkok temple houses a sacred statue, known as the Emerald Buddha

These massive, strong animals are used to plow rice fields

Tuk-tuk

Wat Phra Kaew

These three-wheeled motor vehicles are used as taxis in Thailand

Bangkok

Water buffalo

VIETNAM

CAMBODIA

Islands Andaman

A N D A M A N S E A

Nicobar Islands

Phnom Penh

Ho Chi Minh

Royal Palace

The king of Cambodia and his family live in this palace in Phnom Penh

G U L F O F T H A I L A N D

Ha Long Bay

This bay in northern Vietnam is famous for its dramatic landscape. More than 1,000 small islands, topped by trees, tower above the sea.

THAILAND

Phuket

At 1,483 ft (452 m) this pair of skyscrapers are the tallest twin towers in the world

George Town

MALAYSIA

Petronas Twin Towers

Badminton is a popular sport in Indonesia, which has produced many top-class players

Medan

Putrajaya

Kuala Lumpur

Kuching

Pontianak

Badminton

SINGAPORE

Sumatra

Palembang

SOUTHEAST ASIA

Southeast Asia is a diverse region of many countries and small islands. Much of the mainland is mountainous and is covered with thick forests. The area is the home of fragrant spices and historic temples. The ancient sites and sandy beaches make this region very popular with tourists.

This rain forest flower is the largest in the world, measuring up to 3 ft (1 m) across

Rafflesia arnoldii flower

Jakarta

These ancient ruins in Java form one of the world's greatest Buddhist monuments

Borobudur Temple Compounds

I N D I A N O C E A N

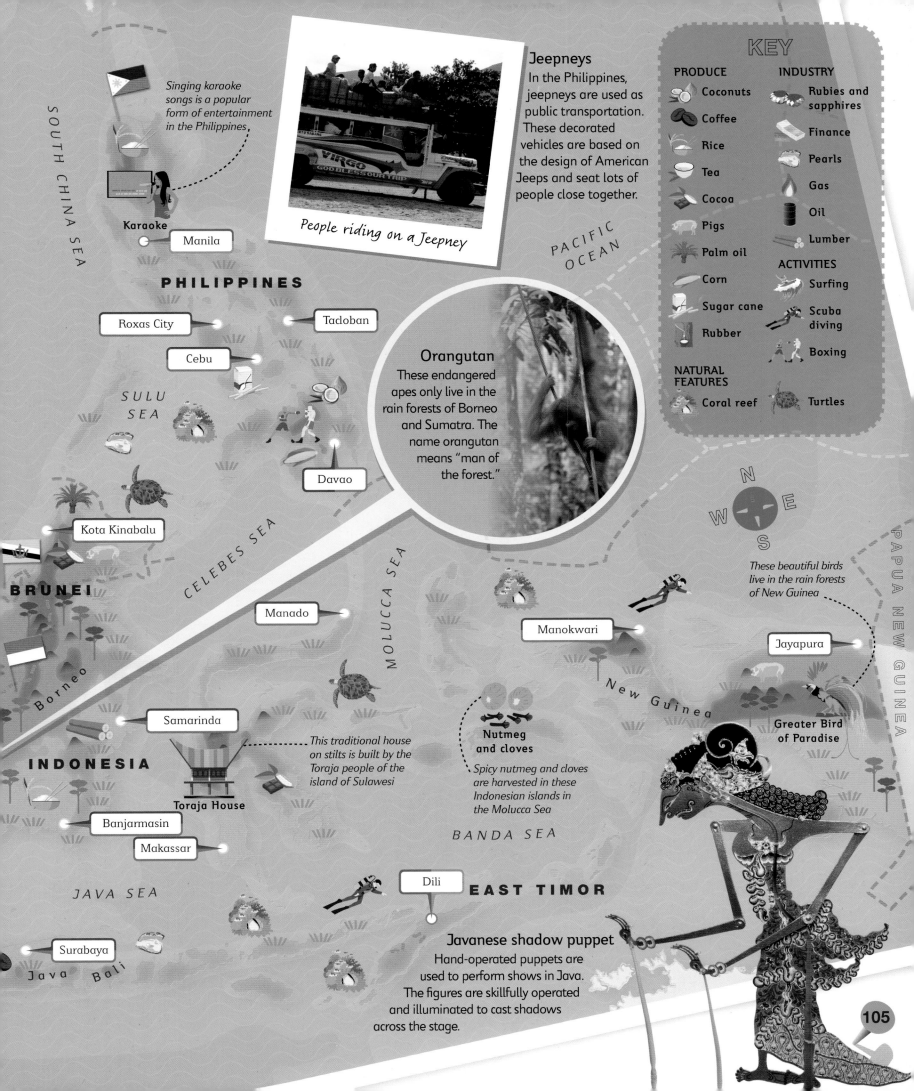

Singing karaoke songs is a popular form of entertainment in the Philippines.

Karaoke

Jeepneys
In the Philippines, jeepneys are used as public transportation. These decorated vehicles are based on the design of American Jeeps and seat lots of people close together.

People riding on a Jeepney

KEY

PRODUCE
- Coconuts
- Coffee
- Rice
- Tea
- Cocoa
- Pigs
- Palm oil
- Corn
- Sugar cane
- Rubber

NATURAL FEATURES
- Coral reef

INDUSTRY
- Rubies and sapphires
- Finance
- Pearls
- Gas
- Oil
- Lumber

ACTIVITIES
- Surfing
- Scuba diving
- Boxing

- Turtles

SOUTH CHINA SEA

Manila

PHILIPPINES

Roxas City

Tacloban

Cebu

SULU SEA

Davao

Orangutan
These endangered apes only live in the rain forests of Borneo and Sumatra. The name orangutan means "man of the forest."

PACIFIC OCEAN

N W E S

Kota Kinabalu

CELEBES SEA

BRUNEI

Manado

MOLUCCA SEA

Manokwari

These beautiful birds live in the rain forests of New Guinea

Jayapura

PAPUA NEW GUINEA

New Guinea

Borneo

Samarinda

This traditional house on stilts is built by the Toraja people of the island of Sulawesi

Toraja House

Nutmeg and cloves
Spicy nutmeg and cloves are harvested in these Indonesian islands in the Molucca Sea

Greater Bird of Paradise

INDONESIA

Banjarmasin

Makassar

BANDA SEA

Dili

EAST TIMOR

JAVA SEA

Surabaya

Java   Bali

Javanese shadow puppet
Hand-operated puppets are used to perform shows in Java. The figures are skillfully operated and illuminated to cast shadows across the stage.

GREAT SITES

Throughout history, humans have built amazing structures and buildings. These great sites were often built to impress people and as a display of power. In the past, cathedrals and castles were among the largest and most awe-inspiring buildings. Today's spectacular buildings and structures include towering skyscrapers and long bridges.

OLDEST BUILDING

The Megalithic Temples of Malta were constructed 5,500 years ago and are among the oldest buildings that still stand today. They were used for religious ceremonies.

Six of the tallest buildings

Tall skyscrapers are built in cities, where land is expensive. Each of these buildings are the tallest on their respective continents. The Burj Khalifa is the tallest building in Asia and the world. It has 163 floors and contains apartments, restaurants, hotel rooms, and offices.

Carlton Centre, Johannesburg, South Africa
732 ft (223 m)
Africa

Gran Torre Santiago, Santiago, Chile, 984 ft (300 m)
South America

Q1 Tower, Gold Coast, Australia
1,058 ft (322.5 m)
Australasia

Federation Towers, Vostok Tower, Moscow, Russia, 1,226 ft (373.7 m)
Europe

One World Trade Center, New York City
1,776 ft (541.3 m)
North America

Burj Khalifa, Dubai, United Arab Emirates
2,717 ft (828 m)
Asia

Five of the longest bridges

Long bridges are built across rivers, lakes, harbors, valleys, and even swamps. Bridges are an important way of connecting communities.

Manchac Swamp Bridge, USA, 22.81 miles (36.71 km)

Lake Pontchartrain Causeway, USA, 23.83 miles (38.35 km)

Bang Na Expressway, Thailand, 34.2 miles (55 km)

Tianjin Grand Bridge, China, 70.6 miles (113.7 km)

Danyang-Kunshan Grand Bridge, China, 102.4 miles (164.8 km)

The Danyang-Kunshan Grand Bridge carries a high-speed railroad over rice paddies, rivers, and lakes.

Ten popular tourist attractions

These 10 great sites are some of the most popular places for tourists to visit. They include historic buildings, religious sites, and ancient monuments.

Golden Gate Bridge, San Francisco, USA

Forbidden City, Beijing, China

Angkor Wat, Siem Reap, Cambodia

Eiffel Tower, Paris, France

Great Pyramid of Giza, Giza, Egypt

La Sagrada Família, Barcelona, Spain

Hagia Sophia, Istanbul, Turkey

Uluru, Northern Territory, Australia

Machu Picchu, Andes, Peru

St. Peter's Basilica, Vatican City

New Seven Wonders of the World

In 2007, an worldwide survey voted the great sites shown here as being the New Seven Wonders of the World. The original Seven Wonders of the Ancient World included the Great Pyramid at Giza, Egypt.

1. CHICHEN ITZA, Mexico

This ancient city was built by the Mayans. It has many great stone buildings, including this pyramid, called El Castillo.

2. MACHU PICCHU, Peru

Nestled in the Andes, this stone city built by the Incas is now in ruins. The name Machu Picchu means "old mountain."

4. COLOSSEUM, Italy

The Romans built this massive, oval-shaped stadium. It could seat more than 50,000 people. Gladiators fought in it.

6. TAJ MAHAL, India

The Taj Mahal means "crown of palaces." It was built as a tomb for Mumtaz Mahal, wife of the Mogul emperor Shah Jahan.

3. CHRIST THE REDEEMER, Brazil

This huge statue of Jesus Christ is 100 ft (30 m) tall. It is carved out of soapstone and looms over Rio de Janeiro in Brazil.

5. PETRA, Jordan

The ancient city of Petra was carved out of rocky cliffs. It is also known as the "Rose City," because of the rock's pink color.

7. GREAT WALL OF CHINA, China

The longest man-made structure, the Great Wall is an amazing sight as it winds its way through the mountains of China.

AUSTRALASIA AND THE POLAR REGIONS

The countries of Australia, New Zealand, and the Pacific Island nations make up Australasia, in the southern half of the world. At the extreme north and south are the polar regions of the Arctic and Antarctic, where few people live because it is so cold.

5. Which Arctic people cut holes in the ice to catch fish?

6. In which country is this building shaped like a beehive?

7. Penguins are found in which polar region?

8. What is the coral reef off Australia's coastline called?

You can find all the answers and more quizzes on pages 120-121.

AUSTRALASIA

The vast region of Australasia contains a wide variety of different landscapes, ranging from the desert that covers most of Australia to tropical islands dotted around the Pacific Ocean, which are fringed with golden, sandy beaches and coral reefs. There are also large areas of dense rain forest in eastern Australia, Tasmania, Papua New Guinea, and New Zealand.

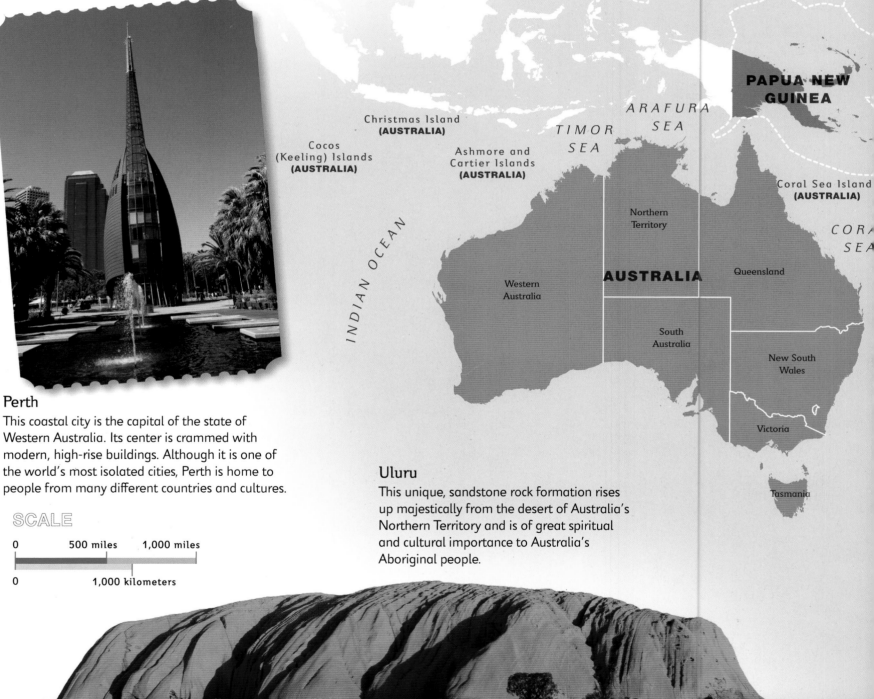

The dotted lines show where these island groups are, as many are too small to see with the naked eye ------

PHILIPPINE SEA

Northern Mariana Islands
(UNITED STATES)

Guam
(UNITED STATES)

PALAU

MICRONESIA

PAPUA NEW GUINEA

Christmas Island
(AUSTRALIA)

Cocos (Keeling) Islands
(AUSTRALIA)

Ashmore and Cartier Islands
(AUSTRALIA)

TIMOR SEA

ARAFURA SEA

Coral Sea Island
(AUSTRALIA)

CORAL SEA

INDIAN OCEAN

Northern Territory

Western Australia

AUSTRALIA

Queensland

South Australia

New South Wales

Victoria

Tasmania

Perth

This coastal city is the capital of the state of Western Australia. Its center is crammed with modern, high-rise buildings. Although it is one of the world's most isolated cities, Perth is home to people from many different countries and cultures.

SCALE

| 0 | 500 miles | 1,000 miles |

| 0 | 1,000 kilometers |

Uluru

This unique, sandstone rock formation rises up majestically from the desert of Australia's Northern Territory and is of great spiritual and cultural importance to Australia's Aboriginal people.

French Polynesia

A group of 118 far-flung Pacific islands makes up this territory that belongs to France, although it is a long way from Europe. The islands have beautiful beaches and coral reefs.

Wake Island
(UNITED STATES)

MARSHALL ISLANDS

Kingman Reef
(UNITED STATES)

Palmyra Atoll
(UNITED STATES)

Baker and Howland Islands
(UNITED STATES)

NAURU

Jarvis Island
(UNITED STATES)

K I R I B A T I

SOLOMON ISLANDS

TUVALU

Tokelau
(NEW ZEALAND)

Wallis and Futuna
(FRANCE)

SAMOA

American Samoa
(UNITED STATES)

VANUATU

Cook Islands
(NEW ZEALAND)

Niue
(NEW ZEALAND)

FIJI

TONGA

French Polynesia
(FRANCE)

New Caledonia
(FRANCE)

Pitcairn, Henderson, Ducie, and Oeno Islands
(UNITED KINGDOM)

Norfolk Island
(AUSTRALIA)

Kermadec Islands
(NEW ZEALAND)

Howe Island
(AUSTRALIA)

PACIFIC OCEAN

NEW ZEALAND

Chatham Islands
(NEW ZEALAND)

Bounty Islands
(NEW ZEALAND)

Antipodes Islands
(NEW ZEALAND)

Auckland Islands
(NEW ZEALAND)

Campbell Islands
(NEW ZEALAND)

cquarie Island
(AUSTRALIA)

SMAN SEA

Coral reefs

Some of the world's most colorful corals and tropical fish live in the warm waters of the Pacific Ocean. The most amazing coral reef is the Great Barrier Reef off the northeast coast of Australia.

Milford Sound

The waters of this beautiful fjord, on the southwest coast of New Zealand's South Island, flow almost 9 miles (15 km) inland from the Tasman Sea. Majestic cliffs sweep up 3,900 ft (1,200 m) on either side. Every year, nearly a million people visit this stunning site.

AUSTRALIA

Australia is a huge island between the Indian and Pacific oceans. The middle of Australia is a vast desert known as the "Outback," which is extremely hot and dry. Most Australians live around the coastal areas, where it is cooler. Here, many people enjoy outdoor activities, such as surfing.

SCALE

0 _____ 250 miles

0 _____ 250 kilometers

KEY

PRODUCE
- Cotton
- Vineyards
- Cattle
- Sheep
- Bananas
- Wheat
- Sugar cane

RESOURCES
- Coal
- Iron Ore
- Bauxite
- Gold
- Silver
- Uranium
- Lumber

ACTIVITIES
- Surfing
- Skiing
- Scuba diving
- Cricket
- Rugby

Kangaroos

Australia is home to many unique animals, including the kangaroo. Kangaroos, like other marsupials, have a pouch in which they carry their young. They move by hopping on their back legs.

A baby kangaroo is called a joey

Surfing

TIMOR SEA

Darwin

This railroad runs from Darwin to Adelaide, a journey of 1,851 miles (2,979 km)

The Ghan Railway

Victoria

Fitzroy

INDIAN OCEAN

G'day! Hello

These desert lizards have thorny scales to defend against predators

TANAMI DESERT

GREAT SANDY DESERT

De Grey

Thorny devil

Fortescue

This distinctive wildflower is found in dry areas

Ashburton

Sturt's Desert Pea

Uluru

Gascoyne

This huge sandstone rock is sacred to Australia's Aboriginals

GREAT VICTORIA DESERT

This passenger railroad links Perth, on the west coast, to Sydney, on the east coast

Kalgoorlie

Perth

Indian Pacific Railway

These huge sharks are found in the seas around Australia

Great white shark

GREAT AUSTRALIAN BIGHT

N W E S

Sun, sand, surf

Australia has long stretches of sandy beaches. People enjoy surfing on some of the world's biggest waves.

Barbecues

Australians love to cook and eat outdoors and barbecuing food, such as juicy shrimp, is very popular. It is also a great way to cook tasty meals.

ARAFURA SEA

PAPUA NEW GUINEA

PACIFIC OCEAN

CORAL SEA

Aboriginal paintings of European ships arriving in the 18th century feature on rocks in this park

Kakadu National Park

This egg-laying mammal is only found in Australia

GULF OF CARPENTARIA

Mitchell

Duck-billed Platypus

All kinds of colorful fish make their home among the corals of the Great Barrier Reef

GREAT BARRIER REEF

Great Barrier Reef
The world's largest coral reefs are off the northeastern coast of Australia. They cover about the same area as Japan and are a great site for scuba divers.

Cairns

AUSTRALIA

Flinders

Townsville

Aboriginals
The Aboriginals were the first people to live in Australia. Some have held onto their traditions and are skilled at finding food in the bush, such as witchetty grubs (larvae of moths).

To reach remote areas, doctors have to travel in light aircraft

Alice Springs

Flying Doctors

SIMPSON DESERT

These bearlike animals live in and eat the leaves of eucalyptus, or gum trees

Digging for food

Australia's national gemstone is found in many bright colors, including green, blue, and yellow

Macadamia trees are native to Australia and their nuts are a tasty food crop

Koala

This bright lighthouse on Australia's easternmost point helps keep ships safe

Opal

These traditional paddle steamer boats still travel on the Darling and Murray rivers

Macadamia nuts

Brisbane

Opera House
Sydney is Australia's oldest and largest city. Its opera house stands in the city's harbor. It is instantly recognizable because of its dramatic shape. The roofs look like the sails of a ship.

Cape Byron Lighthouse

These lakes dry up and disappear in hot, dry months

Darling

This formation of three towering rocks is in the Blue Mountains

Three Sisters Rocks

Paddle Steamer

Murray

Sydney

Adelaide

This sport has two teams of 18 players and is only played professionally in Australia

Australian football

Canberra

This major horse race is one of the biggest sporting events in Australia

Melbourne

Melbourne Cup

TASMAN SEA

Tasmanian devil
These fierce animals are the size of a small dog and only live in the wild in Tasmania. They are named "devils" because of their aggressive character.

This waterfall is in the Tasmanian Wilderness area

Tasmania

Nelson Falls

Hobart

113

All Blacks rugby team

The All Blacks is the nickname of the national men's rugby union team. It is one of the best rugby teams in the world. The men perform a *haka*, a traditional Māori war dance, before each international match.

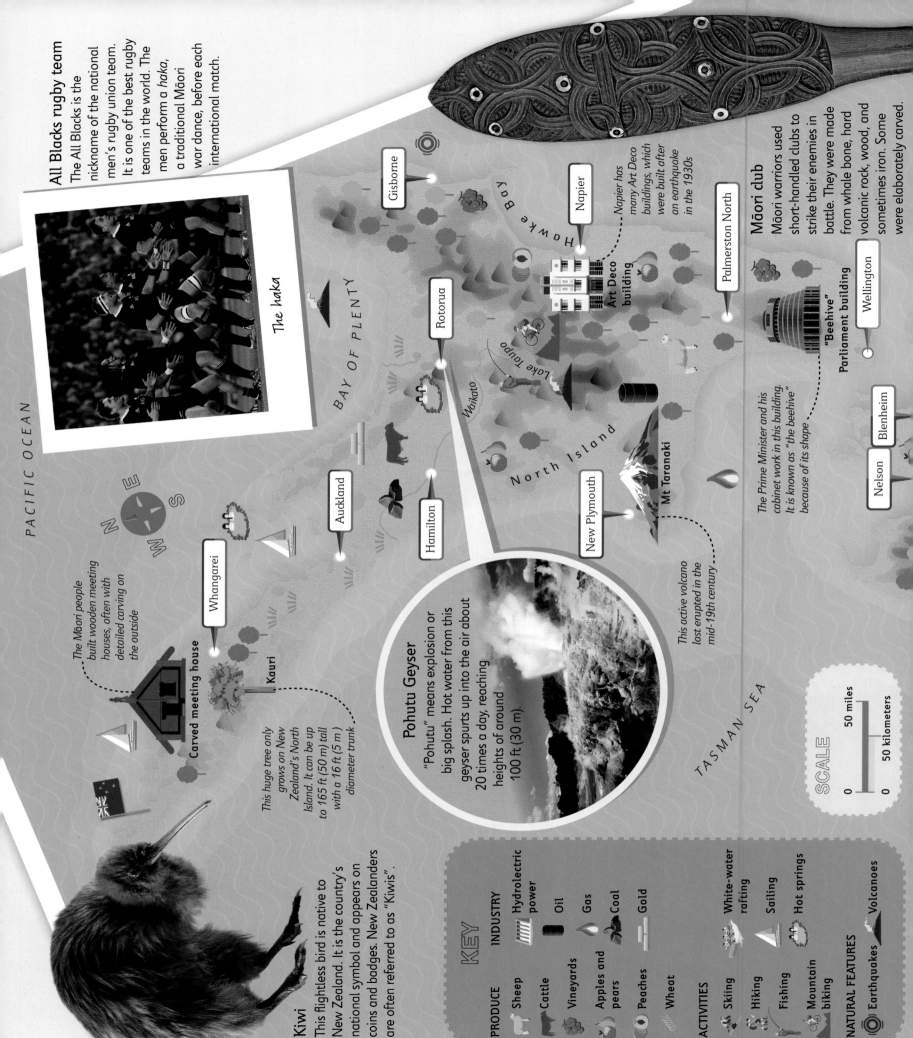

The haka

Kiwi

This flightless bird is native to New Zealand. It is the country's national symbol and appears on coins and badges. New Zealanders are often referred to as "Kiwis".

PACIFIC OCEAN

The Māori people built wooden meeting houses, often with detailed carving on the outside

Carved meeting house

Whangarei

Kauri

This huge tree only grows on New Zealand's North Island. It can be up to 165 ft (50 m) tall with a 16 ft (5 m) diameter trunk.

Auckland

Hamilton

BAY OF PLENTY

Rotorua

Gisborne

Waikato

Lake Taupo

North Island

Hawke Bay

Napier

Napier has many Art Deco buildings, which were built after an earthquake in the 1930s

Art Deco building

Palmerston North

New Plymouth

Mt Taranaki

This active volcano last erupted in the mid-19th century

Pohutu Geyser

"Pohutu" means explosion or big splash. Hot water from this geyser spurts up into the air about 20 times a day, reaching heights of around 100 ft (30 m).

TASMAN SEA

Māori club

Māori warriors used short-handled clubs to strike their enemies in battle. They were made from whale bone, hard volcanic rock, wood, and sometimes iron. Some were elaborately carved.

Wellington

The Prime Minister and his cabinet work in this building. It is known as "the beehive" because of its shape

"Beehive" Parliament building

Nelson   Blenheim

SCALE

0 — 50 miles
0 — 50 kilometers

KEY

PRODUCE

- Sheep
- Cattle
- Vineyards
- Apples and pears
- Peaches
- Wheat

INDUSTRY

- Hydroelectric power
- Oil
- Gas
- Coal
- Gold

ACTIVITIES

- Skiing
- Hiking
- Fishing
- Mountain biking
- White-water rafting
- Sailing
- Hot springs

NATURAL FEATURES

- Earthquakes
- Volcanoes

NEW ZEALAND

New Zealand is one of the world's most isolated countries, being nearly 930 miles (1,500 km) from its nearest neighbor, Australia. It is made up of two large islands and several smaller ones. Farmland and forests cover much of the country. Volcanic activity has created many high mountains and hot springs.

Māori

Māoris were the first people to arrive in New Zealand, nearly 1,000 years ago. Today, they make up less than a quarter of the population, but interest in their culture is growing. Children can now learn the Māori language in school.

Māori dancers

Cardboard Cathedral

An earthquake severely damaged Christchurch's cathedral in 2011. A cardboard, steel, and lumber replacement was built nearby to use while repairs are carried out.

Large numbers of sperm whales feed in the waters near Kaikoura

Sperm whale

Kaikoura

Christchurch

Sauvignon Blanc

New Zealand's climate is ideal for growing grapes for making wine, and the country is famous for its high-quality Sauvignon Blanc wine

South Island

SOUTHERN ALPS

Greymouth

Hello!

Waitaki

This impressive church seats more than 1,000 people

First Church

Dunedin

Clutha

Invercargill

This very rare parrot cannot fly. It is also called the owl parrot, because it only comes out at night

Kakapo

Stewart Island

PACIFIC OCEAN

Milford Sound

FIORDLAND

Despite its remote location, this beautiful fiord is one of New Zealand's most visited sites

Glaciers

New Zealand has many glaciers, mostly on South Island. One of the largest is the Franz Josef glacier, named after an Austrian emperor by a German explorer. This massive block of ice is 7½ miles (12 km) long.

Hiking on Franz Josef glacier

Green-lipped mussels

Kiwi fruit

Farming and fishing

New Zealand exports its produce all over the world. It is famous for its lamb and juicy, green-fleshed kiwi fruit. Large, green-lipped mussels live around the coast and are also farmed.

ANTARCTICA

Antarctica is the coldest and driest continent on Earth. More than 99 percent of the land is covered by a huge ice sheet, which is up to 2¾ miles (4.5 km) thick in places. No people live there permanently, but scientists and tourists visit to study this icy world and its unique animals and plants.

Krill

The cold waters of the Southern Ocean are full of krill. These little shrimplike animals are the main source of food for many birds and whales.

Halley VI dining unit

Antarctic stations

Scientists live and work in Antarctica in research stations. *Halley VI* is a British station that has eight units, which can be moved independently. Each unit sits above the ice on stilts with skis.

Larsen B Ice Shelf

This huge area of ice lying over the Weddell Sea is breaking up and melting. Scientists think this is because the Earth is getting warmer.

Emperor penguins

Penguins cannot fly. Instead, they use their wings to swim underwater to search for krill and fish. Emperor penguins breed on the ice during the winter, with each pair raising one chick.

This species of cod icefish is fished by trawlers from South America

TO AFRICA

Patagonian toothfish

Weddell seals can hold their breath for up to an hour when feeding beneath the ice

This large seabird often robs other birds of their fish catch

San (South Afric

Neumayer (Germany)

South polar skua

Halley VI (UK)

Esperanza (Argentina)

Weddell seal

Capitán Arturo Prat (Chile)

WEDDELL SEA

Belgrano ll (Argentina)

FILCHNER ICE SHELF

ANTARCTIC PENINSULA

RONNE ICE SHELF

Rothera (UK)

Fossil fern

Plant fossils found in Antarctica show that the continent was once much warmer than it is now

TO SOUTH AMERICA

West Antarctica

Icebergs are huge, floating chunks of ice that have broken off ice shelves and glaciers

SOUTHERN OCEAN

Limit of summer pack ice

Limit of winter pack ice

Iceberg

These small whales are at home in the Southern Ocean

SCALE

0	250 miles	500 miles

0		500 kilometers

Minke whale

Maitri
(India)

These ships can break
through ice up to 3 ft
(1 m) thick

Research ship

SOUTHERN
OCEAN

Syowa
(Japan)

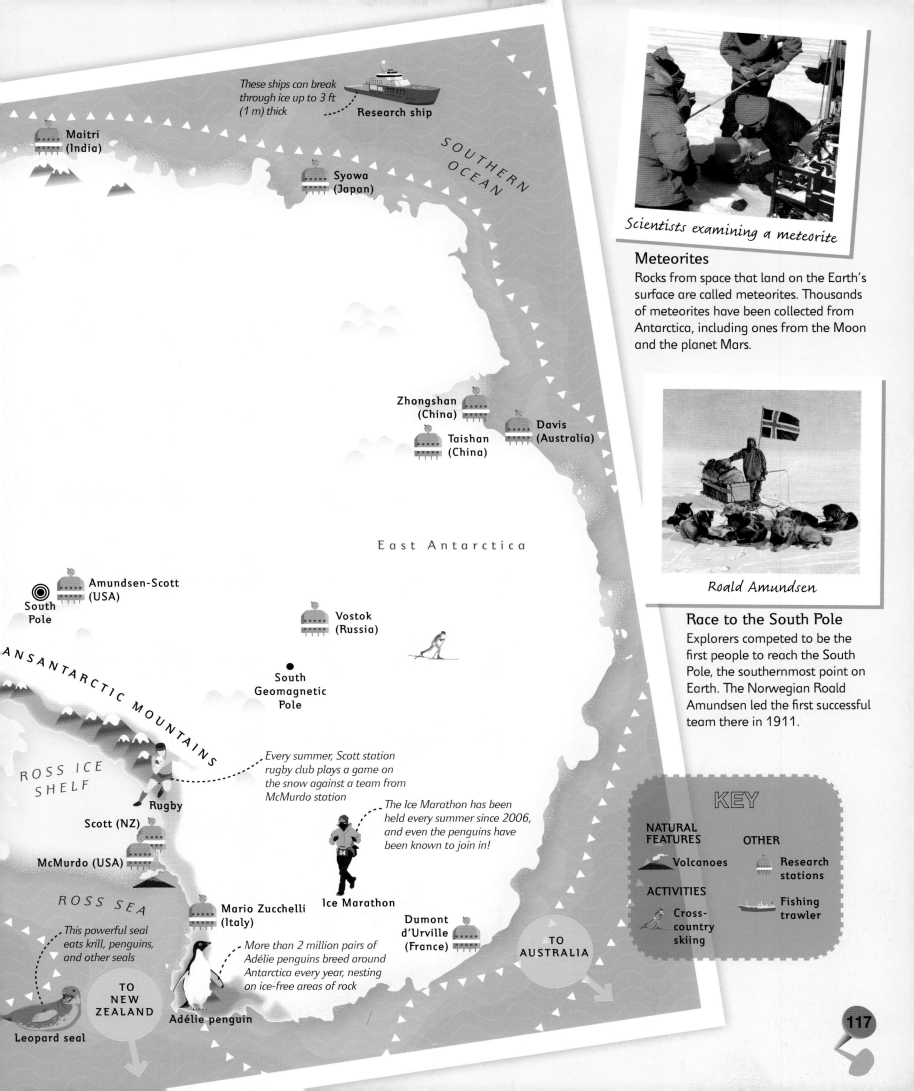
Scientists examining a meteorite

Meteorites
Rocks from space that land on the Earth's
surface are called meteorites. Thousands
of meteorites have been collected from
Antarctica, including ones from the Moon
and the planet Mars.

Zhongshan
(China)

Taishan
(China)

Davis
(Australia)

East Antarctica

Amundsen-Scott
(USA)

South
Pole

Vostok
(Russia)

Roald Amundsen

Race to the South Pole
Explorers competed to be the
first people to reach the South
Pole, the southernmost point on
Earth. The Norwegian Roald
Amundsen led the first successful
team there in 1911.

TRANSANTARCTIC MOUNTAINS

South
Geomagnetic
Pole

ROSS ICE
SHELF

Every summer, Scott station
rugby club plays a game on
the snow against a team from
McMurdo station

Rugby

Scott (NZ)

McMurdo (USA)

ROSS SEA

This powerful seal
eats krill, penguins,
and other seals

TO
NEW
ZEALAND

Leopard seal

Adélie penguin

Mario Zucchelli
(Italy)

More than 2 million pairs of
Adélie penguins breed around
Antarctica every year, nesting
on ice-free areas of rock

The Ice Marathon has been
held every summer since 2006,
and even the penguins have
been known to join in!

Ice Marathon

Dumont
d'Urville
(France)

TO
AUSTRALIA

KEY
**NATURAL
FEATURES**

Volcanoes

ACTIVITIES

Cross-
country
skiing

OTHER

Research
stations

Fishing
trawler

117

THE ARCTIC

The extreme northern edges of the countries of Europe, Asia, and North America lie within the Arctic region. At its center lies the North Pole.

Most of the Arctic is ice, floating above the Arctic Ocean. In summer, the ice shrinks and chunks break off into the ocean. In winter, the ice expands.

Inuit carving

The Inuit are a group of people that live in the Arctic regions of the US, Canada, and Greenland. They have created carvings of animal figures, made from walrus tusks.

Polar bear

The polar bear's thick fur helps it keep warm in freezing Arctic temperatures. It hunts mainly seals, which it catches through holes in the ice. It is also a very good swimmer.

KEY

INDUSTRY

- Oil
- Gold
- Gas
- Copper
- Iron

PRODUCE

- Salmon

ACTIVITIES

- Cross-country skiing

RUSSIA

Lemmings live on the tundra, a treeless area around the Arctic

Brown lemming

Khatanga

Tiksi

Arctic willow

This tiny willow is the northernmost woody plant in the world

LAPTEV SEA

Arctic tern

These birds breed in the Arctic, when it is summer there, then fly to Antarctica to enjoy the southern summer

The Chukchi people of the Russian Arctic depend on their reindeer herds for food and transport

Pevek

Chukchi

EAST SIBERIAN SEA

CHUKCHI SEA

Walrus

Walruses hunt for food in the sea and rest on land or floating ice

The Arctic Circle is an imaginary circle that marks the edge of the Arctic region

ARCTIC OCEAN

Barrow

Prudhoe Bay

USA

BEAUFORT SEA

Inuvik

Musk oxen use their large, curved horns to defend themselves against polar bears and wolves

Musk ox

SCALE

0   250 miles

0   250 kilometers

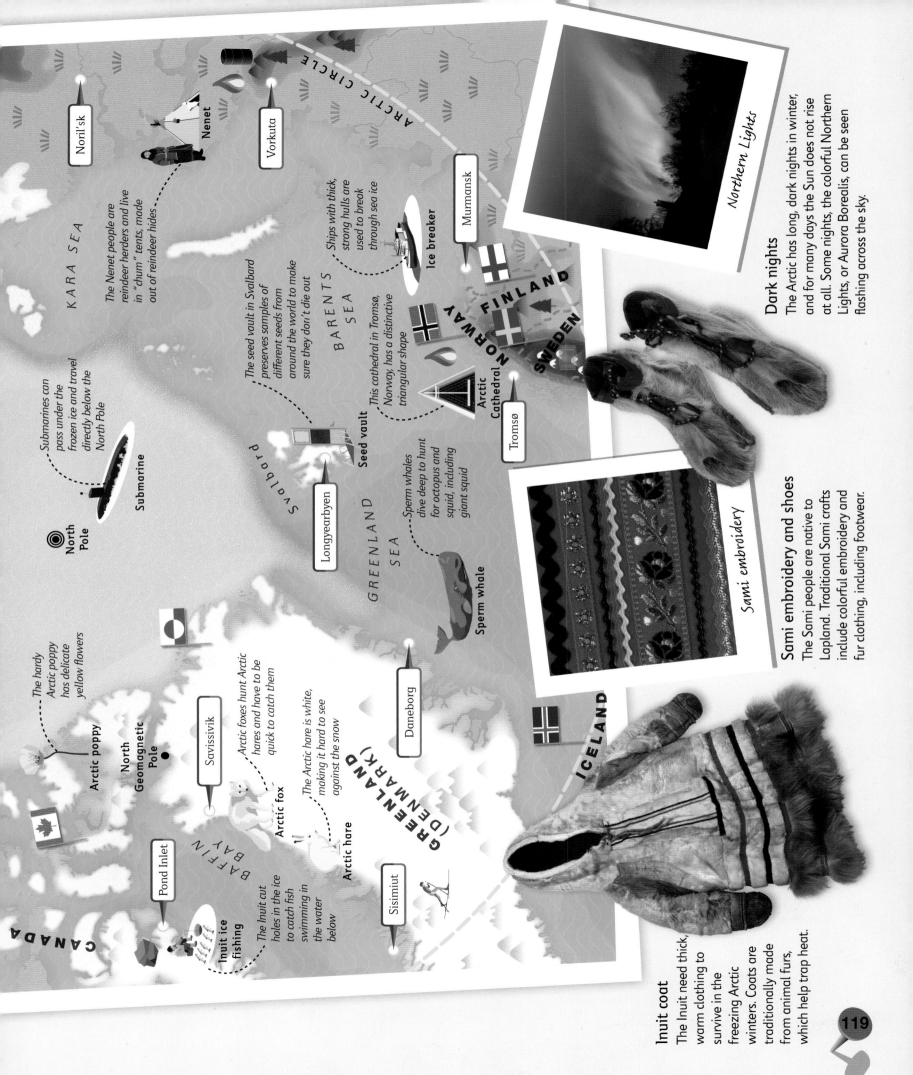

Noril'sk

Nenet

The Nenet people are reindeer herders and live in "chum" tents, made out of reindeer hides

Vorkuta

ARCTIC CIRCLE

KARA SEA

Submarines can pass under the frozen ice and travel directly below the North Pole

Submarine

◉ **North Pole**

The seed vault in Svalbard preserves samples of different seeds from around the world to make sure they don't die out

Ships with thick, strong hulls are used to break through sea ice

Ice breaker

BARENTS SEA

Murmansk

This cathedral in Tromsø, Norway, has a distinctive triangular shape

Arctic Cathedral

FINLAND

NORWAY

SWEDEN

Svalbard

Longyearbyen

Seed vault

Tromsø

Sperm whales dive deep to hunt for octopus and squid, including giant squid

GREENLAND SEA

Sperm whale

The hardy Arctic poppy has delicate yellow flowers

Arctic poppy

North Geomagnetic Pole ●

Savissivik

Arctic foxes hunt Arctic hares and have to be quick to catch them

Arctic fox

The Arctic hare is white, making it hard to see against the snow

Arctic hare

GREENLAND (DENMARK)

Daneborg

ICELAND

Pond Inlet

BAFFIN BAY

The Inuit cut holes in the ice to catch fish swimming in the water below

Inuit ice fishing

Sisimiut

CANADA

Northern Lights

Dark nights
The Arctic has long, dark nights in winter, and for many days the Sun does not rise at all. Some nights, the colorful Northern Lights, or Aurora Borealis, can be seen flashing across the sky.

Sami embroidery

Sami embroidery and shoes
The Sami people are native to Lapland. Traditional Sami crafts include colorful embroidery and fur clothing, including footwear.

Inuit coat
The Inuit need thick, warm clothing to survive in the freezing Arctic winters. Coats are traditionally made from animal furs, which help trap heat.

ATLAS PICTURE QUIZ

1

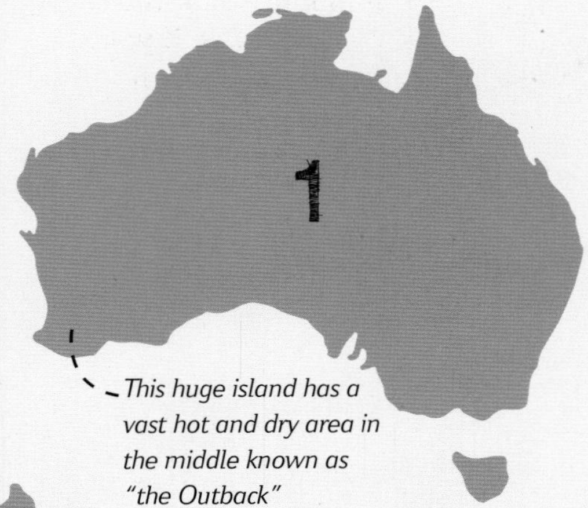

This huge island has a vast hot and dry area in the middle known as "the Outback"

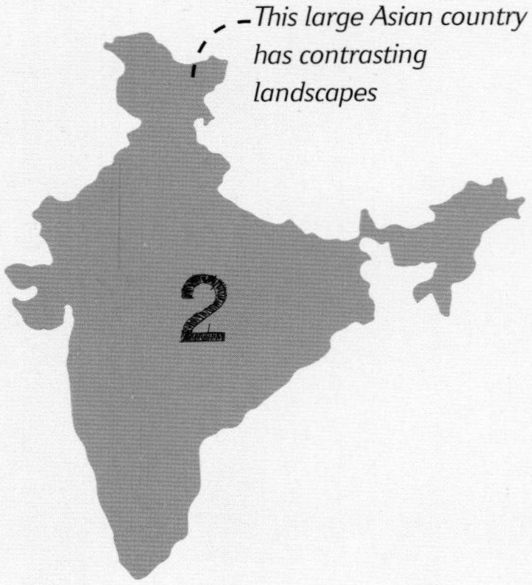

This large Asian country has contrasting landscapes

2

3

This sunny country lies on the edge of Western Europe

4

This icy country is in the far north of Europe

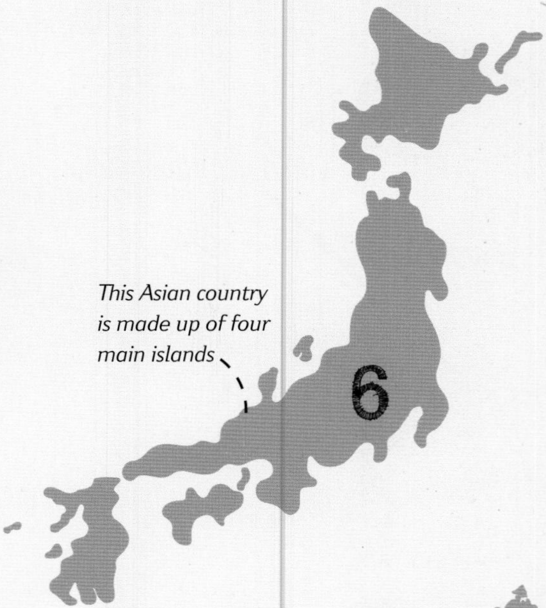

5

NAME THE COUNTRY

Here are the outlines of some of the countries that appear in this atlas. Can you name them? Look at the clues to help you. The answers are on page 121.

This Asian country is made up of four main islands

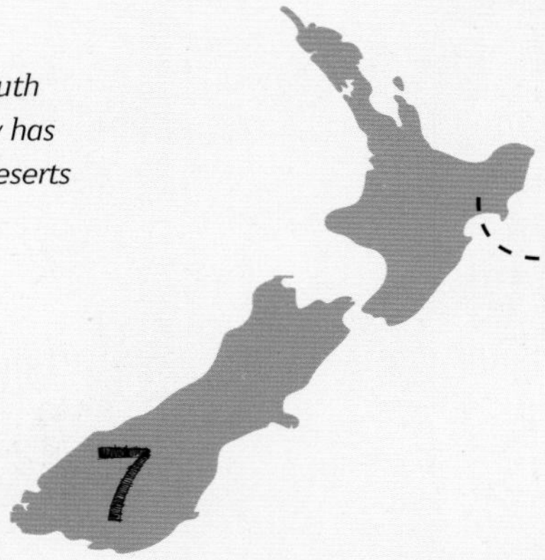

6

This long, thin South American country has mountains and deserts

This fertile country in the southern hemisphere is made up of two main islands

7

9

All kinds of amazing animals are unique to this African island

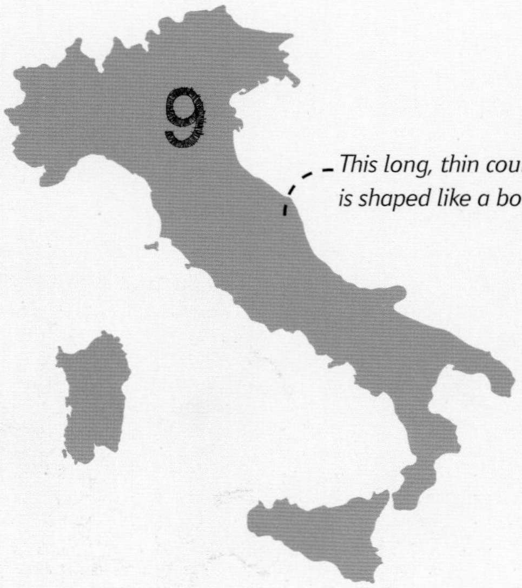

This long, thin country is shaped like a boot

10

This North American country is the second biggest in the world

8

GUESS THE ICON

All these colorful icons appear somewhere in this book. See if you can answer these questions about them. The answers are at the bottom of the page.

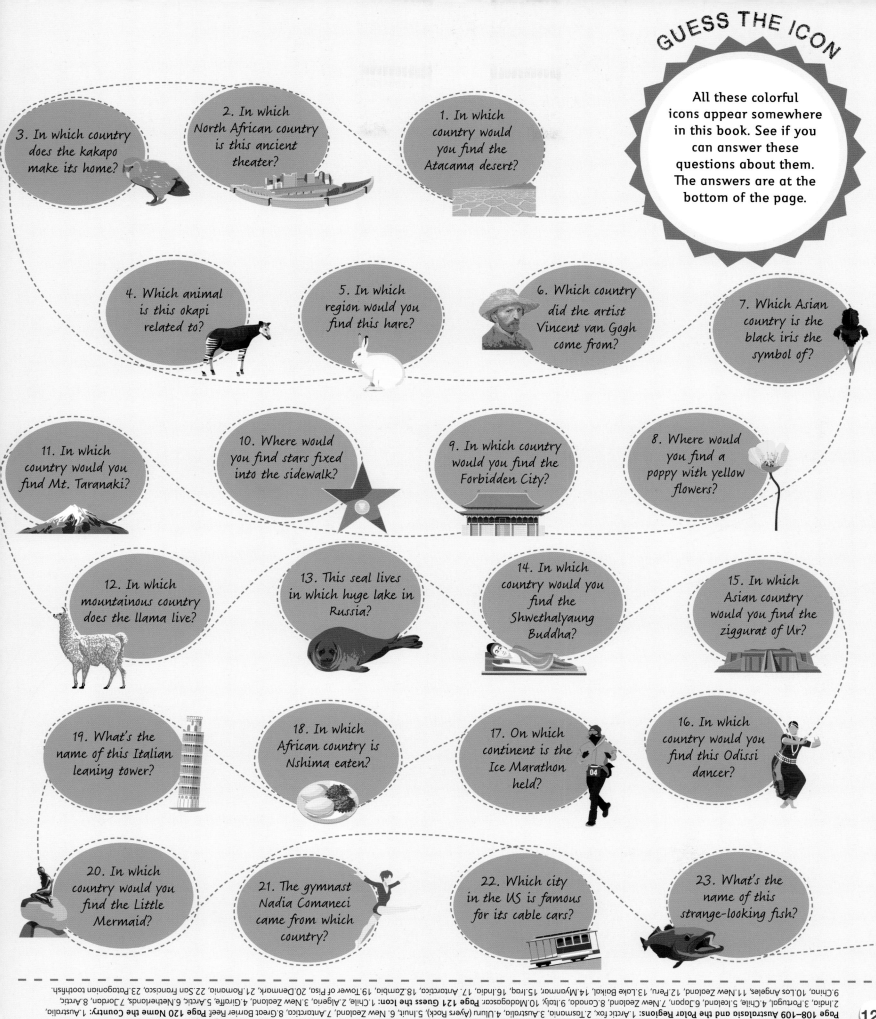

1. In which country would you find the Atacama desert?
2. In which North African country is this ancient theater?
3. In which country does the kakapo make its home?
4. Which animal is this okapi related to?
5. In which region would you find this hare?
6. Which country did the artist Vincent van Gogh come from?
7. Which Asian country is the black iris the symbol of?
8. Where would you find a poppy with yellow flowers?
9. In which country would you find the Forbidden City?
10. Where would you find stars fixed into the sidewalk?
11. In which country would you find Mt. Taranaki?
12. In which mountainous country does the llama live?
13. This seal lives in which huge lake in Russia?
14. In which country would you find the Shwethalyaung Buddha?
15. In which Asian country would you find the ziggurat of Ur?
16. In which country would you find this Odissi dancer?
17. On which continent is the Ice Marathon held?
18. In which African country is Nshima eaten?
19. What's the name of this Italian leaning tower?
20. In which country would you find the Little Mermaid?
21. The gymnast Nadia Comaneci came from which country?
22. Which city in the US is famous for its cable cars?
23. What's the name of this strange-looking fish?

Answers: Page 8–9 North America: 1.Mount Rushmore, 2.Dominican Republic, 3.Toronto, 4.Mexico, 5.New York, 6.Colorado River, 7.Inuit, 8.Panama Canal, 9.China, 10.Los Angeles, 11.New Zealand. **Page 22–23 South America:** 1.Rio de Janeiro, 2.Andes, 3.Colombia, 4.Chile, 5.Brazil, 6.Peru, 7.Spectacled bear, 8.Peru. **Page 34–35 Africa:** 1.Tuareg, 2.Kenya, 3.Libya, 4.Feluccas, 5.Congo, 6.South Africa, 7.Zambia, 8.Madagascar. **Page 50–51 Europe:** 1.Corsica, 2.St. Basil's Cathedral, 3.England, 4.Salzburg, 5.Czech Republic 6.France, 7.Tokyo Skytree, 8.South Korea **Page 80–81 Asia:** 1.India, 2.Tasmania, 3.China, 4.Mongolia, 5.Taiwan, 6.China, 7.Antarctica, 8.Great Barrier Reef **Page 108–109 Australasia and the Polar Regions:** 1.Arctic fox, 2.Antarctica, 3.Australia, 4.Uluru (Ayers Rock), 5.Inuit, 6.New Zealand, 7.Antarctica, 8.Great Barrier Reef **Page 120 Name the Country:** 1.Australia, 2.India, 3.Portugal, 4.Chile, 5.Iceland, 6.Japan, 7.New Zealand, 8.Netherlands, 9.China, 10.Madagascar **Page 121 Guess the Icon:** 1.Chile, 2.Algeria, 3.New Zealand, 4.Giraffe, 5.Arctic, 6.Netherlands, 7.Jordan, 8.Arctic, 9.China, 10.Los Angeles, 11.New Zealand, 12.Peru, 13.Lake Baikal, 14.Myanmar, 15.Iraq, 16.India, 17.Antarctica, 18.Zambia, 19.Tower of Pisa, 20.Denmark, 21.Romania, 22.San Francisco, 23.Patagonian toothfish.

GLOSSARY

aboriginals
Original or first-known inhabitants of a country. It is mainly used to refer to the native people of Australia

artifact
Man-made object, generally of historic or cultural interest, such as a painting or a vase

canyon
Deep, narrow valley with very steep, rocky sides. A stream or river usually flows through it

capital
Country's most important city. It is where the government usually meets and passes laws

climate
Normal weather pattern during the year in any part of the world

continents
Seven large areas of land that the world is divided into: Africa, Antarctica, Asia, Australasia, Europe, North America, and South America

coral reef
Rocklike structure formed by a group of corals (simple sea animals) in the warm waters along tropical coasts. Many fish and other sea creatures live around coral reefs

country
Area of Earth that is governed by the same leaders and has the same flag. Most continents are made up of many different countries

crops
Plants grown to feed people and animals. Crops need the right soil and climate to grow well

culture
Way of life and beliefs of the people of a region or country

delta
Flat land formed from material deposited by a river around the area where it enters the sea or flows into a lake. Soil in a delta area is usually very fertile

desert
Dry region that gets 10 in (25 cm) or less of rainfall in a year. Deserts can be hot or cold. Only a few animals and plants are able to live in desert areas

dunes
Small mounds or ridges of sand that are formed by the wind or flowing water pushing the sand together. They are usually found along beaches or in sandy deserts.

earthquake
Movement of large blocks of rock beneath the Earth's surface. Cracks may open up in the ground, causing buildings to collapse

endangered
Word used to describe a species of plant or animal with only a few living members left

equator
Imaginary line around the Earth, which is exactly halfway between the North and South Poles. Countries close to the equator are hotter than countries that are farther away from it

ethnic group
Group of people who share the same racial, religious, or cultural background

exports
Goods or services that are sold to another country

extinct
Word used to describe a plant or animal species that has no living members. All dinosaurs, for example, are now extinct

fertile land
Land where the soil is particularly good for growing crops on

fjord
Long, narrow bay or inlet, with steep, high, rocky sides. The word is Norwegian and was first used to describe the many deep inlets along Norway's rocky coast

fossil
Remains or shape of a prehistoric plant or animal that have been preserved in rock

game reserve
Area where wild animals are protected from hunters, or where hunting is limited by law. Africa has many game reserves

geyser
Fountain of hot water and steam that shoots up out of the ground. Geysers form when an underground stream flows over hot, volcanic rocks

glacier
Huge, thick sheet of ice moving very slowly, either down the side of a mountain or over an area of land. Glaciers help to shape and form the landscape

grasslands
Open land covered in grass and a few small bushes. Larger plants, such as trees, rarely grow on grasslands. Grasslands are called prairies in the United States

gulf
Large area of sea that is almost enclosed by land, such as the Gulf of Mexico and Persian Gulf

hot (thermal) spring
Place where hot water, heated by volcanic activity, flows out of cracks in the ground

hurricane
Very violent storm with extremely strong winds that can cause a great deal of damage

hydroelectric power
Electricity created by machinery driven by fast-flowing water. Water forced under high pressure through dams built across rivers is often used for this purpose

iceberg
Massive piece of ice that has broken off from a glacier or ice sheet and floated out to sea

imports
Goods or services bought from another country

irrigation
Supplying water to dry areas of land, so that crops can grow there. The water is carried or pumped along pipes or ditches

island
Piece of land that has water all around it. Islands occur in oceans, seas, lakes, and rivers

lake
Large body of water surrounded by land

migrate
Move from one country or region to go and live in another. People migrate for many reasons, such as to find work or escape war

mine
Place where naturally occurring resources (such as coal, iron ore, copper, and gold) and gemstones (such as diamonds and rubies) are dug out of the ground

mineral
Natural substance found in the Earth's rocks, such as metals and precious gemstones, which are removed by mining

monsoon
Strong wind that blows across south and Southeast Asia. It changes direction as the seasons change, causing very heavy rain from May to September.

mountain
Area of land that rises up much higher than the land around it to form a peak at the top. Some mountaintops are so high that they reach the icy cold air far above Earth, and so have snow on them even in summer.

national park
Area of countryside that has been preserved in its natural state by the government of a country to protect the wildlife there and for people to enjoy.

native
Person linked to a place by birth, or whose family are from the original inhabitants of an area.

nomads
People who do not live in one fixed place. Instead they move around an area in search of food, water, and land to graze their animals on

oasis
Area of fertile land in the desert. Plants can grow easily there, unlike in the rest of the desert, because water lies on or very close to the surface

ocean
Very large sea. There are five oceans: Pacific Ocean, Atlantic Ocean, Indian Ocean, Arctic Ocean, and Southern Ocean

pampas
Name given to the vast grasslands found in part of South America

peninsula
Strip of land that is surrounded by water on three of its sides

plain
Area of flat, open land with very few trees. Plains are often covered with grass

plateau
Large area of high, flat land. Some mountains, such as Table Mountain in Cape Town, South Africa, have a plateau at the top

polar region
Area near to the North or South Pole. Polar regions are covered in a thick layer of ice for most of the year and are extremely cold

population
Total number of people living in a given area of land.

port
Town or city on the coast with a harbor, where boats and ships can load or unload goods and let passengers board or get off

province
Officially recognized area of a country or state. Provinces often have their own leaders, although they are still governed by the laws of the country they are part of

rain forest
Dense forest with very high rainfall. Most are near the equator and are also very hot.

rapids
Part of a river that is moving at great speed, because it is flowing over very steep ground.

reservoir
Large natural or artificial lake, where water is collected and stored for people to use in homes, businesses, industry, and farming

river
Large stream of water that flows from a high place to a lower place. Rivers start as small streams high up in the mountains and flow down into the sea

safari
Journey that involves looking at wild animals in their natural surroundings. It usually refers to trips taken in Africa

savanna
Name given to open grasslands in tropical and subtropical countries

sea
Large body of saltwater. Seas (including oceans) cover most of the Earth's surface

sea level
Average level of the surface of the world's seas and oceans. The height of land is given as how far it is above sea level. The depth of a sea or ocean is given as how far it is below sea level

shrubland
Area of land covered in lots of small trees and bushes, as well as different types of grass

species
Distinct group of animals or plants that share similar features

state
Nation or territory that is organized as a community under one government

steppe
Name given to the vast, grassy plains that stretch from Eastern Europe right across central Asia

terrain
Area of land, usually with a particular feature, such as mountains or grassy plains

territory
Area of land that belongs to a particular country or state

tornado
Spinning cloud of very strong wind. Tornadoes will destroy almost anything in their path

tribe
Group of people who share the same culture and history. It usually refers to people who live together in traditional communites, far from cities and towns

tropical
Conditions found in areas near the Equator. Tropical weather, for example, is very hot and wet

valley
Low area of land between hills or mountains

vegetation
Type of plants found in an area of land

volcano
Mountain or hill that may erupt, pouring out hot lava (molten rock) from a crater in its top

wetlands
Land with wet, spongy soil, such as a marsh or swamp. Many animals and plants specialize in living in wetlands

wildlife
Wild animals that live in an area of land

INDEX

CREDITS

Dorling Kindersley would like to thank the following people for their assistance in the preparation of this book: Helen Garvey for design assistance; Emma Chafer, Jolyon Goddard, Katy Lennon, and Kathleen Teece for editorial assistance; Ann Kay for proofreading

Picture Credits:
The publisher would also like to thank the following for their kind permission to reproduce their photographs:

(Key: a-above; b-below/bottom; c-centre; f-far; l-left; r-right; t-top)

10 Dorling Kindersley: Claire Cordier (br); Greg Ward / Rough Guides (cb). **11 Dorling Kindersley:** Ian Cummings / Rough Guides (cr); Rowan Greenwood (tc). **12 Corbis:** PCN (tc). **Dorling Kindersley:** Tim Draper / Rough Guides (cb); The University of Aberdeen (bl, fbl); Paul Whitfield / Rough Guides (cra). **13 Dorling Kindersley:** Tim Draper / Rough Guides (c). **14 Corbis:** Louie Psihoyos (cl). **Dorling Kindersley:** Martin Richardson / Rough Guides (tl). **16 Corbis:** AS400 DB / Bettmann (clb); Mauricio Ramos / Aurora Photos (cla). **17 Corbis:** Juan Medina / Reuters (fcr). **Dorling Kindersley:** Demetrio Carrasco / Rough Guides (c); Thomas Marent (tl). **Dreamstime.com:** Lunamarina (tc). **18 Dorling Kindersley:** Greg and Yvonne Dean (tl); Tim Draper / Rough Guides (tc). **19 Alamy Images:** BlueOrangeStudio (tc). Corbis: EPA / Alejandro Ernesto (cra). **20 Dorling Kindersley:** Rowan Greenwood (cl). **24 Dorling Kindersley:** Tim Draper / Rough Guides (cb); Thomas Marent (bl). **25 Corbis:** Hagenmuller / Jean-Francois / Hemis (b). **26 Alamy Images:** Maxime Dube (bc). Corbis: Philip Lee Harvey (tr). **27 Alamy Images:** Florian Kopp / imageBROKER (bl). **Dorling Kindersley:** Cotswold Wildlife Park & Gardens, Oxfordshire, UK (fcr); Tim Draper / Rough Guides (tl); Hoa Luc (cr). **28 Corbis:** Corbis / David Selman (tl); Robin Hanbury-Tenison / robertharding (tc). **Dorling Kindersley:** Natural History Museum, London (bc). **29 Corbis:** EPA / Marius Becker (bl); Tim Tadder (tc); Tim Kiusalaas / Masterfile (cr). **Fotolia:** Eric Isselee (tr). **Getty Images:** Grant Ordelheide / Aurora Open (bc). **30 Dorling Kindersley:** Tim Draper / Rough Guides (bc). **31 Alamy Images:** Image Gap (bl). **Corbis:** Christopher Pillitz / In Pictures (cr). **Dorling Kindersley:** Tim Draper / Rough Guides (br). **33 Dorling Kindersley:** Tim Draper / Rough Guides (cr). **36 Dorling Kindersley:** Suzanne Porter / Rough Guides (b). **37 Dorling Kindersley:** Rowan Greenwood (tc); Alex Robinson / Rough Guides (cr). **Dreamstime.com:** Roman Murushkin / Romanvm (br). **38 Dorling Kindersley:** Suzanne Porter / Rough Guides (c, fbl). **39 Alamy Images:** blickwinkel / Irlmeier (bc). Corbis: Kazuyoshi Nomachi (bl). **Dreamstime.com:** Gelia (tc). **40 Dorling Kindersley:** Bolton Metro Museum (tr); Eddie Gerald / Rough Guides (clb). **41 Alamy Images:** Andrew McConnell / robertharding (tc). **42 Alamy Images:** Images Of Africa / Gallo Images (br); Paula Smith (bc). Dorling Kindersley: Powell-Cotton Museum, Kent (cr); University of Pennsylvania Museum of Archaeology and Anthropology (tr). **43 Alamy Images:** blickwinkel (bl). Dorling Kindersley: Barnabas Kindersley

(cra). **44 Corbis:** Per-Anders Pettersson (cl); Dr. Richard Roscoe / Visuals Unlimited (tc); Olivier Polet (br). **45 Alamy Images:** Liam West (tr). Corbis: Paul Souders (bc). **47 Alamy Images:** Zute Lightfoot (cra). Corbis: Foodfolio / the food passionates (bl). **48 Alamy Images:** Chad Ehlers (cl); Emmanuel Lattes (crb); robertharding (bl). **Dorling Kindersley:** Greg Roden / Rough Guides (tr); Tim Draper / Rough Guides (clb). **Dreamstime.com:** Bin Zhou / Dropu (br). **Fotolia:** Galyna Andrushko (bc). **PunchStock:** Digital Vision (cb). **54 Corbis:** Creativ Studio Heinemann / Westend61 (br); Dave G. Houser (tc). **Dreamstime.com:** Klikk (cl). **55 Dorling Kindersley:** Roger Norum / Rough Guides (tc); Helena Smith / Rough Guides (cr). **56 Corbis:** Iain Masterton / incamerastock (cl). **58 Dorling Kindersley:** Angus Osborn / Rough Guides (cla). **Fotolia:** Zee (clb). **59 Dorling Kindersley:** Paris Tourist Office (c). **60 Dorling Kindersley:** Herge / Les Editions Casterman (clb); Greg Ward / Rough Guides (bc). **61 Alamy Images:** Realimage (br). **Corbis:** Werner Dieterich / Westend61 (cl). **62 Alamy Images:** Arnt Haug / LOOK Die Bildagentur der Fotografen GmbH (bc); Hans P. Szyszka / Novarc Images (cla). **63 Corbis:** Jon Hicks (tl). **65 Corbis:** Hugh Sitton (bc). **Dreamstime.com:** Netfalls (tr). **66 Corbis:** Rolf Bruderer / Blend Images (br); The Gallery Collection (tl). **Dorling Kindersley:** James McConnachie / Rough Guides (tr); Scootopia (cl). **67 Alamy Images:** amphotos (bc). **Dorling Kindersley:** Jon Cunningham / Rough Guides (c). **68 Dorling Kindersley:** Jon Cunningham / Rough Guides (c); Helena Smith / Rough Guides (cl). **69 Dorling Kindersley:** Barnabas Kindersley (cra). **70 Dorling Kindersley:** Tim Draper / Rough Guides (bl, bc); Eddie Gerald / Rough Guides (tr); Michelle Grant / Rough Guides (fcrb). **71 Alamy Images:** Viktor Onyshchenko (bl). **72 Dorling Kindersley:** Gregory Wrona / Rough Guides (tl, tr). **75 Dorling Kindersley:** Chris Christoforou / Rough Guides (tl); Michelle Grant / Rough Guides (bc). **76 Alamy Images:** Lisovskaya Natalia / The Picture Pantry (tr). **Corbis:** Robbie Jack (bc). **77 Corbis:** Wolfgang Kaehler (tl). **Dorling Kindersley:** Jonathan Smith / Rough Guides (c). **79 Dorling Kindersley:** Roger Norum / Rough Guides (tr). **82 Corbis:** Earl & Nazima Kowall (cl); George Steinmetz (tc); Jochen Schlenker / robertharding (bl). **83 Corbis:** Tuul & Bruno Morandi (tr); Jose Fuste Raga (cr). **Dorling Kindersley:** Tim Draper / Rough Guides (br). **84 Alamy Images:** Nurlan Kalchinov (cl). **Corbis:** Gavin Hellier / JAI (br); Jose Fuste Raga (tr). **85 Alamy Images:** NASA (t). **Corbis:** Robert Jean / Hemis (bl). **Dorling Kindersley:** Blackpool Zoo, Lancashire, UK (br). **86 Dorling Kindersley:** Lydia Evans / Rough Guides (tr). **90 Dorling Kindersley:** University of Pennsylvania Museum of Archaeology and Anthropology (cl, cb/bull, cb/necklace, bc). **91 Alamy Images:** ArkReligion.com / Art Directors & TRIP (cr); Dario Bajurin (br). **92 Alamy Images:** Danita Delimont (clb); George Rutter (tr); Farhad Hashimi (cla). **93 Alamy Images:** Ali Mujtaba (cl). **Dreamstime.com:** Dragoneye (tr). **94 Corbis:** Philippe Lissac / Godong (cl). **Dorling Kindersley:** Dave Abram / Rough Guides (ca). **95 Dorling Kindersley:** Archives du 7e Art / Ashutosh Gowariker Productions / Photos 12 (bl); Tim Draper /

Rough Guides (tl); Gavin Thomas / Rough Guides (ca); Natural History Museum, London (fcr/amethyst). **96 Alamy Images:** Thornton Cohen (fcr). **Dorling Kindersley:** Tim Draper / Rough Guides (tc, fcl). **97 Dorling Kindersley:** Liberty's Owl, Raptor and Reptile Centre, Hampshire, UK (br). **98 Dorling Kindersley:** Karen Trist / Rough Guides (c). Fotolia: Eric Isselee (bl). Getty Images: Ltd, Imagemore Co. (bc). **National Geographic Creative:** O. Louis Mazzatenta (tr). **99 Corbis:** Peter Langer / Design Pics (tl). **Dorling Kindersley:** Alan Hills / The Trustees of the British Museum (tr); Brice Minnigh / Rough Guides (fcrb). **100 Corbis:** KCNA / epa (bc). **101 Dorling Kindersley:** Tim Draper / Rough Guides (tc, br). **102 Alamy Images:** Thomas Frey / imageBROKER (br); Horizon Images / Motion (cl). **Corbis:** Adam / photocuisine (tl); Jeremy Woodhouse / Masterfile (tr). **Dorling Kindersley:** Durham University Oriental Museum (cb). **103 Corbis:** Stefano Politi Markovina / JAI (bl). **Dreamstime.com:** Craig Hanson / Rssfhs (tc). **104 Dorling Kindersley:** Tim Draper / Rough Guides (ftl, fcla). **105 Dorling Kindersley:** Simon Bracken / Rough Guides (tc); Museum of the Moving Image, London (br). **106 Dorling Kindersley:** Sean Hunter Photography (cl). **107 Dorling Kindersley:** Simon Bracken / Rough Guides (crb); Sarah Cummins / Rough Guides (cl); Suzanne Porter / Rough Guides (clb); Jean-Christophe Godet / Rough Guides (bc); Tim Draper / Rough Guides (br). **111 Corbis:** Laurie Chamberlain (br); Frans Lanting (tc); Pete Oxford / Minden Pictures (tr). **113 Corbis:** Claire Leimbach / robertharding (cra). **Dorling Kindersley:** Sydney Opera House Trust / Jamie Marshall (crb). **Dreamstime.com:** Callan Chesser / Ewanchesser (br); Bin Zhou / Dropu (tr). **114 Corbis:** Steve Christo / Steve Christo Photography (cla). **Dorling Kindersley:** Pitt Rivers Museum, University of Oxford (tr). **115 Alamy Images:** travellinglight (tl). Dorling Kindersley: Paul Whitfield / Rough Guides (ca, bl). **116 Dreamstime.com:** Staphy (clb). **Getty Images:** Frank Krahmer / Photographer's Choice RF (fbl). **Science Photo Library:** British Antarctic Survey (fcl). **117 Alamy Images:** Classic Image (cr). **NASA:** U.S. Antarctic Search for Meteorites (ANSMET) (tr). **118 Dorling Kindersley:** The University of Aberdeen (tl); Jerry Young (fcl). **119 Alamy:** Chad Ehlers (tr). **Dorling Kindersley:** Roger Norum / Rough Guides (cr); Pitt Rivers Museum, University of Oxford (br).

All other images © Dorling Kindersley

For further information see: www.**dkimages**.com